THE
NIGHT ATTILA DIED

THE
NIGHT ATTILA DIED

Solving the Murder of
Attila the Hun

Michael A. Babcock, Ph. D.

BERKLEY BOOKS, NEW YORK

THE BERKLEY PUBLISHING GROUP
Published by the Penguin Group
Penguin Group (USA) Inc.
375 Hudson Street, New York, New York 10014, USA
Penguin Group (Canada), 90 Eglinton Avenue East, Suite 700, Toronto, Ontario M4P 2Y3, Canada
(a division of Pearson Penguin Canada Inc.)
Penguin Books Ltd., 80 Strand, London WC2R 0RL, England
Penguin Group Ireland, 25 St. Stephen's Green, Dublin 2, Ireland (a division of Penguin Books Ltd.)
Penguin Group (Australia), 250 Camberwell Road, Camberwell, Victoria 3124, Australia
(a division of Pearson Australia Group Pty. Ltd.)
Penguin Books India Pvt. Ltd., 11 Community Centre, Panchsheel Park, New Delhi—110 017, India
Penguin Group (NZ), Cnr. Airborne and Rosedale Roads, Albany, Auckland 1310, New Zealand
(a division of Pearson New Zealand Ltd.)
Penguin Books (South Africa) (Pty.) Ltd., 24 Sturdee Avenue, Rosebank, Johannesburg 2196,
South Africa

Penguin Books Ltd., Registered Offices: 80 Strand, London WC2R 0RL, England

This book is an original publication of The Berkley Publishing Group.

Copyright © 2005 by Michael A. Babcock, Ph.D.
Text design by Tiffany Estreicher.

First edition: July 2005

Library of Congress Cataloging-in-Publication Data

Babcock, Michael A.
    The night Attila died : solving the murder of Attila the Hun / Michael A. Babcock.—1st ed.
      p.   cm.
    ISBN 0-425-20272-0
      1. Attila, d. 453—Death and burial.   2. Attila, d. 453—Assassination.   3. Murder—Europe.
I. Title.

    D141.B28   2005
    936'.03'092—dc22
    [B]
                                                                                    2005045708

PRINTED IN THE UNITED STATES OF AMERICA

10   9   8   7   6   5   4   3   2   1

For Janel—
ché i he' vostr'occhi, donna, mi legaro.

CONTENTS

Contents

ACKNOWLEDGMENTS

I first got to know Attila—that is, to *really* know him beyond the usual cartoon stereotypes—in a year-long graduate seminar on the Gothic language. My first thanks, then, are appropriately directed to Professor Anatoly Liberman of the University of Minnesota, who introduced me to the sixth-century historian Jordanes. Anatoly's extraordinary mind and even greater curiosity have always inspired his students, including me, to think boldly.

Those who tolerated (and often encouraged) my eccentric research habits as a young scholar also deserve my thanks: Professors Robert Sonkowsky, Kaaren Grimstad, and Evelyn Firchow. In their seminars on Old Icelandic, Old High German, Medieval Latin, and Paleography, I was trained to accept *method* as a gentle leash for my creativity. Where I tug too hard on the leash, the fault is mine. They did their best.

This is a better book because of the encouragement, experience, and judgment of my editor at Berkley, Allison McCabe. I also thank my agent, Ron Formica, for his excellent representation. The whole staff at New England Publishing Associates have been a pleasure to work with.

I thank friends and family who encouraged me by the interest they expressed. I can only mention a few out of the many, but my parents (who always exceed the call of duty) come to mind, along with my colleague David Ehrman; my nephew, Christopher; my cousin, Mary Ruth Santa; my sister-in-law, Mary Jo; and my friend

Rod Parra. With special thanks, bittersweet thanks, I remember my mother-in-law, Helen, who enthusiastically told *everybody* about my book—the hairdresser, the grocery clerk, her Monday-night domino partners—before she lost her long battle with cancer. I wish she could have held this book in her hands.

My children, Wesley and Mary, might have known only that I was writing a book about a "bad man," but the love and joy they bring into my life was a constant source of strength. Most importantly, I express deep gratitude to the love of my life, Janel, without whose support these pages, as well as my life, would be blank.

February 7, 2005
Lynchburg, Virginia

INTRODUCTION

NOBODY today doubts that Attila the Hun died of natural causes. As the story goes, soon after leading his troops home from Italy, Attila took a new wife, a beautiful young woman named Ildico. After a riotous wedding celebration he lay down on his bed, drunk and incapacitated. His sinuses hemorrhaged and he drowned in his own blood. When he failed to stir the following morning, his attendants broke in the door. There were no wounds on the body and no reason to suspect Ildico, who was found weeping beneath her veil. It was the year A.D. 453 and Attila the Hun was dead from a bad nosebleed.

That's the official finding of history—the settled opinion of generations of scholars.

But it's also wrong.

I believe—and I have proof to back me up—that Attila was murdered. This fact is not surprising in itself, since everyone in the ancient world wanted him dead. What is surprising, at least to me, is that history books could be so wrong, so dogmatically and convincingly wrong. It's not that murder wasn't ever *suspected* before; as the last person to see him alive,

Ildico was the first logical suspect. Rumors sprang up immediately that Ildico, a German, must have killed him for some crime he had committed against her people. Medieval poets claimed she killed him out of revenge, and they filled out her character with dark motives and gruesome deeds. By the time the poets were done, she had cut out the hearts of her own sons and fed them to her husband as a delicacy. Then, with a fiendish glint in her eye, she stabbed him and burned down the hall. It's a wonderful story—if you like that sort of thing—but it's pretty far removed from what happened the night Attila died. Historians ignore it altogether. They've got their own story to tell. Not as sensational as the poetic version, but at least it's believable.

But *how* believable is it? My skepticism was first kindled in a classroom on the second floor of Folwell Hall at the University of Minnesota. I was a graduate student in philology, an obscure discipline that a surprisingly high percentage of people seem to think is somehow related to theology. The words sound a little alike—philology, theology. I suppose they might as well be related, even if they're not: both disciplines pursue truth by looking beyond what is visible. Philology is about reconstructing what's been lost through time: bringing dead languages back to life, figuring out the secrets of old manuscripts, and piecing together the legends and myths of our ancestors. Philologists are archaeologists of the word, excavating layer after layer of culture beneath the phonetic and graphic forms of a text. Never satisfied with the text as it is, philologists long to figure out what the text *might* have said, or *must* have said, before it somehow got changed. Before a monk nodded off in the scriptorium and lost a sentence or two from the text he was copying by dictation. Before a Christian scribe took a pagan poem and reworked it to reflect the Church's values. Before a page of vellum parchment was scraped clean and written over with a completely different text. What got scraped away interests the philologist more than what remains. The visible becomes a means of approaching the invisible. Come to think of it, that does sound a lot like theology.

Around a sparse wooden table we sat, five or six of us, parsing our way through Wulfila's fourth-century Gothic translation of the New Testament. At the head of the table was Professor Anatoly Liberman, who corrected our translations with patience and grim humor. He was a brilliant philologist who had written scholarly books in three languages. Under his guidance we were gradually being trained in this arcane method of historical reconstruction. Minnesota was the only place in the United States where you could get a Ph.D. in Germanic philology; only half a dozen of us were studying it when I was there. Five or six of us—a far cry from the days, a hundred years ago, when philology was the only thing to study in the great German universities. There was Jana with her interest in the Old Icelandic sagas; Martha, who inherited from her father (the poet John Berryman) a love of words; Marvin, with his ridiculous fluency in languages; Kurt, with his fascination for obscure linguistic laws that fascinated nobody else. My own interests turned toward the narrative study of Germanic myths and legends. Philology, to me, was like good old-fashioned detective work. Ancient manuscripts, ancient languages, ancient myths—I was hooked. Perhaps it wasn't quite Indiana Jones stuff, but it was discovery nonetheless. I was constantly digging up ancient bodies. They weren't the physical kind that can be subjected to laboratory analysis; but they were bodies nonetheless—bodies of text that hide, and reveal, their secrets.

One of our required readings in Anatoly's seminar was the *Getica*, the so-called *Gothic History* of Jordanes (jor-DAY-neez). The figure of Attila the Hun looms large in this sixth-century Latin text. The first time I read through it, I was intrigued by the dynamic and fully rounded character of Attila that emerged from the pages. The famous account of Attila's death, the one you can find today in any encyclopedia, drew me into its tightly constructed story line and intrigued me with its precise descriptions. Either this was an uncommonly detailed and trustworthy account, I thought, or it was a clever tissue of lies. I learned that this account was written a hundred years after Attila's death, but it was based upon an earlier history written by Priscus, a fifth-century Greek historian and diplomat. Priscus wrote a several-volume history of his times, including an engaging eyewitness account of a diplomatic journey he made to Attila's court in 449. Most of what Priscus wrote has been lost, but this autobiographical travelogue has survived intact. It's a remarkable historical document in which Priscus portrays the events and people of his times, including Attila, in great detail. Historians have been so impressed by the apparent objectivity of his narrative style that they've extended a blanket credibility to everything he wrote, including his account of Attila's death. That account, however, is lost to us in the original Greek that Priscus wrote; we know it only as it was incorporated into later works, such as the *Gothic History* of Jordanes.

So *that's* how we know what we know about Attila's death: not directly from Priscus but secondarily from Jordanes. A hundred years of political and religious agendas separated what *happened* the night Attila died and what was ultimately *passed on* to us in the *Gothic History*. That's when my curiosity really kicked in. I wanted to take a closer look at that lost century and find out what was hidden beneath all the imperial and religious propaganda of the late Roman Empire. And lacking the body of Attila the Hun, there was only one way to uncover the truth: to dig it out of the text.

What I couldn't shake was a hunch: Attila had been murdered.

But is it even possible to pry open the lid on Attila's coffin after fifteen hundred years? It is, if one uses the right tools. And if he was indeed murdered, could I identify his killer after all these centuries? Could a plausible case be made using the scanty evidence that has survived the Fall of Rome in 476, the Fall of Constantinople in 1453, and everything else in between? It was the ultimate cold case—and yet we still have enough evidence to reconstruct the circumstances of his death. More than anything else, I was curious about testing the limits of our historical understanding. If historians are wrong about this, I reasoned, then what can we possibly know about the past?

Knowing what to look for is always the challenge. There's much talk today in public life about "connecting the dots"—of trying to find a pattern, trying to pick out a conspiracy within the innumerable gestures of modern life. It's a difficult thing to do, sometimes impossible, but we don't give up trying. History's like that. We turn again and again to the old books and listen to all the chatter, hoping that we'll pick up something we haven't heard before. Out of all the stories that can be told, we hope we're listening to one that might be true.

This is the story of the night Attila died.

ONE

THE BROKEN BOW

I N the library of the Palais Bourbon in Paris, seat of the French Assembly, Eugène Delacroix painted an image of Attila the Hun that reflects one of the darkest memories of Western civilization. Clad in animal skins and swinging a mace with his right hand, Attila advances on horseback over the bodies of women and children. The sprawling victims, who represent "Italy and the Arts," as the title helpfully informs us, are still trying to pluck out a tune on their harps even while being trampled underfoot. It's appropriate that the painting is a little over the top—literally you have to look up at the ceiling to see it—because the theme is so grand and so dramatic that it can't possibly be right. But it doesn't have to be right—because it's history and it's propaganda.

We're not used to thinking of our histories that way. After all, propaganda is what the other guy writes, or paints. Even Attila the Hun knew how the game was played. In his campaign across Italy in 452, Attila camped for a while in the imperial palace in Mediolanum, the modern city of Milan. He was outraged by what he saw painted on the walls: a depiction of barbarians facedown before the Eastern and Western emperors of Rome. Attila ordered the walls to be whitewashed and repainted. In the new mural, the emperors were to be depicted in the servile act of pouring out gold at Attila's feet. Attila understood that history, like the end of a spear, is how you make a point.

The titanic struggle between Civilization and the Barbarians, which we see depicted so melodramatically in Delacroix's painting, is the historical backdrop for everything we know—and don't know—about Attila's death. The Roman Empire was fighting for its survival, and "truth" was whatever served that noble purpose. For centuries Rome had been the guardian of Civilization; when Rome teetered and fell, the Eastern capital of Constantinople, the Second Rome, became the West's last defense against the Goths and the Huns, and later, the Mongols and the Turks. The Empire (and the Church) were defended by more than armies at this perilous time; they were defended as well by artists and scribes who sometimes told the truth, but more often than not told elaborate cover stories. Some of these stories— press releases, really—were seen as transparent pieces of propaganda from the moment they were written. Others were told so skillfully that they became lodged in the official histories still being written today.

Attila is dead. Nowhere was the news received with more joy than in Constantinople. The relief was felt in every quarter. Everyone knew that Attila the Hun—the Scourge of God and ravager of Civilization—was redirecting his ferocious army from the West to the East. For two years Gaul and Italy had seen his fury. Soon it was to be Constantinople's turn. But then, all of a sudden, he died.

The news would have exploded through every district in the city, Constantinople—a city built for gossip. Ships sailing into the northern harbors of the Prosphorion and Neorion and the southern Port of Julian brought with them news from every corner of the Empire. Merchants from deserted towns on the frontier, overrun decades earlier by Goths and Huns, carried scraps of information along with their goods back into the heart of the city's commercial district. In the marketplace where a dozen languages could be heard, along the docks of the Golden Horn where merchants from Egypt were unloading their grain, in the halls of a palace constantly swarming with intrigue, the words were repeated in a thousand mouths. *Attila is dead.* Blacksmiths and tanners, glassmakers and potters, everyone stopped what they were doing in their shops along the porticoed streets. Outside the public bakeries and inside the taverns, everyone was thinking the same, inevitable thought: *How did he die? And who did it?* Some claimed he was killed by his own bride on his wedding night. Others claimed with equal confidence that divine judgment brought him down at last. The city was alive with rumors.

Scribes, eunuchs, and other bureaucrats huddled in the palace courtyard. All agreed that the news was good, very good—especially for the emperor. Attila had been pressing Marcian hard on the northern borders, threatening a full-scale invasion when spring came around. The list of grievances never changed from year to year. "Return the deserters to me now!" was the terse message brought back from one diplomatic mission. But before Marcian could draft a response, another embassy arrived with a postscript: "And send the gold you owe me!" Nothing peeved Attila more than when the Romans gave safe haven to Hunnish deserters—nothing, that is, except the Empire's refusal to pay the Huns an annual tribute. Every message was accompanied by bellowing threats of war. But all of these threats were drained of their urgency when one breathless sentence was uttered in Marcian's ear: *Attila is dead.*

The emperor was not entirely surprised by the news—or so the evidence would suggest.

A WELL-TIMED DEATH

Attila spent the two years before his death—451 and 452—in disastrous military campaigns.

In 451, as he vacillated between attacking the Eastern Empire (with its vast riches) and the Western Empire (with its open borders), his mind was apparently made up by a bizarre marriage proposal he couldn't refuse. The proposal came in the form of an imperial ring sent to him secretly by Honoria, sister of the Western emperor in Rome. The oldest sibling in a seriously dysfunctional family (even by Roman standards), Honoria despised her brother, Emperor Valentinian III, and would stop at nothing to destroy him. When the family matriarch, Galla Placidia, died, Honoria saw her opportunity to grab power through an alliance with Attila. It's obvious that Honoria had never laid eyes on Attila, or she might have replotted her strategy. Here's the description that the ancient historian Jordanes gives of the man who was "born to shake the nations":

> He was short of stature, with a broad chest and a large head; his eyes were small, his beard thin and sprinkled with gray; and he had a flat nose and a swarthy complexion, showing the evidences of his origin.

But then Honoria wasn't looking for love, she was looking for leverage.

When Valentinian caught wind of her overtures to the Scourge of God, he wasted little time locking her up in a tower. Her fate is unknown, but the scant evidence suggests that she was executed. Her brother probably lost no sleep when he issued the order, especially after witnessing what her scheme had accomplished. In response to her invitation, the most feared man in the world invaded the West, claiming Honoria as his bride and half the Empire as her dowry.

However, somewhere in northern Gaul between the cities of Troyes and Orléans (a place ancient historians called the Catalaunian Plains), the unthinkable happened: Attila suffered his first defeat. His confederation of Germanic and Hunnish tribes was turned back by a Roman alliance commanded by the Western general Aetius (ah-EE-tyus), and Attila barely escaped with his life.

He reassembled his army and returned the following year, 452, this time descending on northern Italy, where he devastated cities from modern Venice to Milan. He approached Rome as though intending to destroy it, when he was met north of the city by an embassy led by the Holy Father himself. Why Attila turned away from Rome and retreated back toward central Europe remains a mystery. Did angels appear above Pope Leo's head, the way Raphael would imagine it a thousand years later? Probably not. By all accounts Leo was indeed a persuasive figure; but then equally persuasive was the pestilence ravaging Attila's troops.

Two campaigns in two years—and two devastating results. The Western Empire lay in ruins, but so did Attila's plans for world domination.

Attila spent the winter of 452–453 waiting for the spring. The West had proved to be a disaster, what one ancient writer called *regio funesta*,[1] a land of death. So he turned his attention to another front, the Eastern Empire and its rich capital Constantinople. Attila renewed his demand for immediate payment of the annual tribute, suspended by Marcian when he came to power in 450. For two years Marcian had watched from a distance as his enemy slowly self-destructed in the West. Marcian knew Attila was vulnerable, but he also understood that he was still dangerous—and he was coming to Constantinople.

Six years had passed since Attila last turned his attention to the Eastern capital in 447, when the imperial purple was worn by Theodosius II. By all accounts, Theodosius II had nothing but a name in common with his grandfather, Theodosius the Great, the last ruler of a unified Empire. Unlike the soldier emperors of old, Theodosius II—described by some ancient historians as effeminate and cowardly—preferred hunting to warfare. This could explain why he built a defensive system of walls and towers (the Theodosian Walls) around the city, the ruins of which can still be seen in Istanbul today. If the city walls could not be breached, there would be no need to meet the enemy in pitched battle. That was the plan anyway; but, unfortunately for Theodosius, a massive earthquake struck the city just as the news arrived that Attila's troops were swarming on the northern border. Fifty-seven towers collapsed and the city was completely exposed. After some initial confusion, the prefect organized brigades that managed—remarkably—to repair the walls within sixty days. The Huns were too far away to capitalize on the disaster; plagued by disease among his troops, Attila turned back toward the Hungarian Plains. The city had been spared.

Farmers harvest their crops near the ruined city walls constructed by Emperor Theodosius II (408–50) around the eastern Roman capital of Constantinople (modern Istanbul, Turkey). The wall was constructed during the fifth century to keep out the raiding army of Attila the Hun. In 447 most of the wall was destroyed by an earthquake. Wall construction began immediately to repair the damage before raiders could attack the city.
Ted Spiegel / CORBIS

While the the emperor and the chieftain waited in their separate capitals through the winter and early spring of 453, Attila took another wife, a Gothic maiden named Ildico. He had just led his Gothic allies into two resounding defeats far from home, and his control over these Germanic tribes was weakened considerably. Ildico was a princess from a noble Gothic family, a pawn in Attila's efforts to patch up the shaky Gothic-Hun alliance.

After the wedding feast, as we have been told by all the best authorities, Attila and his bride retired to their wedding bed. Attila began to hemorrhage while he lay on his back incapacitated from wine. His lungs filled up and he died a bloody, though natural, death—"redundant in blood," as one ancient source puts it. Springtime came and with it the campaigning season, but Attila was dead and buried in a secret grave. The frontiers north of Constantinople were suddenly quiet. It was a well-timed death, at least from Marcian's point of view.

As events go, Attila's death might as well have been scheduled. If nothing else, the convenient timing is enough to prompt questions about what unfolded that night. Yet in the judgment of most historians, the timing was nothing more than a happy coincidence. One scholar has even written that "chance played its part in the providential death."[2] The subtle nonsense of that sentence—what does chance have to do with providence?—reveals an underlying anxiety: the timing *was* just too good to be true. Still, the vast majority of historians have always dismissed the juicier accounts of that fateful evening on the plains in Hungary (murder by a new wife, for instance) as romantic legends, the ancient equivalent of tabloid sensationalism. After all, as much as we might like to improve the story line, we are limited to what the history books have written.

Or are we?

Over the past two hundred years we have learned how to read beyond the text and draw out alternative voices that have long been silenced. Could the settled judgment of fifteen hundred years be wrong about Attila's death? The obscure discipline of philology may finally give us the answer.

QUEEN OF THE SCIENCES

Nietzsche spoke from experience when he described the philologist as one who reads slowly. Most remember Nietzsche as a philosopher, but he was trained as a classical philologist who believed that philosophy should be grounded in the slow reading of the past. Nietzsche's eloquent definition cannot be improved on, so here it is:

Philology is that venerable art which demands of its votaries one thing above all: to go aside, to take time, to become still, to become slow—it is a goldsmith's art and *connoisseurship of the word* which has nothing but delicate cautious work to do and achieves nothing if it does not achieve it lento.

> But for precisely this reason it is more necessary than ever today; by precisely this means does it entice and enchant us the most, in the midst of an age of "work," that is to say, of hurry, of indecent and perspiring haste, which wants to "get everything done" at once, it teaches to read well, that is to say, *to read slowly, deeply, looking cautiously before and aft, with reservations, with doors left open, with delicate fingers and eyes.*[3]

To Nietzsche's "delicate fingers and eyes" we can add "ears," since philologists bend their ears, optimistically, to the many voices that have been silenced in the text.

Later in life, Nietzsche lost his optimism and his mind. He spoke of philology as a discipline to be thrown out along with grandfather's furniture—one more way perhaps in which this brilliant madman predicted the course of twentieth-century culture.[4] Back when Germany invented the modern university, philology was considered the queen of the sciences. One would go to Berlin to study classical philology (the ancient Greek and Latin languages) or Germanic philology (the study of the early Germanic languages). But today almost nobody knows what philology is. I still remember the puzzled expressions when I told people I was getting my doctorate in Germanic philology. "You're studying dramatic theology?" one person asked with genuine interest. Even among academics, there is little understanding and even less interest in what philologists do.

Philology is literally "the love of the word"—an etymology that evokes the classical reverence for written knowledge. In real terms, what philologists work with are ancient languages, ancient manuscripts, and ancient myths. Two types of reconstruction—internal and comparative—make up the toolbox of philology. Looking at the internal consistency of a text is really no different from cross-examining witnesses and poking holes in their testimony; some awkward wording or an outright contradiction in the text may point to the suppression of evidence in the historical record. Comparative reconstruction, the other common strategy, involves analyzing two texts side by side to determine which one is dependent on the other and thereby to reconstruct an earlier version of a story, myth, or language. With these two methods the philologist attempts to recover the lost layers of culture lying beneath the oldest manuscript evidence.

Why would anyone want to do this? Well, at the very least it can provide us with a way to ground possibilities. Sometimes it can even help us sort out what's possible from what's probable. Let's look at an obvious example—the classic task of philology, the reconstruction of ancient languages. Philology's showcase accomplishment was the discovery that most European languages have descended from a common tongue (Indo-European) spoken some five thousand years ago.[5] Not one shred of this original language has survived intact—not one manuscript and not a single place-name on any map. Still, there is no doubt among scholars about the broad outlines of Indo-European grammar and vocabulary. By comparing the languages that *do* survive, and then classifying the consistent ways in which those languages relate to one another, the old mother tongue has been determined with amazing precision. What's been lost has been recovered through what remains.

The most famous philologists were the Brothers Grimm. Some two hundred years ago Jakob and Wilhelm were pioneers of this new linguistic science; but they are most famous, of course, for collecting fairy tales in their spare time. Today we are likely to think of gingerbread houses when we hear their names, but philologists think immediately of Grimm's Law, one of the foundational discoveries of the discipline. Jakob showed, for example, how Latin *pater* and English *father,* Latin *piscis* and English *fish*, are related to each other through a simple, predictable sound change whereby the *p* sound evolved into the *f* sound we have in English and the other Germanic languages. It was a groundbreaking discovery that paved the way for even more linguistic "laws." The credibility of philology as a method for reconstructing the past stands on this impressive foundation.

So what do fairy tales and obscure linguistic laws have to do with each other? And where does Attila's death fit into all this? Fairy tales were not an eccentric pastime for the Grimms, since legends spring ultimately from the same source as language itself—the peasant's mouth—and must be studied with the same tools. Driving the study of both legends and language is the belief that the outlines of a hidden past can be discerned from what has survived into the present. The same methods that have allowed scholars to prove that Latin, Greek, Irish, Sanskrit, Persian, Russian, and English are closely related languages can be applied to written texts, such as the imperial histories authorized by Emperor Marcian, and even the scandalous legends that the Germans told about Attila's death.

The official, imperial histories that document the last days of the Western Roman Empire are ideal candidates for reconstruction. Written in the Eastern capital of Constantinople, these histories are transcriptions, really, of the political agendas of the moment, not reliable accounts of the events as they actually happened. They were written by government bureaucrats who shifted like weathervanes in the political climates of their day. If we know this (and we do), then we cannot approach these histories as accurate accounts of the past. These texts survived not because they are accurate but because they were privileged. They are rhetorical documents, exercises in propaganda, and their whole reason for being is not to enlighten and inform but to suppress and manipulate.

But here's the tricky part: Though not true per se, these histories do *contain* truth. Many times it's a truth arrived at indirectly and revealed only after tough cross-examination; propaganda doesn't give up its secrets easily. If we can accept at the outset, though, that competing versions of the truth were actively suppressed in the service of a ruling elite, then we have taken the first step toward identifying the threads of an alternative history that's been lost. The official histories written in Constantinople are the obvious place to begin looking for the lost history from the last decades of the Roman Empire, and to reconstruct what *really* happened to Attila.

However, Constantinople was not the only rumor mill churning out stories about Attila's death. In small villages along the Rhine and Danube, the story of Attila's last night was told and retold in the accented, alliterative style of Germanic poetry. As far away as Anglo-Saxon England the story of Ætla (as he was called) was widely told. He's little more than a passing reference in Old English literature—*Ætla weold Hunum*, "Attila ruled the Huns"—but it's clear that Attila was an epic hero among the Germanic tribes as famous as Beowulf.[6] The anonymous poets who framed these stories recognized no clear distinction between "history" and "legend." Ancient writings, whether poetry or imperial histories, tend to range freely across the border that (for us, anyway) separates what is true from what is imagined. There is legend in the histories and there is history in the legends. If we're going to get at the "truth" about Attila's death, the biased histories of Rome and Constantinople aren't the only texts to examine. The same philological methods will have to be applied to the legends as well.

And there's plenty of legend to work with. To the medieval Germans in the centuries after Rome fell, Attila gradually developed into "Etzel," a figurehead king in a palace filled with damsels and knights. Over time he would be relegated to a secondary role in the very story that his own life and death had inspired. The medieval Scandinavians who descended from the Gothic tribes once under Hunnish command carried the memory of Attila with them as they migrated over the waves and settled Iceland and Greenland a thousand years ago. In the mouths of Leif Ericsson and his fellow Vikings, Attila had become "Atli," as fierce as the wind and waves of the North Sea. Atli was remembered as a greedy, bloodthirsty chieftain whose German wife wreaked an apocalyptic vengeance upon her husband: she cut out the hearts of their two sons and fed them to Atli on a plate before torching the palace and bringing the story to a fiery end. To the medieval French, Attila was remembered as the *flagellum Dei*, the Scourge of God, the ravager of Gaul's great cities—Orléans, Paris, Troyes—all of which were gallantly defended by brave bishops and virginal saints. To the medieval Italians, Attila was credited with founding Venice (inadvertently) when he destroyed the lagoon city of Aquileia in 452 and forced its survivors to seek refuge in the swamps.[7] To the medieval Hungarians, Attila was canonized as their first king, a wise and valiant leader, a "memory" that required a stunning rehabilitation of his character.

We don't have transcripts, video footage, or physical evidence to rely on as we reopen the case of Attila's death. But truth *can* be salvaged from the fables and myths that Attila's death inspired. It is possible to peel away the propaganda from the historical record, if we follow the lead of Jakob and

Wilhelm Grimm. We don't even have to carry bread crumbs with us. As Nietzsche reminded us, all we need is curiosity and an open mind.

ESCAPE FROM SIBERIA

Among those who have pursued the trail of Attila's death was a twentieth-century Hungarian philologist named Julius Moravcsik. The name became familiar to me, like that of an old friend, during my doctoral studies while scouring footnotes and bibliographies in the basement of the Wilson Library. It appeared often in the German *Zeitschriften* published between the World Wars—the kind of academic publications printed on such cheap acidic paper that they crumble into yellow dust when you take them off the library shelf.[8] But when the name popped up in a Google search—"Julius Moravcsik, Ph.D., Professor of Philosophy, Stanford University"—I took a special interest. Even if I were to adjust for the fabled longevity of philologists, this couldn't be *the* Julius Moravcsik who wrote the definitive study of Attila's death in 1932.[9]

I typed out a short e-mail to the professor, noting that one of the foundational sources in my own research was an article by "a certain Julius Moravcsik" entitled *Attilas Tod in Geschichte und Sage* ("Attila's Death in History and Legend"). "Is Julius Moravcsik, the Byzantine scholar, your father?" I asked, even though the answer seemed obvious enough. It wasn't, after all, a very common name. Two or three weeks later, the philosopher wrote me back.

Dear Prof. Babcock,
the person you mention was indeed my father, and one of the best byzantin-ologists of the past decades. He died some years ago. J. Moravcsik. Philos.

I wrote again, asking if there was any more information he could provide about his father's life and career. I never got a response.

There was much more the younger Moravcsik might have told me. He

Portrait of Jakob and Wilhelm Grimm. Best known for
collecting fairy tales, the Brothers Grimm were pioneers
in the new science of philology (the reconstruction
of texts and languages).
Austrian Archives / CORBIS

might have mentioned, for example, that his father was one of those brilliant
European scholars—a throwback to the days of Jakob and Wilhelm
Grimm—who cut his academic teeth on a dozen languages, rooted out manuscripts in obscure monastic libraries, and managed to advance our understanding of the past without the whole range of digital technology scholars
such as myself take for granted. These scholar adventurers were always on
the hunt for new discoveries—not the kind found in ancient tombs but discoveries teased from lines etched centuries ago on parchment. The popular

misconception that our knowledge of the past lurches forward through breathtaking discoveries is fed by the publicity and lore surrounding all the great archaeological finds of the modern era: Schliemann's excavation of Troy, the tomb of Tutankhamen, the Anglo-Saxon Sutton Hoo ship burial. The truth is far less glamorous and far more difficult to reduce to a headline. It is only through the patient, systematic, and unheralded work of philologists such as Julius Moravcsik that we have come to see the ancient world more clearly.

He was born in 1892 in Szeged on the Tisza River separating Hungary from Yugoslavia.[10] As a youth he would have heard the stories of Attila's death and secret burial that had become the staple of local nationalistic legend. Szeged, in particular, was a breeding ground for Attila legends during the time when Hungarian nationalism reached its peak in the late nineteenth century. Moravcsik went on to the University of Budapest, where he studied Greek, Latin, and Hungarian before furthering his education in Rome, Paris, and Munich. This intense background in languages was the ideal preparation for his life work. His curiosity had been kindled by those legends told along the banks of the Tisza River—legends about Hungary's past and especially Attila's life and death. Over the rest of his career Moravcsik would try to understand those legends within the historical framework of the Eastern Roman Empire.

His academic work was temporarily suspended with the onset of the Great War. All across the Continent a whole generation of young scholars was lost in World War I, but Moravcsik was one of the fortunate ones. He was captured and sent to a prison camp in Siberia, where he simply adapted to his new surroundings and—always the philologist—promptly set about learning Russian, modern Greek, and Turkish. After some time Moravcsik managed a daring escape along with several compatriots. A locomotive driver hid them in the water tanks on both sides of the train's steam boiler. All the way to St. Petersburg, Moravcsik's clothes were singed as he beat back the sparks while clutching the Turkish dictionary he had compiled in Siberia.

Like all the great philologists, Moravcsik viewed the past as a palimpsest that can only be read once the layers are painstakingly scraped away. This is exactly what he set out to do in his essay, "Attila's Death in History and Legend" (1932). But the conclusion he reached was somewhat anticlimactic. Moravcsik studied the texts in their original languages—Greek, Latin, Old Church Slavonic—and concluded that the "official" historical account was indeed correct.

Through the same methodology I have reached a very different conclusion: the official account of Attila's death is an elaborate cover story. How can a "science" yield such different answers? Philology is not a science in the same sense as DNA evidence or ballistics analysis. We've entered instead one of those murky areas, like psychology, where "expert testimony" must be relied on. The evidence never interprets itself. Two experts may weigh the same evidence according to completely different theories. Moravcsik reaffirmed the finding of the history books. Now it's time for the rebuttal.

THE OFFICIAL POSTMORTEM

The basic set of facts has never been in dispute: Attila married a German bride named Ildico, feasted riotously, and died in bed that very night from an internal hemorrhage. This official postmortem rests on an ancient source preserved in the Latin *Getica* of Jordanes.[11] The *Getica*, also known as the *Gothic History*, was written in Constantinople around 550 during the reign of Justinian the Great. It's a remarkably skillful work of propaganda, weaving together the histories of the Gothic tribes from various older sources, recounting their disastrous alliance with the Huns (from the Roman point of view), and encouraging them to embrace their new role as friends and servants of the Empire. The author, Jordanes, had a foot in both worlds—he was a Goth and a Roman citizen—and from that ambivalent position he looks back on the turbulent events of the fifth century. Much of what we know about this highly obscure (and pivotal) century in Roman history we know only from the *Getica* of Jordanes. Where the various chroniclers of the time give us nothing but a single stark sentence—"*Attila occiditur*," "Attila died"—Jordanes gives us the following full-blown account:

> Shortly before he died, as the historian Priscus relates, he took in marriage a very beautiful girl named Ildico, after countless other wives, as was the custom of his race. He had given himself up to excessive joy at his wedding, and as he lay on his back, heavy with wine and sleep, a rush of superfluous blood, which would ordinarily have flowed from his nose, streamed in deadly course down his throat and killed him, since it was hindered in the usual passages. Thus did drunkenness put a disgraceful end to a king renowned in war. On the following day, when a great part of the morning was spent, the royal attendants suspected some ill and, after a great uproar, broke in the doors. There they found the death of Attila accomplished by an effusion of blood, without any wound, and the girl with downcast face weeping beneath her veil.

No journalist today would go with a story that isn't double sourced; we can't be so picky when it comes to ancient history, though. Any source at all is a rare and precious thing, especially one as detailed and convincing as Jordanes appears to be. When we consider how Jordanes divulges his source ("as the historian Priscus relates"), we're led to believe the account is thoroughly reliable; and this is what historians have always concluded, beginning with Edward Gibbon in England and Tillemont in France.[12] Moravcsik, too, confirms its authenticity. But couldn't we just as easily suspect that the story—this single account of Attila's death—is a literary creation? After all, it reads like a dramatic set piece complete with worried palace guards and a maiden "weeping beneath her veil." The moralizing conclusion ("Thus did drunkenness put a disgraceful end to a king renowned in war") is more appropriately suited to one of Aesop's Fables than a sober historical account.

Not everybody has been convinced that the story Jordanes tells us is true. "Can Jordanes be trusted?" asked another great philologist, Frederick Klaeber, who was the world's foremost authority on Beowulf.[13] Born in Bismarck's Prussia, Klaeber took his Ph.D. in Berlin and emigrated to the United States, where he taught at the University of Minnesota from 1893 to his retirement in 1931. By the time I was a grad student at the University of Minnesota in the 1980s, his reputation had not diminished a bit. I remember studying Old English in Professor Kendall's class, where we would open Klaeber's edition to read the poem that begins with that wonderful exclamation *Hwæt!* The word "What!"—meaning, roughly, "Listen!"—was the Anglo-Saxon poet's call for everybody at the dinner table to pipe down and hear the story he was about to tell. "Listen!" could just as easily be what the philologist says as he teases out voices long silent in the text. What Klaeber heard behind the text of Jordanes was the story of Judith and Holofernes. Like Attila, the Assyrian general Holofernes died in a drunken stupor in the company of a woman, the Jewish heroine Judith.

EXHIBIT ONE

The historical version of Attila's death rests upon a single uncorroborated account that has suffered from textual corruption.

Is Jordanes giving us a literary re-creation of this famous story? Perhaps. But Klaeber's question ("Can Jordanes be trusted?") is rarely asked. Historians have always accepted that Jordanes inoculates himself from doubt by referring the facts back to Priscus. After all, Priscus had spent time at Attila's court and had observed him firsthand. The problem with this—and it's a big one—is one I've mentioned already: We don't have the original text Priscus wrote. So we have no way of independently verifying the facts. The history Priscus published in the early 470s was absorbed into a *Gothic History* written around 525 by a Roman aristocrat named Cassiodorus, which was itself absorbed into the abridged *Gothic History* Jordanes wrote around 550.[14] These earlier histories by Priscus and Cassiodorus were neglected and eventually lost as people began to consult the shorter version by Jordanes. The "original" source in Jordanes, then, is actually three steps removed from the actual event:

Attila's death (453) ➡ Priscus (c. 470) ➡ Cassiodorus (c. 525) ➡ Jordanes (c. 550)

Despite these problems, this sixth-century account of Attila's death was endorsed as "history" in the ancient world and has been viewed that way ever since. What we read today in encyclopedias and popular histories ultimately goes back to the *Gothic History*, though the more immediate influence is Gibbon's masterpiece of historical writing, *The Decline and Fall of the Roman Empire* (1776–1788). Gibbon was a great storyteller, and his vivid paraphrase of Jordanes is embellished with the kind of details and character motivations that make the old account more convincing than ever:[15]

> Before the king of the Huns evacuated Italy, he threatened to return more dreadful, and more implacable, if his bride, the princess Honoria, were not delivered to his ambassadors within the term stipulated by the treaty. Yet, in the mean while, Attila relieved his tender anxiety, by adding a beautiful maid, whose name was Ildico, to the list of his innumerable wives. Their marriage was celebrated with barbaric pomp and festivity, at his wooden palace beyond the Danube; and the monarch, oppressed with wine and sleep, retired at a late hour from the banquet to the nuptial bed. His attendants continued to respect his pleasures, or his repose, the greatest part of the ensuing day, till the unusual silence alarmed their fears and suspicions; and, after attempting to awaken Attila by loud and repeated cries, they at length broke into the royal apartment. They found the trembling bride sitting by the bedside, hiding her face with her veil, and lamenting her own danger, as well as the death of the king, who had expired during the night. An artery had suddenly burst: and as Attila lay in a supine posture, he was suffocated by a torrent of blood, which, instead of finding a passage through the nostrils, regurgitated into the lungs and stomach.

What's always most revealing in Gibbon's prose is how he manipulates the facts, how he connects the dots in a way not supported by his ancient source. We are to imagine Attila pining over Honoria and marrying Ildico (on the rebound, as it were) so as to "relieve his tender anxiety" over leaving Italy without his Roman bride. But as Gibbon certainly knew, these betrothals and marriages were nothing but political affairs. Here, as elsewhere, Gibbon is not offering sober analysis. He's simply winging it.

It would seem that Gibbon had personal reasons for connecting the dots the way he did.[16] As a young man in Lausanne, Switzerland, Edward fell in love with a woman named Suzanne Curchod. He later described in very simple terms what had happened to him: "I saw and loved." Edward promised Suzanne that he would return to marry her, as soon as he had informed his father back in England and secured his approval. The young man's joy turned to sorrow—"tender anxiety," we might say—when his father refused to bless this "strange alliance" between foreigners. Edward never married. In his *Autobiography*, Gibbon looked back at this and noted pithily: "I yielded to my fate: I sighed as a lover, I obeyed as a son." In a historical sense it is preposterous to imagine Attila ever "sighing as a lover," the way Gibbon has presented him. But then Gibbon is doing much more than writing history. He's investing this historical event with his own personality and inscribing himself into the story he's telling.

More embellishments follow. When Attila's door is broken down the following morning, Gibbon reports that Ildico is not just "hiding her face with her veil" (this much the ancient source relates); now she's "lamenting her own danger, as well as the death of the king." Reasonable inferences, perhaps, but these are judgments not expressed in Gibbon's source. Drawing out these inferences makes the historical account seem more plausible, more true to life, fleshed out with actual emotions, reactions, and responses. This is the temptation, of course, in all historical writing, especially the really good kind of writing that Gibbon gives us. The will to narrate sweeps aside the nagging question: *How do we know this is what really happened?* In telling a good story—and telling it well—the historian tries to navigate between a dry, excruciatingly accurate style with ponderous footnotes on the one hand, and (on the other) a fictionalized, romanticized history with its pre-ciosities, anachronisms, and at least one "she exclaimed with a sigh" on every page.

Gibbon's weaknesses are well known to scholars, but not so well known to a public that reads the various popular histories filtered through his in-fluential prose. One of these histories is Will and Ariel Durant's eleven-volume *The Story of Civilization*. These readable volumes entered middle-class American life in 1959 as the standard historical reference work—a new-subscriber premium for joining the Book-of-the-Month Club. (When I joined the Club in the late 1970s, I opted for the compact version of the *Oxford English Dictionary*, the kind that takes a special magnifying glass to read.) We probably shouldn't hold the Durants to a very high standard, saddled as they were with the burden of narrating *all* of history. Nonethe-less, here's how Attila's death comes off in their account:

> Meanwhile he [Attila] consoled himself by adding to his harem a young lady named Ildico. . . . He celebrated the wedding with an unusual indul-gence in food and drink. On the morrow he was found in bed beside his young wife; he had burst a blood vessel, and the blood in his throat had choked him to death.[17]

The Durants do not cite Gibbon, but they should have, since they cribbed his account. Instead, they follow Gibbon's lead by footnoting Jordanes, even though it appears they never consulted the original source. Gibbon's finger-prints are everywhere. What gives them away is the opening statement that "Attila consoled himself by adding to his harem"—an anachronistic inter-pretation not found in Jordanes but which is a loose paraphrase of Gibbon's self-indulgent prose. The Durants seem not to have noticed that Edward is still thinking about Suzanne.

Since we can never read the mind of an author, we've got to settle for the next best thing: reading the mind of the text. The side-by-side comparison of these two modern texts—Gibbon and the Durants—has given us a simple example of how the philological method works. Whether we're reading an-

Portrait of Edward Gibbon (1737–94), British historian best
known for *The Decline and Fall of the Roman Empire.*
Bettmann / CORBIS

cient texts (the usual object of philological study) or modern ones such as
these, the goal is always the same: to reconstruct the circumstances that produced the text as we have it. Of course, we can't say with certainty that Gibbon is transcribing his own life into his account of Attila; but we do know
that historians carry all sorts of personal, social, and political baggage into
everything they write. And though we can't be dogmatic, we can tease out
plausible reconstructions that take us beyond the naive acceptance (on the
one hand) of a reader who resists "reading between the lines," or the agnostic resignation (on the other hand) of a scholar who believes that the past is
irretrievably lost. The philologist's goal is always to reconstruct an older
form of the text, because we are certain that an older form exists. We know

that something else lies behind the text, motivating it and providing a context for its interpretation. That "something else" might be the propaganda machine of a decaying Empire (Jordanes), the memory of a woman in Lausanne (Gibbon), or the sloppiness of authors who copy another historian without checking the original source (the Durants). Comparison and reconstruction—what Nietzsche called "slow reading"—is the stuff of philology, and it's the stuff that will help us identify Attila's killer.

MARCIAN'S DREAM

It would seem that the Latin of Jordanes is as close as we can get to the night Attila died: one hundred years and three historians removed from the facts. But the tools of philology make it possible for us to figure out what Priscus originally wrote in his Greek history. In doing this, we'll discover that Priscus did, in fact, write the account that Jordanes has attributed to him. But here's the caveat: *Priscus also knew more, and wrote more, than Jordanes has chosen to preserve.* Priscus related a far more sensational account of Attila's death, one that was later suppressed when Jordanes drafted his abridgement of the *Gothic History*. In the following chapters, we'll be looking over the shoulder of the Greek historian, reconstructing what he knew and when he knew it.

The American historian Carl Becker observed that "every age is bound, in spite of itself, to make the dead perform whatever tricks it finds necessary for its own peace of mind."[18] That probably explains the curious story that forms an addendum to the ancient account of Attila's death. On the night Attila died, Emperor Marcian had a dream. Here's how Jordanes relates the event:

> Moreover a wondrous thing took place in connection with Attila's death. For in a dream some god stood at the side of Marcian, Emperor of the East, while he was disquieted about his fierce foe, and showed him the bow of Attila broken in that same night, as if to intimate that the race of the Huns owed much to that weapon.[19]

Marcian, we can be sure, dreamed no such thing. (Ancient histories are full of timely dreams like this.) And yet Jordanes refers us back once again to the authority of Priscus, just as he did with Attila's death. "This account," Jordanes writes, "the historian Priscus says he accepts upon truthful evidence." The story of the broken bow was propaganda, one of many flattering stories Marcian apparently sponsored during his reign.[20] But beyond the story's obvious function in enhancing the emperor's prestige, it may also serve as an unintended confessional. Of course, Marcian would have had advance word of Attila's death, if he planned that death in the first place. Though the story is probably not historical, it does show Priscus tipping his hand, pointing us to the one person who had the most to gain from Attila's death.

Since Priscus was willing to be Marcian's mouthpiece in this case, why should we accept at face value what he tells us about Attila's death? Historians have been too ready to impute a modern journalistic mind-set to the Greek historian, as, for example, when Julius Moravcsik approvingly noted "the objective voice" of Priscus.[21] But Priscus would not have remained long on the imperial payroll if he had not demonstrated a flair for propaganda. What we need is a more sophisticated view of this ancient historian, one that can accommodate both the accuracy of an eyewitness account and the slanted judgments of a Byzantine bureaucrat.

Dredging up those questions of *how* and *who*—questions first asked in the shops and warehouses and palaces of Constantinople—might be a futile exercise if it weren't for one simple fact: the official version of Attila's death cannot be trusted. Of course, we cannot rule out that the account *might* be true: Attila *might* have died from a nosebleed. But the historical "certainty" of this rests upon a very narrow ridge of evidence: a single account by one man whose job description (in part) was to make the emperor look good. Though an eyewitness to Attila and his court, Priscus was not an eyewitness to his death. Whatever he knew of the night Attila died he would have culled secondhand from the rumor mills of Constantinople. And what Priscus ultimately chose to write down, once he had sorted through the competing stories available to him, would have served the larger goals of the Empire. Serving the goals of the Empire is exactly what Priscus was doing when Attila died. In 453 this mild-mannered but ambitious clerk was far away in Egypt on a diplomatic mission—one that nearly took his life.

TWO

FROM THE WOMBS OF WITCHES

OR the first time in his young career, Priscus was entirely alone—disturbingly so—as he stood on the streets of Alexandria in the middle of a riot, watching the Temple of Seraphis burn to the ground.[22] It was a bad time and a bad place to be a Roman diplomat, considering that Roman diplomats inside the temple were being burned alive. A more experienced ambassador, like Maximin, would probably know what to do. But Maximin was dead. His secretary, Priscus—who was more comfortable reading Herodotus than negotiating for his life—would have to figure this one out on his own.

A BADLY RUN MUSEUM

The career of this unlikely diplomat began four years earlier, somewhat abruptly, when Maximin invited Priscus to come along on a sensitive mission far to the north. Priscus agreed to go, and after that first unforgettable trip to Attila's court in 449, he stayed on as Maximin's secretary and personal assistant. Maximin was a senior diplomat of the Eastern Roman court in Constantinople, a roving ambassador, and so Priscus found himself in an unusually privileged position to witness history. And not just to witness history but also to shape how the history of his times would be written.

They made an interesting team: The older man was experienced in war and peace, the younger man in rhetoric and philosophy. Maximin was a retired general whose reputation as a diplomat rested on a single spectacular success: negotiating peace with the Persians back in 422. But he never lived up to that first big impression, and in his final missions—the ones Priscus witnessed—he comes off as a prime example of the Peter Principle: Maximin had risen to his level of mediocrity. At least that's how Priscus portrayed his boss in the tell-all history he published some twenty years later, the insider's memoir that is our major source of information about Attila the Hun. This history has come down to us in fragments, but there's enough left to give us a fairly good portrait—if only in the nuances of the text—of all the principal characters in this story. The portrait of Attila is famous for good reason; as a contemporary eyewitness description of a barbarian, it is perhaps without parallel in ancient literature. Less well known, but no less important to cracking the case of Attila's murder, are the portraits of the minor characters that emerge from this history—the close-up look we get at Priscus himself, of Maximin, and of the whole imperial bureaucracy in which they served.

Take Maximin. He seems to have been a genial and well-intentioned old man who plodded along in the best interests of the Roman Empire. His biggest shortcoming may have been his utter guilelessness, a *really* serious deficiency if you were working within a Byzantine court. Everyone else in the court was plotting, not *plodding*, and if you couldn't see that, then perhaps you'd end up exactly as he did in 449 when he and Priscus stood before Attila, completely unaware that they were there to assassinate the Hun. But more about that later.

Needless to say, Maximin's diplomatic missions never failed to become improvised adventures somewhere along the way. This trip, which landed Priscus in front of a burning temple, would be no exception. It had started when Emperor Marcian sent the diplomatic partners, Maximin and Priscus, to Damascus in 451 or 452. Their assignment was to bring a little finesse to the ongoing efforts at pacifying the local Arab population, the Saracens. Ardabur, a highly decorated Roman general, had already defeated the Saracens in battle and was wrapping up a peace treaty by the time Maximin and Priscus arrived. There was little left for them to do, which must have annoyed Priscus deeply. Why else would he go out of his way to describe Ardabur as an effeminate, dissolute ruler, once valorous in battle, but who had now settled into the easy life of a provincial ruler whose only aspirations (according to Priscus) were to lounge around eating grapes and watching jugglers all day?

Actually a very good reason comes to mind, and it has nothing to do with sour grapes in Damascus. Priscus is describing this event, as he would also describe the death of Attila, from a distance of twenty years. His history was published sometime in the early 470s, years after Emperor Marcian's death and during the reign of Leo "the Butcher." Leo earned his nickname by killing his rival, Aspar, in the palace and slaughtering his whole family, including his son, Ardabur. This would be *the* Ardabur from Damascus. The unmotivated criticism that Priscus levels at Ardabur probably reflects the fact that Priscus wasn't too upset by what Leo had done. After all, Leo was a problem solver, like Marcian before him, and sometimes solving problems means killing one's enemies. (Attila comes to mind.) As he looked back on his time in Damascus, Priscus didn't remember the general who served the Empire with honor. He remembered instead a pansy with a weakness for jugglers. This ancient historian, whose "objectivity" has so impressed the modern scholar, managed to get his digs in.

Since Ardabur clearly had the situation in Damascus under control (the jugglers testified to that), Maximin and Priscus were dispatched to the Empire's next hot spot, Egypt. A conflict had been brewing on the upper Nile; the local population east of Thebes, the Blemmyes, were protesting the Roman occupation.[23] In truth, they posed no real military threat to Rome—they were simply cattle raiders and worshipers of Isis—but any instability in the Empire's bread basket was a matter of grave concern.

Once home to the pharaohs, Thebes had become a dingy outpost on the fringes of the Roman Empire, a remote museum of antiquities. The magnificent temples and obelisks built in the distant past were still standing, but no one could read the peculiar stone markings any longer. At some point in the fourth or fifth century the hieroglyphic art was lost to Egypt's scribes, not to be recovered until Champollion cracked the code of the Rosetta Stone in 1822. The ancient world was passing away, and its languages, mysteries, and secrets would remain hidden for centuries until another group of scribes, modern philologists, would come along and try to piece that lost world together again. How successful we've been at doing this is a matter of considerable debate. But there can be little doubt that a young historian such as Priscus would have understood that deep desire to connect ourselves to the distant past. He felt it too. It's not hard to imagine him gaping wide-eyed at the wonders of Egypt as he sailed down the Nile. He knew Herodotus well—he quoted him often—and Priscus must have felt that he was retracing the steps of the original scholar-adventurer who had marveled at these very sights some nine hundred years before.

When Maximin and Priscus arrived in Thebes, they found a city overrun by swamp disease and squabbling pagans. Desert monasteries had been springing up left and right throughout the Nile region of southern Egypt. As Christian hermits moved into the caves and mountains around the Valley of the Kings, one culture gradually supplanted another. The worship of Isis was giving way to the worship of Christ, and the Blemmyes were the only holdouts in this slow war of attrition. After intense lobbying by St. Ambrose, Theodosius the Great had outlawed the worship of all pagan gods back in 392. But fifty years later, the tribesmen who controlled the vast stretches from the Nile to the Red Sea were stubborn in their unbelief. Each year these recalcitrant pagans would leave the hills of Ethiopia and journey to the Temple of Isis at Philae. On this island in the Nile the ancient priesthood and its hieroglyphic script were kept alive by their patronage. Two years after Theodosius had issued his injunction, the Blemmyes made their annual pilgrimage. A young man named Nesmeterakhem, who described himself as the son of a priest and "the Scribe of the House of Writings," picked up his

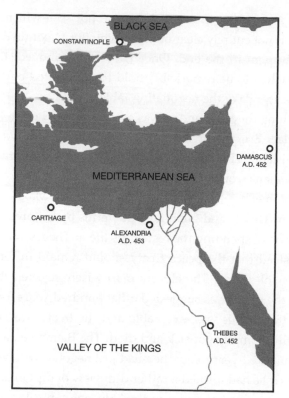

A reconstruction of the diplomatic journey of Maximin
and Priscus south from Constantinople in A.D. 452
Maximin died in Thebes, Egypt. Priscus continued the
journey north to Alexandria, where he would have
learned the news about Attila's death.
Map by Matthew Pamer

chisel and hammer and commemorated the visit in hieroglyphics on the
wall of the Philae temple. It was August 24, 394. This would be the last
recorded instance of hieroglyphic writing in the ancient world.[24]

Fifty-eight years later the Christians tried one more time to close down
the Temple of Isis. The imperial mood certainly favored a crackdown. Religious councils were in full swing in Constantinople, and Emperor Marcian
was prosecuting heresy and paganism with a vengeance. The Blemmyes re-
sisted violently and Maximin was sent south. He was sent either as a general

to fight or as a diplomat to negotiate, we're not sure which. The account Priscus wrote is not entirely clear on this point. But Maximin did end up negotiating with them in the end. Once they were subdued, the Blemmyes showed themselves to be remarkably bold for a defeated party, presuming even to set the agenda at the negotiating table.

The one thing they demanded was access, free and clear, to the Temple of Isis at Philae. Every year they came with their gifts and were ferried across to the island. They would be very happy to stop harassing the Romans if the Romans would just leave them alone. As for how long the treaty should remain in effect, the Blemmyes suggested that Maximin should take up residence in Thebes and guarantee the terms by his presence. Maximin had no intention of spending the rest of his life in Thebes, so the barbarians suggested instead that the peace treaty should remain in force as long as Maximin was still living. The elderly man wisely rejected these terms as well. Finally, the Blemmyes suggested a flat hundred years for the duration of the peace treaty. This was acceptable and the treaty was signed, whereupon Maximin promptly got sick and died. The Blemmyes wasted no time voiding the hundred-year treaty they had just negotiated. One could hardly blame Priscus if he had formed a rather dim view of diplomacy by now.

Today, on the island of Philae in the Nile, one can still read the faint inscription that was made December 19, 452, when the treaty was signed. On the roof of the temple's porch, under a drawing of a pilgrim's feet, the inscription simply reads: "The feet of Panakhetet the lesser." It is written in demotic, a commercial script widely used in ancient Egypt.[25] This reference to Panakhetet's feet is the last known instance of demotic writing—a humble ending (a footnote, as it were) to thousands of years of continuous Egyptian history. Ancient Egyptian writing, both hieroglyphics and demotic, reached the end of the line here at Philae, and that end coincided, curiously, with the diplomatic mission of Maximin and Priscus. This last living monument of ancient paganism, the Temple of Isis at Philae, survived the pharaohs, the Greeks, the Romans, the desert monks, the rise of Islam, the Ottoman Empire, the British and French occupations—only to be threatened with destruction in the 1960s when the Aswan Dam was built. For five years

Christians and Muslims joined in their efforts to take the temple apart block by block and reassemble it on higher ground nearby. Thus, access to this pagan shrine has been assured, for tourists if not for votaries. In the end, the original terms of Maximin's treaty have been honored.

MISSION TO ALEXANDRIA

What happened next we don't know. Maximin was dead, and it's tempting to conclude from the textual silence that Priscus just threw up his hands and caught the first boat north. It's more likely, however, that we've hit one of those blank spots in the fragments—a gap in the text, or a lacuna, as philologists call them—where what Priscus wrote has not survived. Somehow, though, toward the end of 452 he ended up in the coastal city of Alexandria where things were just as chaotic as they were in the south. The local bishop, Dioscorus, had been removed from his office the year before by the Council of Chalcedon. Under the patronage of Emperor Marcian and his wife Pulcheria, bishops had gathered in Constantinople from all across the Christian world in 451 to decide once and for all the Church's position on the nature of Christ. For several weeks the delegates wrangled over which Greek preposition best captured the divine mystery—the "hypostatic union" of God and man. We look at this now as a red-letter event in the history of the Church; Emperor Marcian saw it as a political mess and a headache that wouldn't go away.

How did Chalcedon play back in Alexandria? For the man on the street, it all came down to the principle of the thing. Not that the average Alexandrian cared a whit for the theological intricacies that led the council to label the popular Dioscorus a heretic and remove him from office. The principle that really set them off was a political one: The Empire had no business meddling in their hometown affairs. Riots ensued. The Roman officials sought to control the crowds by suspending chariot races and closing down the public bakeries. It was a bad call. Now with a whole host of grievances—specific theological positions ranking fairly low on the list—

the rioters chased the Romans into a temple and burned them to death. That's about the time Priscus arrived on the scene. He had come straight from the disaster in Thebes, and found himself in immediate peril of his life.

The surviving account is short on details. From what can be gathered between the surviving lines, Priscus sensed that the local Roman ruler, Florus, needed all the help he could get and was fortunate to have such a talented young man as Priscus show up in the nick of time. Priscus advised Florus to reverse the hard-line policy in classic Roman fashion ("Give them bread and circuses"), and civic order was soon restored. It was the obvious thing to do, not a stroke of diplomatic brilliance, and the idea must already have occurred to Florus. The political logic went something like this: The people had started off being angry that Dioscorus was fired. Then they got even angrier when their bread and circuses were taken away. Give them back the bread and circuses and they'd forget about Dioscorus. Advantage Empire.

In a curious, offhanded way Priscus tells us that Florus decided on this policy change "at the emperor's suggestion." It's an odd detail to include when so much else has been omitted. Considering that the emperor was in Constantinople and the riot was spiraling out of control across the sea in Alexandria, it wouldn't have made sense to wait two or three weeks for instructions to arrive by ship. It must have been Priscus, then, who urged Florus to resume the public services, and the phrase "at the emperor's suggestion" merely conveys that he was acting in the official capacity of a diplomat. Obviously, it would be too bold to credit himself directly. But by dropping into his text the superfluous phrase, "at the emperor's suggestion," Priscus guarantees that we'll see *him* behind the action. The young diplomat was hitting his stride, seizing the initiative, and even managing to do what Maximin could never quite master: the fine diplomatic art of taking credit for a sure thing. Somewhere between Thebes and Alexandria, this once reluctant secretary had been promoted to ambassador, either officially or unofficially, after Maximin's sudden demise. Priscus would make the most of this opportunity as he emerged from the shadow of the great diplomat who (truth be told) had been irrelevant in Damascus and ineffective in

Thebes. The contrast between the two diplomats is striking: Priscus was decisive when he acted and deliberate when he wrote. In this minor episode we get a first glimpse into his mind; we see Priscus demonstrating the canniness and resourcefulness that would shape his famous account of the night Attila died.

EXHIBIT TWO

Priscus was not an objective narrator but a government employee who was skeptical, inquisitive, self-serving, and rhetorical.

In light of these biographical and historical factors, it's hard to justify the certainty so often expressed that "Attila died thus and so." Priscus eventually wrote down the details of an event that he "witnessed" only from a great distance. He was constrained by his position within the imperial bureaucracy. He was possessed of an inquisitive and skeptical personality. That's why he is such a pivotal witness in this case—one we must question very closely. Not only does the historical account of Attila's death rest entirely upon his word (as preserved by Jordanes), but it also turns out that he's an ironic (which is to say, not entirely trustworthy) narrator. To be sure, Priscus was a skilled propagandist who towed the party line; but he drops clues into his text that often point us toward very different conclusions. Maximin had towed the party line as well; but, judging from what Priscus says, he didn't have an ironic bone in his body. In this mission to Alexandria we watch a young diplomat who is growing into his job. We also see a scholar and historian who, like Edward Gibbon, ended up producing a document that was almost as much about himself as the events he purported to describe.

After the smoke settled and the riots died down, Priscus stayed on for several months in Alexandria. Florus no doubt had more work for Priscus the diplomat, but Priscus the scholar was himself in no hurry to leave a city that was synonymous with the life of the mind. This was not just the city of Alexander, Julius Caesar, and Cleopatra, it was also the city of Euclid and Archimedes, Manetho and Philo. The libraries back in Constantinople might have been good, but this one was *great*. Everything that had ever been written was here, rolled up in individual scrolls and catalogued neatly on shelves. And when he strolled down to the harbor, Priscus could see ships coming into port from all over the world, drawn like magnets to the lighthouse—*the* Lighthouse, one of the Seven Wonders of the Ancient World, as tall as a forty-story building. Thirty-five miles out at sea, sailors could see the light reflecting off the mirror that was mounted, along with Poseidon, at the top of the tower.

Then one day an ordinary ship from Constantinople arrived in the harbor. It carried an extraordinary message.

In a scene that was reenacted dozens of times across the Empire, the crew disembarked and the news spilled out onto the dock and into the streets. *Attila is dead.* Priscus must have rushed down to the dock when he heard the news. The spell of antiquity was broken, and Priscus was brought back to the here and now, back to a story he was personally invested in. Everyone knew the terrible name, but Priscus was the only one in Alexandria who had ever met Attila, sat across the dinner table from him, and scrutinized the very lines in his face.

One can imagine Priscus tracking down the ship's crew and pumping them for details. The accounts he heard were a bundle of fragments and contradictions, rumors that were well on their way to becoming the legends of medieval poetry. Priscus knew he'd have to get closer to the scene if he wanted to pursue the truth of the matter. His trusted sources in Constantinople would have to be interviewed and travelers from the North would have to be debriefed. All the evidence would be carefully weighed, and then something would be written down for posterity. We now read his account through the fog of fifteen hundred years. But we're pretty much in the same position as Priscus when he looked out across the sea and tried to grasp the meaning of this latest twist in the story of his times. Though he had more immediate resources at his disposal, Priscus would still have to plow through the fog of initial reports. He would return to Constantinople and there continue to write his history.

The narrative Priscus wrote of his life and times is one of the most remarkable documents that has come down to us from the years known as late antiquity. Priscus takes one of history's most notable tragedies—the Fall of the Western Roman Empire—and wraps it up within a hundred comic moments, none of which is of any great importance by itself. We read of blustering generals, incompetent bureaucrats, petty tyrants, and powerful matriarchs. It's practically Shakespearean, though without the poetry. What holds it all together are the experiences and impressions of one insignificant man, a bureaucrat—a clever one, but a bureaucrat nonetheless.

As he sailed back to Constantinople, the old city of Byzantium, Priscus was looking out on a world that was crumbling. In another time and place, W. B. Yeats described a world in which "things fall apart," a world in which "the center cannot hold." Certainly Romans viewed their own times this way. Priscus had seen "mere anarchy" loosed upon the streets of Thebes and Alexandria. As he sailed out of the harbor, past the great Lighthouse and toward the Bosporus, he was sailing toward a future he had already glimpsed in Egypt: a shrinking Empire, religious factionalism, diplomatic impotence, and the loss of ancient knowledge. Rome had retreated from Britain, the Vandals were poised to sack the Roman capital in 455, and (in the centuries to come) the destruction of Alexandria's fabled library would be complete. In every way imaginable, his world was changing.

THE WORLD IN A.D. 453

In order to wrap our minds around the chaotic world of 453, we must first set aside the popular image of Rome as a single Empire stretching outward from the Italian peninsula. In reality, Rome had long since become two political entities— a Western and Eastern Empire with separate capitals in

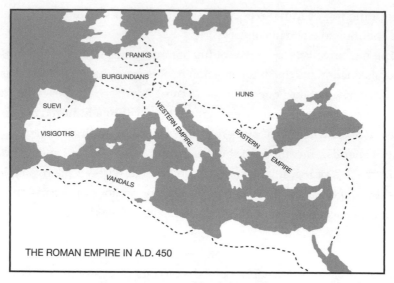

THE ROMAN EMPIRE IN A.D. 450

In A.D. 450 the Roman Empire was governed by separate emperors in the east and west. The Western Empire was gradually being lost to the barbarian tribes and would ultimately succumb in 476. The Eastern Empire would survive (as the Byzantine Empire) until 1453.

Map by Matthew Pamer

Rome and Constantinople. Connected by imperial bloodlines and a common history, the two halves of the Roman Empire would gradually diverge toward very different destinies.

In the year Attila died, the imperial purple was worn by Marcian in the Eastern capital. The Eastern Empire would quickly forget its death struggle with Attila, surviving him by exactly one millennium when Constantinople was finally overrun by the Ottoman Turks. In the Western half of the Empire, however, Rome was quickly heading toward the "ash heap of history." The emperor in the West, Valentinian III, occupied an office that boasted an impressive history but no longer wielded any real power. Valentinian and his court shuttled back and forth between Rome and Ravenna, unaware that their world was coming apart and impotent to do anything about it. With a mere twenty-three years left to stand, in 453 the Western Empire was in its last generation, at least by Edward Gibbon's reckoning.

Not much was left in the West to defend besides the Eternal City herself. One by one the provinces were being abandoned to barbarian tribes. In Britannia, for example, Saxon keels in 453 were bringing German immigrants to the British coast. The Roman armies that had occupied the island for over four hundred years were withdrawn in the early fifth century, never to return. The Roman capital was now threatened, and the remnants of Rome's military machine were pulled back toward Italy in one final effort to save the Empire. Left behind in Britain were the settlers, of Roman stock but now fully "British," native generals such as Ambrosius Aurelianus whose exploits in facing down the Anglo-Saxon invaders would be remembered in centuries to come as the adventures of King Arthur and his knights.[26]

In that same year, 453, a young priest in Ireland named Patrick was alive and "flourishing," as old history books used to say, plucking clovers from the field and holding them up to illustrate the inscrutable doctrine of the Trinity. By 453 the Merovingian dynasty was becoming established in Gaul; Clovis, who is sometimes called the first king of France, would be born just a few years later. And in Germania, in the valley of the Rhine, the story of a minor war twenty years before (the so-called Fall of the Burgundians) was well on its way to becoming the national legend that would capture Wagner's imagination. In 453 Rome was dying; but in the Roman provinces and beyond, the great nations of Europe were being born, and with them their historical and legendary heroes—Arthur, Patrick, Clovis, Siegfried. The split between East and West was now final, and Constantinople would have to muddle on by itself, which it did rather gloriously for another thousand years.

Looking back, it all seems inevitable. As early as the reign of Marcus Aurelius (161–80), thoughtful Roman leaders—and there were a few—had worried about an overextended Empire and had been tinkering with various forms of joint rule. These experiments would continue for another three hundred years, symptoms that Rome had become ungovernable. Emperor Diocletian took the boldest step toward reining in the unwieldy Empire. His great innovation was the "tetrarchy," a system instituted in 286 in which authority was shared between two or among four emperors, each one responsible for one of Rome's frontiers. The Empire could thus respond more quickly to the threats of invading barbarians or ambitious usurpers. At least that's what Diocletian claimed.

But there was a downside to the reforms. Political power became so decentralized by the end of the third century that Rome was no longer the nerve center of the Empire, though it remained the most prestigious city, the symbol of Rome's history and destiny. There were now many capitals—wherever a given emperor happened to set up his office: Thessalonica, Nicomedia, Trier, Milan, Ravenna. Emperors seldom lived in Rome any longer, and the ancient city on the Tiber ceased to function as the Empire's capital in any meaningful sense. Early in the fourth century the Empire once again began to coalesce around a new center of power in the East. Constantine relocated the imperial capital to a city that he named after himself. The new capital of Constantinople would be built on the thin strip of land where Europe and Asia come together along the Straits of Bosporus. This old Greek settlement of Byzantium underwent major building projects in the early fourth century and soon lived up to its reputation as the New Rome. The prestige of Rome itself would endure, but from this point on Constantinople would be the Empire's most important city.

The last man to reign unchallenged over a united Roman Empire was Theodosius the Great (379–95), so named for his dogged defense of the Church against the Arian heresy and his military successes against Goths and Huns. Before his death in 395, Theodosius had come to the sad realization that neither of his two young sons shared his genius. Once again the old formula of joint rule was put into effect. Arcadius would rule in the East and Honorius in the West. The division of the Empire was now formalized as a political reality. Neither son proved his father wrong. Where their father had held the Empire entirely in his grip, each son was unable to control effectively the half that had been entrusted to him. Honorius had the hardest time of it in the West, presiding over insurrections and the first sacking of Rome by the Goths in 410.

All the political skills that Theodosius had possessed directly bypassed the men and went straight to the women of the family. These daughters and granddaughters were the natural-born leaders, capable and strong, unafraid of taking risks. Foremost among them was Galla Placidia, who was probably the best-connected woman in all of Roman history. She was a daughter of the great Theodosius, but she was also a granddaughter, niece, grandniece, second cousin, aunt, wife, and mother of Roman emperors. As the mother of Valentinian III, Galla Placidia practically ruled the Western Empire from 425 until her death in 450.

In the East, a granddaughter of Theodosius would similarly dominate the political scene in Constantinople. Pulcheria was the daughter of Arcadius, the granddaughter of Theodosius, and the sister of the hopelessly inept emperor Theodosius II.[27] When her brother died in 450, Pulcheria became the empress in the East, ruling for a month until, for propriety's sake, she submitted herself in marriage to a distinguished old senator named Marcian. The House of Theodosius finally had a strong male leader once again, even if he had been acquired through an expedient marriage. Marcian was a pragmatist with a keen strategic eye. His wife was a saint—literally—who had taken a vow of perpetual virginity and was on a career track toward canonization.

Thus Marcian entered the family business. In the half century following the death of Theodosius in 395, the politics of East and West would be shaped largely by the fortunes of the bloodline of the great Theodosius. This dynasty is central to the story of Attila's demise, since maintaining the Empire intact became the chief mission of the Theodosian House for two generations. Even after the royal line had died out, the desperate men who battled for power in the West grasped for any connection, however slight, to the name of Theodosius. There was political capital, instant legitimacy, to be gained from the lingering mystique of Rome's last great imperial family.

But the house did die out and the West was lost. The last scenes of this protracted drama were playing out when Priscus published his narrative in the early 470s. The center of political gravity had now shifted entirely to Constantinople, completing a process begun almost two centuries before. This eastward shift of Roman power has major implications for how we understand the death of Attila. In the popular imagination Attila has always been pictured with Rome squarely in view: the symbol of Western civilization under the shadow of the world's preeminent barbarian. And though the Western Empire does play a significant role in the historical account, Attila's threat was just as often directed toward the East. If we are to understand Attila's death as history, not fiction, then we must look at the facts from an Eastern perspective, reliving as best we can what we find in the first-person narrative of Priscus.

PRISCUS OF PANIUM

Priscus was born early in the fifth century in Panium, a small town in Thrace, a Roman province that corresponds more or less to modern-day Bulgaria.[28] Thrace was a land of rich coastal plains and rolling hills, known in ancient times for its wine and gold. It was also the birthplace of one of the world's great storytellers, Aesop, and one of its greatest philosophers, Aristotle. Priscus, too, was a storyteller and a philosopher of sorts, though his fame rests upon the last-minute decision he made to accompany Maximin on an official expedition north from Constantinople, beyond Thrace, far into the land of wolves and witches. Edward Gibbon judged that Priscus "deserved, by his eloquence, an honorable place among the sophists of his age."[29] But in reality his place in history was assured only by the striking eyewitness account he wrote of this one trip.

This highly personal account places Priscus among the rarest of ancient historians—one who emerges flesh and blood from the scant fragments of parchment and ink. The history that he wrote of his life and times stands in sharp contrast to the dull registers of doubtful facts so characteristic of his age.[30] Priscus had an eye for the kind of vivid, realistic detail we expect from a Charles Dickens novel: Attila eating from a wooden bowl, the wool mats covering the floor of the queen's hut, the white linen canopies held aloft when Attila passed by. The fresh immediacy of his style, as though he were feeding text right into an Internet blog, has made him the darling of modern historians. An "acute journalistic account" written with "real dramatic power" is how the authoritative 1911 edition of the *Encyclopedia Britannica* describes his style. Clearly, the style of writing is seductive—and misleading. Just because Priscus felt the world deeply doesn't mean that he was impartial. If anything, it means just the opposite. The starting point for Priscus was always what could be filtered through his own experience, and the death of Attila was no exception.

Like every other Roman citizen, Priscus asked the same predictable questions when he first heard the news: *Who killed Attila, and why?* Everyone else returned easily to the mundane concerns of life, especially in the distant regions of the Empire, like Alexandria, where Attila was just a name in a headline. This was no idle speculation for Priscus, though. It was more like an obsession, something he kept mulling over in his head. *Who killed Attila?* After all, he had gained crucial inside knowledge on his first diplomatic trip to the North. The trip had been a colossal failure as events spun wildly out of control. Good training, as it turned out, for what would later happen in Egypt. Now, while sailing back home from Alexandria, he replayed that first trip in his mind, certain that the truth could be found in the details he had witnessed and the characters he had observed.

The year was 449.[31] "By his entreaties," Priscus wrote, "Maximin persuaded me to set out on this embassy with him." Was Priscus truly reluctant? Or is he plugging his own importance, making himself appear (as he remembers it twenty years later) to be an indispensable member of the delegation? Maximin had been personally recruited by the emperor, Theodosius II, to head up the diplomatic team going north. It was a risky gamble sending Maximin, for though he was a long-standing and high-ranking member of the bureaucracy, he did not hold the lofty rank of consul. This might be a problem, since Attila had often shown himself to be a little testy in negotiations. It didn't take much to set him off. The usual tirade would begin with accusations of Roman disrespect, and would end with the assertion that "Attila, too, is the son of a king."

It's not clear what Maximin hoped to gain by asking Priscus along. By training and temperament Priscus was a thoroughly intellectual type—a "rhetorician" and a "sophist," as he's called in the old Byzantine source-books, which translates roughly into our vernacular as "geek." He had composed a work known as the *Rhetorical Exercises* (thank God this didn't survive) as well as numerous letters. Regrettably, we have none of the letters; but we do have enough fragments from his eight-volume *History* to give us a good peek inside his mind. His career as a historian—and one of the most important historians of late antiquity, at that—may have been something he stumbled into, much like his diplomatic career. Perhaps Maximin was grooming him for the foreign service. Or he may have wanted a trustworthy companion who could carry on a good conversation around the campfire. It may have been that Maximin had already pegged Priscus as a savvy problem solver whose unique skills might be needed in a pinch. Whatever the reason, Maximin did ask, and Priscus did hem and haw (or he pretended to) before offering his talents to the Empire. For all we know, he might have had his bags packed all along.

If Priscus had stayed home, we might never have known his name. He would have sunk into the nameless ranks of the Byzantine bureaucracy. But he couldn't have been thinking of us when he decided to go. So what did he hope to gain? Why did he leave the comfort and security of urban life to rough it in the uncharted North? The spirited nature of his story gives us a clue: Priscus loved a good adventure. As it turned out, this trip to Attila's court would be the seminal event of his career, the one that catapulted him into literary prominence. Among all the things he wrote, the extended narrative of his journey to Attila's camp has survived in one piece even while the bulk of his history has been lost.[32] Too bad for us the whole thing didn't survive, considering the rich resources Priscus had at his disposal: his own personal adventures, the deep political contacts he had fostered, and all the material (now lost) that was in the imperial archives. Fortunately, later writers did quote Priscus at length, the way college freshmen drop whole chunks of books into their research papers. We call it plagiarism, but that's how books were written in the ancient world.

Was Priscus a pagan? What about Maximin? It's long been assumed, without any evidence at all, that if one man was a pagan, then the other man must have been as well. The evidence is sparse. It's worth noting, though, that Maximin was promoted by Emperor Marcian, who was no pagan, but a Second Constantine and the husband of a saint. In Marcian's administration, Maximin became a grand chamberlain, one of the four top ministers of the government—an unlikely position for a pagan.[33] On the other side of the ledger, some have sensed that Maximin was tolerant of the Blemmyes because of his own pagan convictions. Edward Gibbon "suspected" that both men were pagans, and Thomas Hodgkin called them "worshipers of the Olympian gods."[34] But then others have noted that Maximin and Priscus turned up in Rome in 450, hand delivering letters to and from Pope Leo. This might suggest, though not necessarily, that they were Christians. A certain amount of religious ambiguity was typical of the late Roman world. It is probable that neither man was very religious at all, and that when Maximin was dying in Thebes, he really didn't care if he went to heaven or the Elysian fields. But when they set out to meet Attila, Priscus and Maximin might have wished, despite their religious ambivalence, that the Church's missionaries to the Huns had been more a trifle more successful over the years.[35] The Huns had been as hard to convert as the Blemmyes, but they were considerably more disagreeable.

A WHIRLWIND FROM THE LOFTY MOUNTAINS

Somewhere in the Carpathian Basin, in a vast region that includes Slovakia, Romania, and Hungary, the heart of the Hapsburg Empire and the home of Count Dracula, a land of horsemanship and the white stork—somewhere in this land of one hundred thousand square miles lived Attila the Hun. Today, the territory that was the main stomping ground of the horse-bound Huns is a fairly bleak track of land from Budapest due south to Szeged, Hungary.

Archaeologists have not been able to tell us where his camp was located. But Roman ambassadors knew how to find him. Go north and ask for directions. It was all Attila's land.

When I traveled this stretch by train in 1995, I was struck by its barrenness and desolation, and by the endless fields of corn and the few signs of productive life. Before the Huns appeared in the late fourth century, this had been one of the Empire's most remote provinces, Pannonia, or modern-day Hungary. The provincial capital of Aquincum was a flourishing city on the Danube, the ruins of which are located in and around modern Budapest. Founded in the first century A.D., Aquincum in its heyday boasted all that a Roman city could want: aqueducts, sewers, paved streets, public baths, a large forum. There was even an amphitheater that could accommodate several thousand spectators, and where today, among the ruined arches, the homeless now sleep.

One senses, however, that despite the usual Roman amenities, Aquincum remained something of a frontier town, dangerously close to the precipice where Civilization officially came to an end. The city had become largely depopulated in the fourth century after being repeatedly attacked and ransacked. It was simply too far from Rome to be defended adequately. By the time Attila came to power in the 430s, Aquincum had been a ghost town for decades; its walls were crumbling and its artisans, merchants, and vine growers had long since disappeared. A well-established Roman population continued to live throughout the region under Hunnish rule, among whom was a man named Orestes, best known for fathering the last of the Western emperors, the hapless Romulus Augustulus. Orestes was also one of Attila's top lieutenants and, though official history has not recorded it, he was probably complicitous in Attila's death.

Long before men spoke of werewolves and vampires, this land had become a place of brooding mystery, darkness, danger, and witchcraft. After the Romans abandoned Pannonia in the fourth century, the Huns moved in and settled on the plains between the Carpathian Mountains of Transylvania and the Danube River. We know today what no Roman historian understood: that the Huns had come from much farther away, far beyond the

Carpathian Mountains, from the steppes of Central Asia.[36] Turned back by the Great Wall of China, the Huns migrated westward until they reached the outskirts of Roman cvilization. From their foothold in the North, the Huns would descend time and again upon the Empire to raid border towns and extort "protection money" from the survivors. Writing in the late fourth century, Ammianus Marcellinus recorded the first shock of terror when "a race of men, hitherto unknown, suddenly descended like a whirlwind from the lofty mountains, as if they had risen from some secret recess in the earth, and were ravaging and destroying everything which came in their way."[37] You almost want to tell Ammianus to take a deep breath, but you just couldn't breathe easily when *these* people were camping on your doorstep.

But were they even people? Ammianus had his doubts. "They are certainly in the *shape* of men," he hedged, though they might easily be confused for a "low-legged beast." Other Roman propagandists would claim that the savage invaders had lumps for heads, pinholes for eyes, and had dropped from the wombs of witches.[38] One might have tolerated them in the neighborhood if they had just kept to themselves. But what made them really terrifying was the way they fought—on horseback, with lightning speed. The Romans marched in a straight line and were sitting ducks each time the Huns swooped in, riding their tough little horses at full gallop. Their skill as horsemen came from practically living on horseback—eating, sleeping, negotiating, making love—*living* on horseback, according to Ammianus. Such was life on the move that they didn't even bother to cook their meat; they just warmed it up a little (so we're told) by placing it between their thigh and the horse's back.

So where in all this propaganda is the truth? We shouldn't take Ammianus too literally, since we're pretty sure that Attila died on his wedding night in bed, not on horseback. The point of the exaggeration, as with all propaganda, is to emphasize the differences, to depict the Huns as "the Other" against which the Romans defined themselves. The Huns were restless and could never settle down into anything approaching a civilized life. Romans knew that civilization started in the field—that "agriculture" is the foundation of "culture"—which is why Ammianus stressed that "none of them plow, or even touch a plow handle, for they have no settled abode, but are homeless and lawless."

Nor were the Huns tempted by the luxuries of urban life. Aquincum remained uninhabited throughout the Hunnish period. They were content to live according to the austere ways of the steppes. And while the image of Huns living on horseback is clearly not accurate, there can be no doubt that they lived and traveled on the cheap—the original "Europe on five dollars a day" philosophy. One of the most puzzling things to the Romans was that the Huns extorted Roman wealth on the one hand while renouncing Roman luxury on the other. That simply made no sense. What in the name of Jove was wealth for if you didn't enjoy it? One more reason to be repelled by these people.

SILK GARMENTS AND INDIAN GEMS

"For the man who travels lightly," Priscus wrote, "it takes thirteen days to reach Sardica." Though he's using a figure of speech, this must also have been the plan—to travel lightly—as Maximin and Priscus headed northwest in 449 to the city we know today as Sophia, Bulgaria. They did take a caravan of provisions with them and plenty of diplomatic gifts; perishable foods would be procured along the way. The ambassadors would be well provided for as long as they were in Roman territory. But once they crossed the border—wherever that was, it was always shifting—they would have to rely on the kindness of strangers. The route they traveled from Constantinople to Sardica can still be traveled today, by car or train, from Istanbul to Sophia, which is roughly the last leg of the fabled Orient Express, traveled in reverse. The fertile plains of ancient Thrace on the lowest tip of the European continent are still dotted with small villages, much as they were hundreds of years ago.

On the way to Sardica they passed through Adrianopolis, which was where the Empire suffered its first great loss to the Goths in 378. It had been a stunning defeat. Emperor Valens fell in battle and his body was never recovered. Gone forever was the idea, carefully cultivated for centuries, that Rome could not be beaten. But Adrianopolis, and other Thracian cities along the way, are passed over without comment. Priscus tells us nothing of the first two weeks of travel. The first inkling that something was very wrong with this trip came when they reached Sardica, about three hundred miles to the northwest. At this point in the narrative, Priscus slows the story down and describes the characters with subtle detail. Maximin and Priscus were accompanied by a diplomat of lesser rank, a court insider named Bigilas (BIG-uh-lus) who couldn't keep his mouth shut. There were a few tagalongs as well, such as a Roman named Rusticius, who, though a translator like Bigilas, was making the trip for purely personal reasons. Also traveling with the party was one of Attila's top ministers, a barbarian named Edecon (EE-duh-con) who couldn't be trusted, and another one of Attila's chief advisors, a Roman native of Pannonia named Orestes (o-REST-eez), who suffered from petty bouts of jealousy. This explosive combination of impulsiveness and deceit would make for an interesting trip—and some lively conversation along the way, especially when they stopped at Sardica for the night.

The city was ruined. At every point along this journey they would be reminded of the brutal pounding the once flourishing cities of the Balkans had endured. These had been beautiful cities—miniature Romes with villas, forums, and public baths. But after a decade of continuous attack, no city north of Constantinople had been spared the devastation. Those who had survived the slaughter lived in and around the ruins, suffering under deplorable conditions and waiting in vain for the emperor to rebuild and refortify their homes. In these parts at least, the Huns had earned every ounce of their reputation. The intensity of the Hunnish destruction would be remembered for centuries to come in a proverbial saying still heard in modern times in Bulgaria and Serbia: "The grass will not grow where Attila's horse had trod."[39]

Though they traveled as a party, the Romans and barbarians kept separate quarters and prepared separate meals. Once they reached Sardica, however, the Roman ambassadors "thought it well," as Priscus put it, to invite

Edecon and his compatriots to dinner. Priscus is suggesting that this was a diplomatic decision and that the mere invitation itself conveyed an unmistakable message. Though the place was in shambles, essentially abandoned to its own fortunes by an Empire in retreat, Sardica was still a *Roman* city. If anyone were going to host a dinner, it should be the rightful occupants of the town: Romans.

Thanks to the generosity of the locals, Maximin was able to put a respectable dinner on the table: some beef stew, perhaps, and lamb cutlets prepared with oil and wine.[40] After the pleasantries and the small talk, the dinner took an ugly turn when the barbarians began to sing their chieftain's praises. Bigilas, who couldn't keep his mouth shut, jumped in with this retort: "How can one possibly compare a man to a god?" Attila was the man, of course, and Theodosius was the god. Bigilas had seen Attila in all his glory during an earlier negotiation, and he wasn't anything to write home about. The insolence of the barbarians was hard to understand; they had just come from Constantinople. They had seen the splendor of the city and the royal court. What did Attila have that could compare to this? The only proper response of a barbarian should be awe. The Gothic king Athanaric had reacted properly, with awe, when Theodosius the Great invited him to visit the capital. "Now I see what all the fuss has been about," he said. Jordanes recorded the scene: "Turning his eyes hither and thither, he marveled as he beheld the situation of the city, the coming and going of the ships, the splendid walls, and the people of many nations gathered like a flood of waters streaming from different regions into one basin." And then, when Athanaric saw the emperor's armies, he declared, "Truly the Emperor is a god on earth."[41]

Now, *that* was the right response. What Bigilas heard from Attila's men could not go unanswered. Tempers flared. But before things got physical, the ambassadors managed to change the subject and everybody calmed down. Just to make sure nothing was left unsettled, Maximin produced some parting gifts for Edecon and Orestes: silk garments and Indian gems. The altercation must have seemed odd to Priscus, since this is the only event he recorded from the first thirteen days of the journey. Why had Bigilas been so cocky? It might have been the wine, but it was probably more than that, certainly much more than Priscus could have known at the time.

Later on as the party was breaking up, something else occurred that made no sense at all to the ambassadors. Orestes pulled Maximin aside and complimented him. "You did a fine diplomatic job," Orestes said, "unlike those offensive toads back at the imperial court." Maximin was confused. "Excuse me?" he said. Holding up the garments and gems, Orestes explained that it was proper for the ambassador to give gifts equally to himself and Edecon. Back in Constantinople, however, he had been slighted. Edecon had received the royal treatment—wined and dined, pampered with gifts, and invited to the private quarters of the grand chamberlain himself. And what did Orestes get? Absolutely nothing. "This speech was meaningless to us," Priscus wrote.

What are we to make of this little dispute? It wasn't the jostling and jealousy between Attila's lieutenants that puzzled Maximin and Priscus—that much could be expected. Among the Hun's inner circle, a current of ambition was flowing beneath the surface, held in check only by the force of Attila's personality. The ambassadors saw the same thing back in the imperial palace. (The eunuchs were the *worst*.)[42] What puzzled them, instead, was the obvious breach of protocol in the capital. Orestes had a legitimate gripe. After all, Maximin's instinct as a diplomat was to honor both men with an equal distribution of gifts. Why would Edecon have been treated with greater deference? The ambassadors asked Orestes repeatedly for an explanation of why this had happened, but Orestes had nothing more to say.

The next morning they packed up and set out from Sardica. Maximin and Priscus were still talking about the odd exchange they witnessed the night before. They mentioned it to Bigilas. "What right does Orestes have to be angry?" he fumed. Bigilas pointed out that the two men technically were not of equal rank. Edecon was a Hun and a key military advisor to Attila. Orestes was just a Roman secretary, one of Attila's hired men, a servant. The men had been treated, then, in exact accordance with their rank. No protocol had been violated.

This answer must have satisfied their doubts, but Bigilas wasn't finished yet. He brought the subject up again later on that day. "Edecon wasn't happy when I told him about the conversation," he said. Bigilas assured Maximin, however, that he had smoothed things over with Edecon. Presumably, this was an effort to silence the ambassadors, to keep them from probing any further into the matter. Under the pretext of not ruffling Edecon's feathers, Bigilas was trying to keep Maximin and Priscus from discovering the true reason why Edecon had been treated so well back at the palace. Behind the fence-mending, then, was the dark design of a conspiracy that Bigilas was trying hard to keep under wraps.

Bigilas had started a chain reaction that would unravel a secret plot.

Historians have seldom pointed out the intricate pattern of causation Priscus is implying.[43] We can piece it together, though, from the mundane details in the text. This first plot to kill Attila was doomed from the moment Theodosius paired an obnoxious fool (Bigilas) with an experienced diplomat and his clever assistant. Maximin was the consummate diplomat who understood protocol. Priscus was skeptical, inquisitive, and tenacious in his pursuit of answers. The dinner at Sardica provided a setting for these personalities to interact—finally, after thirteen days on the road. The plot began to unravel and Priscus was busy taking notes.

Everything had started with a single impulsive comment: "How can one compare a man to a god?" Bruised egos had to be assuaged, and so Maximin doled out the gifts—silken garments and Indian gems. No doubt he was already planning to end the dinner this way—protocol demanded it—but Priscus implies that Maximin was especially generous because of the argument. Maximin was evenhanded in his liberality, something the sensitive Orestes could not fail to notice. When Orestes turned a compliment of Maximin into a *complaint* about the court, all kinds of red flags went up. Bigilas only made things worse by talking to Edecon. By this time everybody was suspicious of everybody else, and the plot was bound to fail.

These intricate details are classic Priscus. As he looked back on the failed plot of 449, Priscus must have identified the seeds of a second conspiracy, which succeeded in 453. Perhaps the rivalry between Orestes and Edecon was ultimately exploited to the Empire's advantage. Perhaps they were convinced to partner together as coconspirators before dividing the spoils of victory and going their separate ways, enemies once more. Twenty years later, when Rome was falling, these two men would still be at each other's throats, though by then they'd be competing by proxy through their sons. The son of Edecon, Odovacer (odo-VAH-Ker), would depose the son of Orestes (Romulus Augustulus), and the line of Western Caesars would forever come to an end.

If only Bigilas had kept his mouth shut.

THREE

DINNER WITH THE BARBARIANS

O N the second floor of the Kunsthistorisches Museum in Vienna you can see the so-called Holy Lance of Longinus, also known as the Spear of Destiny. First mentioned in tenth-century records, the gilded lance became associated in legend with the spear that pierced the side of Jesus on the cross. Many great kings and conquerors supposedly had possession of its mystical powers over the centuries: Constantine, Alaric, Charles Martel, Charlemagne, Barbarossa, and Kaiser Wilhelm. Yes, even Attila the Hun at one time had possession of it, so the legend goes, and fearing its great power, relinquished it at the gates of Rome. "It is no use to me," he said, "since I do not know him who made it holy." In 1912 a young art student named Adolf Hitler would go to the museum, gaze at the artifact in its glass case, and dream that he, too, would one day wrap his fingers around the lance and wield its power.[44]

Also in Vienna at the time was a young doctor named Sigmund Freud who could have told Hitler what he was really dreaming about. Freud himself was a collector of ancient artifacts—his office was a virtual museum—

and he understood how objects hold a mystical power to conjure up our deepest longings. Twenty-six years later German troops marched into Vienna, and Hitler went back to the museum. He was drawn magnetically to artifacts like this, especially when they held the promise of unbridled power. Attila, too, was a superstitious man, and a collector of artifacts. Priscus tells the story of how an old sword found in the field became a potent symbol of world domination.[45] When a shepherd noticed that one of his heifers was limping and bleeding, he followed the trail of blood. He found a rusty sword sticking out of the ground and took it to Attila. It was surely the ancient sword of Mars, Attila said, and it meant that he would rule the world.

Sometimes a sword is just a sword. But not this time. Weapons attached themselves to Attila's reputation—the sword of Mars, the spear of Longinus, the broken bow—evidence once again of how easily ideas can triumph over facts. For modern Hungarian patriots, Attila's sword has represented the destiny of a nation. But within the ancient historical record, these weapons, especially the legendary "sword of Mars," pointed to an unbroken trail of blood that began with a limping heifer and ended in a wedding bed.

THE TRAIL OF BLOOD

A gruesome execution north of Constantinople in 435 was the first indication that a trail of blood had been inaugurated. Every traveler along this highway north of the capital must have heard the story. Though Priscus was too young to have witnessed it himself, he heard about it like everyone else back in the capital. He even remembered the names of the two young men, Mama and Atakam, who were impaled on stakes and left to die in the Thracian city of Carsum (modern Harsova in Romania). They were Huns, of royal lineage, and though Priscus calls them children, we're meant to understand that they were teenagers. Attila had staged this scene for maximum effect. He succeeded spectacularly, for Romans still talked about the horrible event fourteen years later. This was the first time the Romans had seen the new chieftain up close and personal. Everyone agreed: He made a strong first impression.

It was already clear by 435 that the Huns were an especially difficult variety of barbarian. All the more reason to engage their king in dialogue, Theodosius believed, and try to figure out what Rua (ROO-uh) wanted. Ambassadors traveled back and forth between the palaces of Constantinople and the log huts of Hungary. What the Romans learned was alarming: The Huns sought nothing but unimpeded access to the treasure-houses of the Empire. These people who wheeled their wagons across the steppes and across the Caucusus a mere two generations before had some nerve (the Romans thought) to issue demands to an Empire that had stood for a thousand years! Celebrations, then, were in order when the news arrived in 435 that Rua was dead. A fifth-century church historian, Socrates Scholasticus, recorded that Rua was struck dead by lightning during an invasion of Thrace;[46] but this sounds too conveniently like divine judgment to be trusted. As we will soon see, the Eastern Romans had a way of turning the deaths of Hunnish leaders into sermon illustrations.

Rua was the last member of a powerful ruling clan; his brother Octar had ruled jointly with him until his death in 430.[47] Another brother, Mundiuch (MOON-dyuk), must have died years before since the only thing we know about him is that he had two sons, Bleda (BLAY-duh) and Attila. Rua was succeeded by his two nephews (which suggests Mundiuch had been the oldest sibling), and they carried on the practice of jointly ruling the loose confederation of tribes who looked to the Huns as overlords. Few could predict in either Roman capital what this would mean for the Empire. The only high-ranking official who had any inside knowledge at all was the Western general Flavius Aetius. As a young man he had lived as a hostage among the Huns—a diplomatic hostage—and it's always been assumed that he personally knew Attila from his youth. After his rise to power, Aetius would maintain an extensive spy network throughout Hunnish territory that funneled fresh intelligence back to Italy. Not even Aetius, though, could have known that the fate of the Empire would come down to a face-off, some sixteen years down the road, between boyhood friends. Aetius and Attila had hunted together in the woods and fields of Hungary, but they would fight to the death in the woods and fields of France.

For the time being, there was no sense of urgency in the West, where the Huns had been kept in check through alliances. The Eastern court in Constantinople, however, was deeply worried. A high-level delegation was assembled, led by a distinguished diplomat named Plinthas who had been opening up diplomatic channels to the Huns before Rua's death. It was important to get an early read on who these new rulers were. Perhaps they would be easier to negotiate with than their uncle Rua had been. Who knows? Perhaps a new era of cooperation might even be ushered in. The nephews, too, must have known how important this first encounter was. They wanted to make a fresh start with the Eastern Romans, to strike the right tone and convey just the right message. Hence the crucifixion. It was probably Attila's idea. He understood that it was better to be feared than loved. Mama and Atakam had abandoned their posts in an earlier skirmish and sought refuge among the Romans. Their punishment would speak louder than any boasts or threats. This was a new regime, and Attila would command both the loyalty of his subjects and the respect of his foes.

The Huns and Romans met outside Margus, a settlement on the Danube not far from modern Belgrade. It was a frontier town protected by a Roman fort on the opposite side of the river. Not far away, the barbarians had put down their own stake in the community—royal tents to house their ambassadors and other visiting dignitaries. Margus was thus a cosmopolitan town, a crossroads of cultures, and it had become an important center of trade. A bazaar flourished along the banks of the river, a duty-free zone both sides were keen to maintain. For the Huns especially, trading posts like this facilitated their transition from nomadic life to a more settled existence.[48] At this little outpost of civilization, the Huns and Romans approached each other warily on horseback. Attila and Bleda refused to dismount. Unsure what to do next, the Romans decided to stay mounted as well. This may be one of the few things we can trust Ammianus about—the Roman propagandist who claimed that the Huns did *everything* on horseback. It does appear that negotiating in the saddle was a Hunnish practice, a way perhaps of keeping their options open. The talks went quickly and the two sides rode away.

What had been accomplished? Quite a lot—the seeds of every major conflict Constantinople would face during the next twenty years had been planted. Emperor Theodosius II, grandson of "the Great," had given away the company store. Attila wanted the "annual tribute"—what the Romans euphemistically called an honorarium—doubled from 350 to 700 pounds of gold. Plinthas agreed. Attila wanted all Hunnish expatriates to be denied asylum and returned immediately. Plinthas agreed. Attila wanted the commercial district in Margus to remain open for free trade. Plinthas agreed. Attila insisted that the Romans make no alliances with any people who set themselves against the Huns. Plinthas agreed. When Plinthas brought the Treaty of Margus back to the capital, Emperor Theodosius must have rejoiced that peace had been achieved in their time.

From this point on, diplomatic relations between the Huns and Romans would boil down to two simple demands: return the hostages and pay us the gold. The fugitives were returned, as the treaty stipulated, and they were promptly executed; among them were Mama and Atakam, who were crucified close enough to the capital to send a chilling message. Thereafter, the annual "honorarium" was always on time. The Romans were a quick study, and it must not have taken them long to conclude that assassination was the only sure way to deal with a man this ruthless. He was impossible to negotiate with; he merely dictated terms on horseback. And if those terms were rejected, if they were violated, if they were even delayed, then you could expect to see dust billowing on the horizon and hear the distant pounding of horses' hoofs.

The encounter in Margus occurred almost two decades before Attila's death, but it holds a big clue to how his life would end. When Plinthas arrived in Margus in 435, he negotiated on horseback with two leaders. Whatever happened to Bleda? The answer will prove instrumental in demolishing the textbook account of Attila's death.

A TOUR OF RUINED CITIES

After the Treaty of Margus we hear nothing of Attila and Bleda for five or six years. And when they do burst back on the scene with a vengeance in 441, their return has everything to do with Margus once again. A new bishop had arrived in town. He recognized the wealth of the Huns and it grieved him to see such resources wasted in the burial chambers of their kings when he could put it to much better use. The bishop of Margus sneaked over into Hunnish territory and began despoiling their burial sites like a nineteenth-century archaeologist, going straight for the gold and tossing everything else aside. The bishop's greed has been imitated so many times throughout the centuries that almost every visible trace of these consummate plunderers has been looted, ironically, out of existence. (This is why when you squint to read those little labels in museums, you find so few that are labeled *Hunnish, Vth Century*.)

It's a little hard to picture what supposedly happened—a bishop rifling through graves and stashing gold vessels in the folds of his robe. And yet the story must be true, in some sense at least. Rome had a problem in the fourth and fifth centuries with bishops who moonlighted as grave robbers. An imperial edict in 347 describes the clergy prying open tombs with iron tools and "bringing to the sacred altars of the Church hands that are polluted by the contagion of the ashes of the dead."[49] The "truth" of the story, however, may lie not in its specific allegations about the bishop of Margus but in its broader awareness that this kind of pilfering did occur. The story reads like a simplification of something much greater and may be intended as an ecclesiastical warning against heresy and luxury among the priestly ranks. The patriarch in Constantinople, St. John Chrysostom, had frequently condemned these violations of the tombs. As the bishop's indiscretions would prove, the fight against the Huns would have to rely on more than walls and weapons. The Empire's safety was ultimately tied to the Church's purity.

In any event, the Huns were outraged by the sacrilege. They responded by attacking the Roman fortress across the river and then slaughtering the merchants whose buying and selling had been guaranteed by the treaty. The Romans, in turn, protested what they saw as a premeditated violation of the commercial agreement. The standard response of the Huns—"You started it"—always had an ominous edge to it. Whatever you started, the Huns were sure to finish. All they needed was an excuse to escalate an uneasy detente into full-scale war. The Huns would act first and ask questions later. (Usually, they never got around to asking questions at all.) They demanded the bishop's surrender. The battered bodies of Mama and Atakam immediately sprang to the bishop's mind and—since he lacked "the spirit of a martyr," in Edward Gibbon's piquant phrase—he decided to turn sides and save his skin.[50] He gave himself up and promised to deliver his flock to them, the town of Margus, if the Huns would only spare his life. They agreed and the bishop opened the gates. Thus began the horrible Balkan campaign of 441. City after city fell as the Huns went on a rampage. The bishop's greed had been the flashpoint, but the Huns had been spoiling for a fight.

The year 442 saw another tentative truce put in place, but in 443 the Huns struck again. During these turbulent years, Emperor Theodosius vacillated between risking war and simply draining the treasury upon demand. Usually he endorsed the latter policy, which imposed severe wartime conditions on the privileged classes of Constantinople. In order to pay the war tax, proud members of the aristocracy could be found hocking the family's jewelry and furniture in the marketplace. Historians estimate that as much as 22,000 pounds of gold were doled out to Attila during the 440s.[51] Ensconced within the Grand Palace and surrounded by sycophants, Theodosius was insulated from the hard realities of his appeasement. But the man who succeeded him in office, Marcian, saw it clearly enough; he was a senator, and these were *his* friends, *his* colleagues, who were paying the price for the emperor's foolish capitulations. Every ounce paid to Attila became one more reason to kill him.

Perpetual war in the Balkans served Attila's larger interests. During these years he managed to consolidate his base and gradually extend his control over what had been a loose confederation of stubborn, nomadic raiders. Others, such as Bleda, must have argued for a policy of moderate aggression balanced by cooperation. Domestic politics among the Huns, however, is a mystery to us; as little as we know about policy making inside the *Roman* court, we know even less about the inner circles of the Huns. But we get some interesting hints. Bleda ruled in the eastern half of the Hun Empire; he must have favored a more cooperative approach, leveraging from Constantinople as much wealth as possible. Attila ruled in the west and favored an aggressive policy of intimidation, conquest, and plunder, though you wouldn't necessarily know this from his actions. Things were relatively quiet in the west during these years, as Attila negotiated with the Romans, visited the Italian border region to receive ambassadors, and exchanged gifts with General Aetius. The balance of power between Bleda and Attila appears to have shifted toward the end of their joint rule, during the time the Balkan wars were fought in 441 and 443. During the campaign of 443, a number of Hunnish warriors (members of the royal family, Priscus tells us) refused to serve under Attila and fled instead to the Roman side just as Mama and Atakam had done eight years before.[52] Small details like this point to an ongoing power struggle among the Huns, and it must ultimately have involved Bleda himself, Attila's older brother. He died mysteriously in 445 and the Balkan war raged perilously close to Constantinople in 447 before Attila retreated.

Two years later, in 449, Maximin and Priscus were traveling the Thracian highway—now a tour of ruined cities and abandoned fortresses—carrying with them letters from the emperor and a secret they knew nothing about. We left them in Sardica in the last chapter, where Bigilas had ruined dinner with his big mouth. After a few more days of travel, the ambassadors reached Naissus, one hundred miles farther west. Naissus was famous as the birthplace of Constantine the Great. Outside the city stood a magnificent palace, once a summer residence for emperors, now only a heap of ruins. (The palace was attacked once again, inadvertently, when NATO planes bombed it in 1999.) As the ambassadors entered the outskirts of the city, they began to see the full extent of the devastation Attila had wreaked on Constantine's hometown; the banks of the river were so littered with

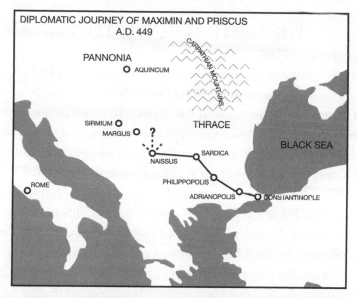

A reconstruction of the diplomatic journey of Maximin and Priscus
in A.D. 449. The ambassadors traveled in a northwesterly direction from
Constantinople; their specific itinerary after Naissus, however, is unclear.
Scholars do not know where Attila's headquarters were located.
Map by Matthew Pamer

bones that the Romans had a hard time finding a clear spot to pitch their tent.

The next day Maximin delivered his orders to the local military commander. The last five of the seventeen fugitives demanded by the Huns were under the commander's protection; these were to be turned over to the Roman delegation for safe delivery to Attila. They would face certain execution. All that remained now was to head due north, past Margus, across the Danube, and into the wilderness. Some friendly barbarians gave them passage across the river in their dugout canoes. Shortly thereafter, Edecon's group separated and went ahead to announce their arrival. The Romans were told to stay put and await further instructions. It seems that Attila was in the neighborhood.

THE MEETING IN THE TENTS

Late that afternoon they heard horses in the distance and looked up from their dinner. Two Huns whom they had never seen before rode up. "Attila bids you come along," they said. It was too late to travel farther, so they set out the next morning for Attila's camp, a vast collection of unmarked tents. Lots and lots of them. Maximin and Priscus began setting up their own tent on a slope, but they didn't get very far before an angry Hun told them to stop. Attila's tent was on low ground, they were told, and no one could presume to pitch his tent higher than the chieftain's. This is another one of those little details Priscus amplifies out of proportion, a means of commenting, perhaps, on the vanity and arrogance of Attila. Yet he manages to say just as much about himself. You can almost see Priscus bristling as he looked around and saw tents everywhere. "It turned out that he had many of them," Priscus wrote flatly. They all looked alike. Who could tell which one was his? "We lodged where it seemed best to the Huns," Priscus wrote.

There was no time for rest as a delegation of Huns soon appeared outside their tent. Their traveling companions, Edecon and Orestes, appeared, along with a high-ranking Hun named Scottas who had led embassies to Constantinople earlier in the Balkan wars. "We are here to inquire as to the purpose of your mission," they announced in what Priscus characterizes as a formal, stilted manner. Priscus and Maximin looked at each, deeply puzzled. Bigilas, too, must have wondered what was going on. Both Edecon and Orestes had traveled with them for several weeks, and even shared meals with them along the way! They *knew* what the purpose of the mission was— the broad outlines, at least—these missions were always the same, always about fugitives. The agenda hadn't changed since the Treaty of Margus, fourteen years before. What *was* clear, though, was that they were now asking for specifics—*How much gold? How many fugitives?*

"It would not be proper to tell you," Maximin replied. The letters bore the imperial seal and were intended for Attila's eyes only.

"Do you think we're making this up ourselves?" Scottas said, enraged. "Don't you think Attila sent us here to ask you this?"

Maximin held his ground; if there was one thing he couldn't stand, it was a lack of protocol. He may have been in the middle of nowhere, far from the culture and comforts of home, but by God, he was *still* a Roman.

The conversation ended abruptly and the Hunnish delegation returned to Attila's tent—whichever one it was.

Then they returned moments later without Edecon.

Point by point, Orestes and Scottas laid out the whole agenda of the trip, right down to the last detail. "Your business is concluded," they said. "You should pack up and head home immediately unless you have something you'd like to add."

Maximin and Priscus were confused and Bigilas was depressed. How did the emperor's private letters become revealed? And were they now to turn around and go home, having accomplished nothing? They had hostages to deliver and gold to be paid, and it confused them that Attila was suddenly interested in neither. Bigilas was depressed, since the assassination plot could not go forward if the diplomatic mission were scuttled. It never occurred to Bigilas that Edecon might have told Attila everything about the plot.

The ambassadors began packing their bags, but Bigilas wasn't ready to give up. "It would be better to take our chances with a lie than to go home empty-handed," he said. "Why didn't you tell them you had some other matter to take up with Attila—something they didn't know about? Something to pique their interest and secure an audience with the king?" Priscus relates how Bigilas railed on and on, stressing how tight he was with Edecon and what a great impression he had made on Attila in an earlier round of negotiations.

Night had fallen, but since the animals were already loaded down with their baggage, they decided to get an early start for home. They hadn't gone but a few paces when some Huns caught up with them: Attila wanted them to stay overnight because the hour was late. Shortly thereafter, some more Huns arrived with an ox and some river fish—compliments of the king. The sudden attention was flattering, especially to Maximin; he was finally being treated like an ambassador. They had no idea, however, that they were the necessary stooges in an imperial plot—a plot that had just failed—to assassinate Attila under the cover of a diplomatic mission. Attila *did* know, and now he was toying with them like a cat with a mouse. Later it would all make sense to Priscus as he looked back on the odd events:

the boasting of Bigilas in Sardica

the peevishness of Orestes at having been slighted at the palace

the unpredictability of Attila not receiving the ambassadors

the urgency of Bigilas to complete the mission

Edecon had betrayed the conspiracy (that's why he had gone ahead to "announce" their arrival);[53] Bigilas would be hung out to dry. Maximin and Priscus wouldn't know any of it until they returned to Constantinople—how Edecon had agreed to assassinate his chieftain, how Bigilas had been commissioned to pay Edecon the blood money once Attila was dead. We'll come back to the conspiracy behind this failed assassination attempt; but for now we'll follow the ambassadors in their blissful ignorance.

The next morning brought no progress. The Huns arrived again with the same brusque message: *Get out of town—that is, unless you have something more to say.* And then we arrive at one of those distinctive "Priscus moments" in the narrative, in which the young man (or the old man remembering himself as a young man) pushes himself into the foreground of the story. All along Priscus has been referring to himself and Maximin collectively as "we." *We* said. *We* replied. Maximin hardly registers as a separate identity apart from his young companion. But now Priscus takes charge; he looks around and sizes things up. Maximin was dejected; he had hoped that a new day would find Attila in a better mood. More than anything, Maximin just wanted to complete his mission. It was a terrible embarrassment for an official of his stature to be rebuffed in this manner, and he was thinking no doubt of how his influence would sink back at the capital.

So Priscus the rhetorician sprang into action. He would try his own hand at diplomacy. He asked Rusticius to join him, a Roman who was fluent in the Hunnish language, and the two of them headed up the path to see Scottas—the influential Hun they had just met, rather unpleasantly, outside the tent. Rusticius had traveled with them from the start, not as part of the official entourage but because he had personal business with an old friend of his, an Italian named Constantius who was serving as Attila's secretary. Why didn't Priscus take Bigilas along as his translator? More than likely Priscus had grown weary of the translator's constant nagging. Priscus was also freelancing—the kind of improvised diplomacy that would later save his skin in Alexandria—and it made sense to use an unofficial member of the team so as to limit his liability should things go badly. But things went well. It was only by his boldness and initiative (he implies) that the mission was turned around from failure to success. Perhaps that's really true; or perhaps this is more proof that Priscus was a sophist and a rhetorician, and that far from being a reliable witness, empty words were often his specialty.

"Maximin has many gifts for you," Priscus began, "which are now packed up and heading for home. He'd be happy to unload them for you if you would arrange a meeting with your king." Scottas appeared interested and so Priscus continued. "And not just for you but also for your brother Onegesh (OH-nuh-gesh). I noticed that he is absent. Too bad. There are gifts waiting for him as well. The emperor specifically asked if Onegesh would come to Constantinople and negotiate a peace treaty between us. Imagine how disappointed your brother will be when he learns how he's missed out on the emperor's generosity." Priscus wasn't finished. Now he appealed to the Hun's vanity. "Like your brother, you have quite a reputation," Priscus said. "I've been told that you have Attila's ear. I wonder what would be said about you if people heard that you couldn't secure an audience."

Scottas stiffened. "You will soon see," he replied, "that I hold equal rank before Attila with my brother Onegesh." And then Scottas galloped off toward Attila's tent, somewhere in the large sea of tents before them.

Priscus isn't modest about his success. He was a rhetorician—one who *does* things with words. "Prepare some gifts!" he announced to his companions when he returned to camp. Maximin and Bigilas had been lying dejectedly on the grass, but they quickly jumped up. At this point our eyewitness—the dispassionate Priscus whom scholars have transformed into a tape recorder and a camera lens—gives us this "objective" piece of information: "They applauded my ingenuity."

They were still rustling up gifts when Scottas arrived to lead them to Attila, who was sitting in his tent on a wooden stool. Maximin approached the king, greeted him, and handed over the letters from Theodosius. "The emperor prays that you and your followers are safe and sound," he said. Everyone knew that *that* was a lie. Attila's response was ironic: "The Romans will have what they wish." He then looked past Maximin and straight at Bigilas. "You worthless beast," he said. "How dare you come into my presence without all the fugitives you promised! Those were the terms of the treaty that we negotiated." It was a complete turnaround from how Attila had treated Bigilas the last time they had met.

"Every fugitive has been accounted for," Bigilas said weakly. "There are no more in Roman territory."

"Liar!" Attila was now shouting. "If it weren't a violation of custom, I'd crucify you right now and let the birds peck out your eyes. I *know* there are fugitives that have not been surrendered." And then Attila gestured to an aide who produced a list and read off some names. "Go home and get me an answer. Will the Romans surrender these fugitives or will they risk war over a few pathetic cowards?" Attila acknowledged the gifts and abruptly dismissed the Roman delegation.

Back in their tent, the Romans pursued a trivial conversation that contributes nothing to our historical understanding. Why then does Priscus devote a paragraph to it when he passes over whole weeks without comment? "We got along so well in our earlier meetings," Bigilas said. "I have no idea why Attila treated me so harshly."

"Perhaps," Priscus noted, "some of the Huns told him what you said back in Sardica. You remember, don't you, that reckless comment about comparing a man to a god?" Maximin agreed that this was the likeliest explanation, but Bigilas wasn't convinced. "No one would dare speak such words in Attila's presence," he said.

Again, there's no obvious reason to include this exchange, except that Priscus is interested in the story itself. Once you've taken on the intricate challenge of making sense of the world, substance and method (or, the "truth" and how you arrive at it) become nearly indistinguishable. The story *does* become about storytelling. Each of the Romans was trying to figure out what had just happened in Attila's tent. Priscus plots a story to explain it: word had reached Attila that Bigilas had spoken rashly about him. It was a plausible theory, but it wasn't right. *Nobody* got it right. Bigilas couldn't see beyond his false assumptions, and the ambassadors were limited by incomplete information. And that sums up our predicament, too, as we look back at these events.

While they were discussing these things, Edecon showed up at their tent and called Bigilas outside for a private discussion. It seemed to be an urgent matter, and Bigilas was in a much better mood when he returned. "Edecon was just explaining why the king was so upset," Bigilas said. "He's pretty bothered about the fugitives." Bigilas would later tell Priscus what Edecon had *really* said—how he falsely assured him that the plan was a "go" and that he should bring back the gold to bribe Attila's bodyguards.

SOME DANGLING SOCKS

This first meeting with Attila—the "meeting in the tents"—was held near the Danube along the southernmost region of Hunnish territory. Why was Attila so far south? Perhaps he was there to shore up his base. Perhaps he had traveled south because he was about to marry a new wife, which was one of the ways he shored up his base. Or perhaps he had been preparing for another Balkan campaign, should the ambassadors not bring a favorable response from the emperor. Attila had already shown that he could negotiate without dismounting from his horse. Now he was letting it be known that he could stretch things out for weeks on end if it suited his purposes to do so. Maximin and Priscus were to accompany him as he journeyed back north to his headquarters. Bigilas, meanwhile, was to return to Constantinople.

The ambassadors traveled with Attila's band for a few days until they were ordered to take an alternative route with their guides. Attila was turning aside into a small village where he was planning to take another wife, the daughter of a certain Escam. Though Priscus describes how they journeyed through plains and across rivers, the descriptions are so generic historians have been unable to reconstruct the route. Along the way they stayed in Hun villages where the locals provided them with millet and mead (barbarian beer). After one particularly long day of traveling, they came upon a lake. It was dusk and the lakeshore would be a good place, they thought, to set up camp; but a violent storm came up suddenly and blew their tent and supplies into the water. The scene Priscus describes is one of spontaneous panic. Everyone was in the dark, in a blinding rainstorm with lightning flashing all around them. They scattered in different directions, shouting for help and taking whatever path they could find. Even the levelheaded ambassadors got separated in the chaos. Hearing all the racket, the Huns lit their torches and guided them to the shelter of their own huts, which were squalid hovels made of mud and straw.[54] Priscus doesn't say so, but he implies that this was a remarkable gesture of hospitality for such an uncivilized people.

The mayor of the village was a noblewoman. When she learned that Roman dignitaries had stumbled into her village in the rain, she sent food to their hut and shapely young women to their beds. They accepted the first while declining the latter. After dismissing the young women—"We refused them intercourse," Priscus is quick to point out—the ambassadors slept soundly that night as guests of Bleda's widow. It was a chance encounter occasioned by a sudden storm, but it must have reminded them of Attila's brutal rise to power. What had happened to Bleda, after all? Four years later, Priscus would be asking that question about Attila; on this trip, however, he had every reason to be thinking of Bleda. They couldn't have crossed the Danube, near Margus, without recalling the two brothers on horseback, dictating the terms of a humiliating peace. And now in an obscure village visited by accident they find his widow—or one of his widows, anyway—holding a position of honor as though Bleda were still alive. It must have seemed as though the ghost of Attila's brother was lurking everywhere they went. They would come across still more traces of Bleda's life and legacy, and only then would Priscus begin to form some idea of the intricacies of Hunnish politics. Priscus was always looking for causes and effects; he would think long and hard about Bleda on this trip, and would eventually link the deaths of these brothers, who had been locked in an intense sibling rivalry.

Fourteen years earlier Rua had been succeeded by his two nephews, though it's not entirely clear what the political arrangement was. It's been described as a coregency—Bleda ruling in the eastern half and Attila in the west—patterned perhaps on how the Romans had divided their Empire.[55] But these are only hunches. The only time we see them "side by side" is during the negotiations at Margus in 435, and even this Priscus only implies. We're fairly certain that Bleda was the older brother;[56] less certain (though we can demonstrate it from scattered historical clues) is that Bleda was in charge and Attila was his subordinate. In the cultural memory of the West, however, Bleda will forever stand in the imposing shadow of his younger brother. The story of how Bleda ended up that way, murdered and forgotten, is more than just an interesting subplot; it will turn out to be a significant link in the chain of evidence pointing to Attila's eventual murder.

We'll begin unraveling the details concerning Bleda's fate in the British Isles, where Roman troops had been withdrawn in the early fifth century. Less than a century after the death of Attila, a British monk named Gildas wrote a contemporary history known as *The Fall of Britain*.[57] Gildas relates that the haggard remnant of Romans still residing in Britain in the 440s had sent a letter to Agitius, "a man holding high office in Rome," urgently requesting help as they sought to defend themselves from the Scots and the Picts. The letter began: "To Agitius, in his third consulship, come the groans of the Britons." They were between a rock and a hard place—or, as the letter put it, "the barbarians press us into the sea and the sea pushes us back upon the barbarians, such that either way we are dead."

Another two centuries passed, and "the Venerable Bede"[58] paraphrased Gildas in his *Ecclesiastical History of Britain*, adding that Agitius never responded with aid since he was "engaged in the most serious wars with Bleda and Attila." Here's where Nietzsche's "slow reading" will serve us well, as we reconstruct how Bede was thinking his way through some textual and historical problems in this passage. Bede knew his Roman history well. He obviously had access to older sources now lost to us, and, using that knowledge, he annotated Gildas in important ways. For example, he was the first to identify Agitius as Aetius, the Western Roman general. Bede also noted that the "third consulship" of Aetius began in 446, which would date the events of the letter to 446 or 447. And then Bede went on to add that Bleda had actually died the year before, "murdered by the treachery of his own brother Attila." Finally, Bede tried to tie the two things together—that is, to explain how Aetius could be battling against "Bleda and Attila" if Bleda had been killed the year before. This posed a real chronological problem that required an explanation. Bede wrote: "Yet Attila remained so intolerable an enemy to the Republic, that he ravaged almost all Europe, attacking and destroying cities and castles." The phrase "yet remained" is Bede's solution to the problem. The fact that Bleda was dead was a mere technicality. There was no change in policy. Forget the fact that there *was* a change in policy—that's why Attila killed Bleda in the first place.[59] Bede's only interest is to squeeze some sense out of the passage, even if he has to force it in the end. The passage is what scholars call a crux, an unstable intersection of meanings in the text that invites commentary.

Bede is a careful and conservative historian, preserving what his source has given him but trying at the same time to reconcile apparent contradictions. These are the most telling moments in an ancient text, where reverence for the written word collides with the rational need to explain a semantic problem in the authoritative source. The solution? Pencil in some commentary, as Bede has done. The semantic tensions here between Gildas and Bede point clearly to the understanding—in some ancient source now lost, probably Priscus—that Bleda had ranked higher than Attila. The fact that Bleda is mentioned first in Bede's acount ("Bleda and Attila") is an obvious reference to this original pecking order, preserved out of a conservative deference to what his source had told him.[60]

Were Bleda and Attila joint rulers, or was Bleda the first among equals?

Priscus probably asked these questions as he journeyed through barbarian territory; unfortunately, what he wrote about this has survived only in filtered form, as preserved by Jordanes. Here's what we can read in the *Gothic History*:

> Now this Attila was the son of Mundiuch, and his brothers were Octar and Rua who are said to have ruled before Attila, though not over quite so many tribes as he. After their death he succeeded to the throne of the Huns, together with his brother Bleda. In order that he might first be equal to the expedition he was preparing against the Romans, he sought to increase his strength by murder. Thus he proceeded from the destruction of his own kindred to the menace of all others. But though he increased his power by this shameful means, yet by the balance of justice he received the hideous consequences of his own cruelty. Now when his brother Bleda, who ruled over a great part of the Huns, had been slain by his treachery, Attila united all the people under his own rule.

Scholars agree that Priscus stands behind the bulk of what Jordanes has to say about Attila's life and death. But how many of these words by Jordanes can we place in the mouth of Priscus, and how much is later commentary?[61] Did Jordanes do what Bede did and amplify his source with explanatory material? Actually, he did just the opposite—he condensed Priscus, and didn't do a very good job of it. After telling us Attila "succeeded to the throne of the Huns," Jordanes includes the phrase, "together with his brother Bleda," as though the older brother were secondary to the younger. Bleda has been reduced to an afterthought—a necessary afterthought, since the older source (Priscus) must have written of him in the lost text. And though Bleda is described as "ruling over a great part of the Huns," we don't get the sense from this passage that he's Attila's superior, or even his equal. The text is schizophrenic, and it got that way because Jordanes has cut material about Bleda that would have clarified his actual role.

This is a classic philological problem. When you find these wrinkles in a text, you've found something that has a story behind it, something that's crying out for reconstruction. It's like packing a suitcase, and after it is shut noticing there's a sock sticking out of the side. The scholar is interested in that sock—the one thing that's not right—because that's how he or she is going to get into the suitcase. (I used this illustration once, and my teaching partner later stopped me in the hallway. "You've got to be kidding," she said. "A sock?" I admit now, as I admitted then, that it's a clumsy illustration. But it gets my point across.)

The sock sticking out of *this* suitcase is Bleda, and he has an interesting story to tell. It's a story of treachery; the actual position of Bleda in the Hunnish command was gradually obscured by later copyists of Priscus, as their own versions of history emphasized the world-historical significance of Attila. Though Bleda was never completely forgotten,[62] what did get lost over time, especially in the historical record, was the sense of how important he actually was, of why it was necessary for Attila to kill him, and how that treacherous act in 445 prefigures how Attila himself died in 453. Fortunately, a residue of the old text of Priscus remains, just enough—like a tiny swab of DNA—to yield some surprising evidence.

EXHIBIT THREE

Attila's death in 453 is connected in some way
to Bleda's death in 445.

Let's look again at what Jordanes wrote, remembering all the while that Priscus is the source behind what we're reading. "Attila sought to increase his strength by murder. Thus he proceeded from the destruction of his own kindred to the menace of all others. But though he increased his power by this shameful means, yet *by the balance of justice he received the hideous consequences* of his own cruelty." Jordanes goes on to say even more explicitly that Bleda was "slain by the treachery of his brother." Most historians don't doubt the claim that Attila killed his older brother; what *has* always been overlooked is how this particular fact is couched within a highly rhetorical style. Bleda's death is not reported as a brute fact but as a fact that has special significance in the larger scheme of things. He tacks on a comment that looks far ahead to the end of Attila's life: "Yet by the balance of justice Attila received the hideous consequences of his own cruelty." Bleda's death and Attila's death are somehow linked. We can attribute this conclusion to Priscus.[63] He's the rhetorician, after all, the historian who's grappling with motives and seeking rational explanations for human events. Remember that trivial conversation in the tent? Remember how Priscus reached back to find a cause (the argument in Sardica) for an effect (Attila's harsh treatment of Bigilas)? He's doing the same thing here.

All stories do this—assemble facts in ways that construct meaning. That's the whole point of histories, religious texts, urban legends—to make sense of things by relating one fact to another. Nietzsche wrote that facts don't exist at all unless they're first given meaning. As a storyteller, Priscus seems to understand this intuitively, since Bleda's death for him comes freighted with meaning. Bleda's death helps explain Attila's life ("Thus he proceeded from the destruction of his own kindred to the menace of all others"). More significantly, it helps explain Attila's death. We're given two criteria by which to understand this event: *equivalence* ("balance of justice") and *causality* ("hideous consequences"). Just as Bleda died treacherously, betrayed by those closest to him, so also—"by the balance of justice"—Attila died, betrayed and treacherously slain by his own followers.

And the hideous consequences?

He who lives by the sword dies by the sword.

EXHIBIT FOUR

Priscus originally wrote a second version of Attila's
death in which the Hun died violently.

Yet if we flip ahead a few chapters in Jordanes's *Gothic History* to read
how Attila died, we find no treachery and no violence; just a bad nosebleed. Where's the balance and where's the justice? Where's the sense of
cause and effect? The Latin word Jordanes uses to describe Bleda's
death—*fraudibus*—means "by fraudulent means." Jordanes uses this
same word three more times in his *History*, always referring to tricks,
plots, and conspiracies.[64] According to Jordanes, what was Attila to expect
from his treacherous murder of Bleda? A "deformed exit"—*deformes
exitus*—expressed more idiomatically as a "dishonorable death." The root
word *deform* is used extensively by Jordanes, almost always to refer to
moral deformity, dishonorable or shameful behavior. The Roman general
Stilicho, for instance, ambushed the Goths in what Jordanes described as
an act of treachery, a blot of dishonor on his character. The consequence
of his dishonor, too, was a dishonorable death—he was betrayed and
murdered.

Now we've got a big sock—a big, polka-dotted sock—hanging out of the
suitcase. The Russian playwright Chekhov used a different metaphor when
he advised young writers to deliver what they promise. "If you put a gun on
the wall in the first act," he said, "make sure it goes off in the third." Jordanes fails to deliver, and there's only one good reason why. Remember that
Jordanes is abbreviating his source. He has copied what Priscus wrote about
Bleda's death (that's the gun in the first act). But when he shortens what
Priscus wrote about Attila's death, he effectively writes the gun out of the
third act. Priscus must have known more about Attila's death than Jordanes
has conveyed to us. Priscus must have originally included another account
of the death—an account of murder, *fraudibus*, "by treacherous means." Jor-

danes took that version out when he packed his suitcase.[65] Along the way we've lost the gun, but we've gained a dangling sock.

THE CASE OF THE PURLOINED VASES

In the little village ruled by Bleda's widow, the ambassadors were very wet and very tired. At first light they went searching for their baggage. It was all there, strewn around on the bank and soaking wet, but salvageable. The rest of the day was spent drying out their things and repacking for the journey. Before leaving, they paid a quick visit to the widow's hut and thanked her profusely for her kindness and generosity. Maximin presented her with silver drinking bowls and a few delicacies such as Indian peppers and exotic dried fruits. It would have been improper for Priscus to grill her about Bleda, as much as he might have wanted to. But their guides were Huns and Goths, and there's plenty he might have picked up along the way from casual conversation.

Seven more days of traveling, ever deeper into Hunnish territory, and they were ordered to stop in a certain village lying at the junction of several roads. Attila would be passing by this way in a few days and it was not right that they should precede him. It didn't take long to find out that they weren't the only Romans in town. A high-level delegation from Rome had also been ordered to wait. The local tavern must have become a little oasis of civilization for these ambassadors—a place where they could compare notes, exchange imperial gossip, slap each other on the back, and remind one another that even in this godforsaken place there were other Romans like themselves. These were the moments Priscus lived for as a writer, moments when the geopolitics of his world could be reduced, over a sour mug of Hunnish mead, to a single vivid story of greed and revenge. And, boy, did the Italians ever have a story to tell.

They were an impressive bunch. Romulus was a count. Promotus was a governor. Romanus was a duke. Their political connections were equally impressive. Romulus was the father-in-law of Orestes; Tatalus, the father of

Orestes, was also traveling with the embassy, though not in an official capacity. Attila's secretary, Constantius, must have been in Italy on business as he, too, was returning with the Western ambassadors. Priscus reminds us that Constantius was sent to Attila by Aetius. In addition to being hand-picked by the Western general, Constantius was well acquainted with the Roman diplomats, having known them all back in Italy. It was a tightly knit group.

The Italians told Priscus and Maximin a peculiar story about Attila's secretary, Constantius. This was not *the* Constantius who was now traveling with them. It was a story about the secretary who served before Constantius, *also* named Constantius and also sent to Attila by Aetius. Even Priscus seems to have been confused at first, since he stresses that these were two different men who happened to share similar profiles. A name and a patron was all that the second Constantius was hoping to share with the first, as the first Constantius had been crucified. That was the best that Constantius could hope for once Attila and Bleda found out what he'd done. The whole thing happened a number of years before, but the scandal was never resolved to Attila's satisfaction. He was still plenty worked up over the golden vases that ended up in a pawnshop in Rome.

Back in the early years of the Balkan wars, in 441 or 443, the Pannonian city of Sirmium was under attack by the Huns. The local bishop wrapped up some golden vases and spirited them off to Constantius for safekeeping. If the city should fall, then the gold could be used to ransom the bishop, or (in the event of his death) any other citizens taken hostage. It was meant to be an insurance policy. The city fell, of course, but Constantius turned his back, walked away, and abandoned the bishop to his fate. The first chance he got, Constantius packed the hot property off to Rome. A certain Silvanus, described as a banker, took the vases and gave him a loan that was to be paid back with interest. Details are lacking, which probably means that even the Italians didn't fully know what the secretary was doing. Perhaps Constantius was using the money as venture capital in some scheme and had every intention of coming back for the vases and later presenting them to Attila, having made for himself a tidy little profit on the side. Whatever was going on, Attila and Bleda were suspicious and decided to crucify him—just in case he was a spy. Better safe than sorry.

Nor does Priscus tell us how Attila found out that some of *his* property (as he believed it to be) was sitting in a pawnshop in Rome. Attila learned the specifics only after Constantius had been impaled, and so his motives, whatever they were, died with him. The vases were later given to the Church, but that didn't stop Attila from demanding them back. Destruction was the better part of ownership. He had destroyed Sirmium, so he owned the city and everything in it. Silvanus was a thief who should be turned over immediately *or else*—and the usual threats followed. To their credit, the Western Romans saw this as a simple matter of justice and held firm in their refusals. Silvanus was innocent. It would be dreadfully wrong to turn him over to the Huns. Gold could be given, perhaps—that could always be arranged. But the life of this man was nonnegotiable. And that's where things stood.

Like a good classical rhetorician, Priscus could see "the whole in the part"—or, as the textbooks described it, *pars pro toto*. This may explain the fascination Priscus had for these personal encounters. It's as though the whole sorry geopolitical mess Rome found herself in was bound up in the greedy motives and petulant claims of this one tawdry scandal. This was more than a good story for Priscus. He must have seen in the close connections of these Western Romans the fertile grounds for a conspiracy. Orestes and Constantius served in the Hunnish high command; but they were *Romans*, and they could be convinced to betray Attila.

KULTUR IN PANNONIA

When Attila had finished celebrating his nuptials, he passed by the village where the Eastern and Western ambassadors were waiting. They fell in line and followed him across "many rivers" (all unnamed) until they reached a large village. A throng of maidens in elaborate formations came out to welcome the king. They held white linen sheets up over their heads as they danced and sang. Attila's procession then entered the village and stopped first at the house of Onegesh, Attila's prime minister and the brother of Scottas. Here Priscus witnessed a formal welcome as Onegesh's wife led her servants from the house, bearing trays of delicacies and goblets of wine. Attila remained seated on his horse and took a ceremonial nibble of the food and a sip of the drink. After the formalities, Attila proceeded to his palace, which (Priscus noted) was situated at the highest point of the village. Maximin and Priscus remained as dinner guests of Onegesh and his wife. The host couldn't stay for dinner, however, as he had just returned from a diplomatic mission himself and Attila had not yet heard the outcome of the trip—not to mention the broken arm that Attila's son had suffered on the journey. It had been an accident—he tripped and fell—but Onegesh wanted to tell Attila about it personally since he had been entrusted with the welfare of the king's son.

Onegesh's house was the second-most impressive in the village. Attila's palace, the most impressive, was just a stone's throw away. Both structures were made entirely of wood that was highly polished and precisely fitted together. Both structures were enclosed by wooden walls. Attila's walls even had little towers, features that were intended, Priscus notes, "not for safety, but for beauty." Onegesh had a Roman bath, built out of stone by a Roman hostage captured in the Balkan wars. (The unfortunate man told Priscus how he had labored long and hard to build this exquisite indulgence for Onegesh, believing that freedom would be his reward. But Onegesh liked his work so much that he kept him on as his family's bath attendant.) These little touches of comfort and beauty were not what the Romans expected to find. Culture had been found in the barbarian capital after all, even if it was culture with a capital *K*.

What Priscus relates next has raised questions about his reliability as an eyewitness. Maximin sent Priscus to Onegesh's house the following morning to present gifts from the emperor and to schedule a formal audience with Attila. While waiting outside the door and pacing back and forth, Priscus encountered a man who was dressed like a Hun but who greeted him with the Greek salutation *"Chaire!"* or "Hail!"

"I was surprised to hear a Hun speaking Greek," Priscus writes. Gothic and Latin were frequently spoken in the Hunnish camps, but Greek was almost never heard. They struck up a conversation and Priscus learned his life story, how he was a Greek and a merchant. How he had been captured in a city along the Danube and wound up as part of Onegesh's household. How he had fought for the Huns as a slave in their battles against the Romans and eventually won his freedom. How he had chosen to remain in Hunnish territory, married a barbarian woman and had children. How he now ate at Onegesh's table and how his life was far better than when he was a Roman. Priscus listened politely while the man enumerated the simple virtues of Hunnish life. When the Huns are done fighting, the man said, they know how to enjoy their lives. They live and let live. For the Romans, however, war means the uncertainties of serving under cowardly generals. Peace means high taxation and a corrupt legal system that provides relief only for those wealthy enough to bribe the right people.[66]

If for no other reason, the story is suspicious because it goes on for several pages. It's a transcript, far longer and more detailed than any other episode in the journey narrative. It reads like a staged piece of propaganda, the sort of thing the ancient Greek historian Thucydides would write when he wanted to make a point. Priscus listened, and then he presented his rebuttal. He offered a spirited defense of the Roman constitution, of its guarantees to individuals and its checks and balances between civil and military officers. Even with all its faults, Priscus argued, this system was far superior to what the barbarians had achieved. By the time he was done, the Roman expatriate had been reduced to tears.

"It's true," the man confessed. "The Roman system is much better." And then he gave the rhetorical game plan away: "Roman officials are ruining the Roman state," the man said, "by not following the example of their noble forefathers."

Priscus could have told him, "You took the words right out of my mouth," since that's exactly what he was doing. No doubt Priscus did in fact meet a fellow Greek outside Onegesh's house. No doubt they did speak of his life and briefly discuss the relative merits of Hunnish and Roman society. But the long dialogue between them exists not because it's "true" but because it advocates a conservative political position that Priscus wholeheartedly endorsed.

Scholars have treated this passage as though it's somehow unique, as though you could isolate a single biased passage in a "historical decontamination booth" and safely remove it from all the direct, unbiased observations that make up the rest of the narrative. That's naive. Whether he's saving the day in Alexandria, or demonstrating his cleverness by twisting the arm of Scottas, or tipping his hand when he connects Bleda's death to Attila's, what we've got here is a thoroughly engaged writer who has filled the narrative with *himself*. We don't have to choose between a historian and a propagandist. He's both. The windy conversation outside Onegesh's house is but one example of an active personality who is behind the text, shaping its every detail. Why shouldn't he dress up the dialogue? He was a rhetorician, and a patriotic partisan. Whether the conversation occurred or not is beside the point. It gives him the opportunity to criticize Roman politics on the one hand while vigorously defending the Roman system on the other.

After the "conversation" ended, we learn that the doors to the enclosure were opened and Onegesh came out with his attendants. Priscus ran up to him and announced he had personal gifts to present from Maximin, as well as the official payment of gold from Theodosius. Onegesh received the deliveries and told Priscus he would come by shortly to meet Maximin at their tent. Maximin was ready with an offer when Onegesh came by moments later. There were many gifts and much honor waiting for Onegesh in Constantinople, Maximin began, if he would cross over the Danube on an embassy to the emperor. Certainly Onegesh could apply his great talents to the intractable problems between the Huns and the Romans. Onegesh was suspicious of the flattery and asked whether this was just a clumsy bribe. "Do you think I will be seduced by Roman wealth, abandon my upbringing as a Hun, and leave my wives and children?" Onegesh had a question for the ambassador as well. "The king wants to know why a diplomat of consular rank wasn't sent." Maximin must have winced at that. "Attila wants your assurances that the next embassy will be headed by a man of sufficient dignity, such as a consul," and then he listed two or three names that the chieftain would find acceptable.

The next day, Priscus was sent out again with gifts, this time to the house of Attila's favorite wife, Kreka. It would be his first peek inside Attila's private compound. Priscus was admitted to the queen's house, where he found her reclining leisurely on a cushioned floor with servants tending to her every need. The encounter was short and sweet: a formal greeting, the presentation of gifts, and a swift departure. A crowd was gathering around Attila's house, so Priscus walked over to see what all the excitement was about. The king was going to hold court, hear disputes, and issue his judgments. The guards recognized Priscus and left him alone as he mingled among the crowd. Suddenly, the doors opened and Attila emerged "with a haughty strut, looking around here and there." Onegesh was at his side.

Once again we find ourselves under the spell of an eyewitness account that sounds convincingly real. But how real is it? Another historian earlier in the fifth century, Olympiodorus of Thebes, had recorded a similar description of a Roman general, Constantius—not to be confused with either of Attila's two secretaries: "He was a man with large eyes, long neck, and broad head, who bent far over the neck of the horse carrying him and *glanced here and there out of the corners of his eyes* so that he showed to all, *as the saying goes*, 'an appearance worthy of a tyrant.' "[67] Glancing to either side, as both Attila and Constantius did, may have been a stylized affectation, the universal body language of absolute power that the poet Shelley described as "the sneer of cold command." The fearsome gazes of Sargon the Great, etched in stone, come to mind. Or the drawings made by a British explorer in 1860 of the central African monarch Mutesa, strutting like a lion along the banks of Lake Victoria. It's not hard to imagine Attila strutting and glancing as well, since that's what tyrants do. But the description may depend more on a prefabricated stereotype ("as the saying goes, an appearance worthy of a tyrant") than it does on anything Priscus actually observed.

In other words, we can't stop asking questions, and we don't have to trust everything we read.

As the impromptu court session unfolded, the Italian diplomats walked up and joined Priscus. Rusticius was with them. (He's the translator Priscus had taken along when he went to see Scottas.) "Have you been dismissed yet?" he asked Priscus. "Or are you being prevented from leaving?" Priscus told them he would have an answer as soon as could speak with Onegesh again. And then Priscus turned to the Italian diplomats. "How are things going with you?"

"Badly," Romulus replied. "So far, we've had no success. Attila keeps threatening war if we don't hand over Silvanus or the gold vases."

Everyone agreed that Attila was being especially unreasonable, but nobody could figure out why. Romulus speculated that Attila's head had become so large that he couldn't even think clearly. No barbarian before Attila had ruled a unified nation the way he did. "He won't stop," Romulus said ominously, "until he controls everything. He's going to turn his army toward Persia next." Priscus thought very highly of Romulus, describing him as "an ambassador experienced in many affairs." The dark warnings about Attila—what his real intentions were and the folly of trying to placate him—must have made a deep impression on him.

"I hope," Priscus said, "that he does indeed turn his attention toward Persia. Better them than us." But everyone knew that even a Persian campaign would not protect them in the long run. Everyone knew about the ancient sword recently found by a shepherd, who noticed one of his calves limping and bleeding. The shepherd followed the trail of blood and found a half-buried sword, which he immediately brought to Attila. The discovery was proclaimed to be the fabled "sword of Mars," the god of war, and the omen could only signify one thing: Attila was destined to conquer the world. Stop at Persia? Not a chance.

FOLLOW THE DWARF

Already it had been a busy day for the Roman ambassadors, but there was much more to come. A messenger arrived with a dinner invitation from Attila.[68] "You are to come this evening to a banquet," he said. "Be there at three in the afternoon." So they were there at three in the afternoon, milling around outside the wooden enclosure along with the Italians, waiting to have dinner with the barbarians.

One of the first things Priscus noticed as they were ushered into the large dining hall was the bed. You couldn't miss it. It sat in the middle of the room and was surrounded by a canopy of white linens. Apparently, the banqueting hall doubled as Attila's bedroom.[69] Cupbearers presented the ambassadors with a ceremonial drink and directed them to their seats. Chairs were ranged along the sides of the hall. Attila sat on a couch in front of his bed. Priscus looked around and took in the whole scene. The position on Attila's right hand was the place of honor. Here Onegesh sat with two of Attila's sons. On Attila's couch, at the far end, sat Attila's oldest son. All three sons spent the evening looking at the ground, never daring to make eye contact with their father. On Attila's left, the next-highest place of honor, sat one of his honored advisors, Berica, a Goth. The diplomats were also seated here.

EXHIBIT FIVE

Priscus describes Attila's character in terms that
contradict the official account of his death.

The feast began with an elaborate toast ceremony. Each guest had his own cupbearer. Attila's cupbearer stepped forward and offered him a sip of wine. The king then saluted the highest-ranking official, Onegesh, who stood up and remained standing until the king had tasted. Each of the guests was so honored, all the way down the list. After this, the food was brought out and placed on several tables in the center of the room to be served family style. Various meats and bread were carried in, course after course of "sumptuous food," as Priscus calls it, each course punctuated by another round of toasts to the king's health. The food was served on silver platters—*Roman* platters—no doubt looted from the various cities and towns of the Balkans. All of the Hunnish officials drank from golden goblets, while Attila drank from a wooden mug. He ate very little—just some meat. His clothing was plain, with none of the jewels and embellishments that his lieutenants wore. Everything about him was simple and fastidiously clean. He was the picture of sobriety and self-control, quite different from the gluttonous and drunken chieftain portrayed in the story of his death.

Darkness had now fallen and pine torches were set ablaze to light the hall. That must have been the cue for the entertainment portion of the program to begin. Two singers presented their own compositions, martial chants about the greatness of Attila. Priscus looked around and observed the rapt attention of the guests. He noticed particularly the old men "whose bodies were weakened by time and whose spirits were compelled to rest." The old veterans wept as they remembered glorious battles from days of yore.

The mood was quickly broken by the next act. Priscus describes him as a crazy Hun who babbled unintelligibly and had everyone in stitches. But even that was just a warm-up for what followed. The hall exploded in laughter at the very sight of him hobbling toward the tables, dressed like a miniature warrior. He was a Moor, a hunchback and a dwarf, and his name was Zerko. His feet were large and his nose was flat. He lisped when he spoke. His stand-up routine consisted of a comic monologue in three languages—a mishmash of Hunnic, Gothic, and Latin. Priscus was fascinated by the grotesque figure before him and so he leaned over to ask a dinner companion what the dwarf's story was.

Zerko was a man without a country, a man without dignity, and a man without a wife. Seventeen years earlier he had been a young man in North Africa, where his unusual physiognomy had fated him to a life of privileged ridicule among the rich and powerful. In 432 a Roman legion under the command of General Aspar was in Libya trying without success to root out the Vandals from the North African provinces. (This is the same Aspar who would become a major force in Eastern politics and who would be slaughtered along with his family by Leo "the Butcher" in 471.) Priscus tells us that

Zerko was presented as a gift during the time Aspar was in Libya, though we're not told anything about the dwarf's previous owner.

The Libyan campaign was a memorable defeat. Even though the Romans would be humiliated by Gaiseric—the Vandal who went on to bigger and better things (he sacked Rome in 455)—there was a glimmer of Roman greatness in the desert sands. One of Aspar's lieutenants was a talented young man named Marcian, who was to be the future emperor of the East. The sixth-century historian Procopius, whose stories are generally deemed unreliable, tells us what happened.[70]

Marcian was among the defeated Romans who were herded into an open courtyard, an improvised slave market, where the soldiers awaited their fate beneath the Libyan sun. As the sun beat mercilessly on their heads, Marcian lay down and fell comfortably asleep. Above his head an eagle hovered in the air, floating up and down with outspread wings to shelter the young man from the heat. Gaiseric looked out a window, saw the sleeping man and the hovering eagle, and put two and two together. This was the imperial eagle of Rome. The young man was marked out for a great career. Who could challenge what the gods had decided? So Gaiseric, "being a quick-witted man," let Marcian go, but only after the future emperor swore an oath never to wage war against the Vandals.[71]

In this story Procopius was spinning a tale of destiny, the grand destiny of one man, Marcian, chosen by God to save the Empire. Marcian's life would be defined by these omens, these moments of divine favor. You will recall that when Attila died, Marcian dreamed of a broken bow in the sky—an improbable story, a piece of propaganda, related by Priscus. The barbarian who clutched the sword of Mars, who was called to a great purpose by the pagan gods, had met his match in the Second Constantine. Marcian's God was greater than Attila's—a point the imperial propaganda copied by Procopius and Priscus serves to emphasize.

In the Libyan desert Aspar had lost the war, but he gained a dwarf. Zerko appears next in Thrace, the province north of Constantinople, where Aspar lost another war—and this time lost the dwarf, too. During the Balkan campaigns in the early 440s, Zerko was captured and taken to the

Hunnish kings. Attila couldn't stand the sight of the hideous man, which is a sweet irony, since that's exactly how the Romans viewed Attila. Bleda, on the other hand, could hardly contain his mirth at the curious find and treated him like a pet. Zerko accompanied Bleda wherever he went, at feasts and on the battlefield. A special suit of armor was made for him, so that the stresses of battle could be relieved by a simple glance at the ridiculous little warrior. Perhaps the whole point about the armor was to suggest—it was a joke, of course—that Zerko was their secret weapon against the Romans. Who wouldn't die laughing to see what the Huns were sending against them? But Attila never saw the humor.

Zerko finally reached the point where he had suffered these indignities long enough. He ran away the first chance he got. Bleda was beside himself. "Bring me the dwarf! I want the dwarf!" It didn't matter that several other captives had fled as well. *They* were dispensable, but the dwarf could never be replaced. It was an act of extreme desperation for Zerko to flee, since everyone knew how the Huns punished deserters. The message had been repeated with every crucifixion: you can run, but you cannot hide. Sure enough, Zerko was caught. Though he was angry, Bleda immediately burst into uncontrollable fits of laughter all over again when he saw the dwarf being led back to camp in chains. Priscus gives us a "transcript" of the encounter:

"Why on earth did you flee?" Bleda laughed. "Is life here so intolerable that you prefer what the Romans can give you?"

Zerko looked up. "Perhaps the Romans could give me a wife."

That was not what Bleda had expected to hear.

"What I did was wrong," Zerko said. "But all I really want is a wife. Just give me a wife."

"A wife?" Bleda asked incredulously, and then doubled over again in laughter.

"Yes," Zerko repeated. "Give me a wife."

And that's what Bleda did. One of the noblewomen of the queen's retinue had recently fallen out of favor. She was now to be Zerko's wife. But Zerko's good fortune would soon end. When Bleda died, Attila sent the dwarf—without his wife—as a gift to Aetius. To be sure, the sober-minded Attila seems to have had little interest in supporting a court jester; but his decision to send Zerko to Rome may signal something more than his strong personal distaste for the dwarf. In divesting himself of a gift that had been given to Bleda by a Roman general, Attila was declaring his sovereignty—his authority to dispose of Bleda's possessions in a dismissive way. The dwarf was not sent back to Aspar, whom Bleda had defeated in the East, since that might be interpreted as a sign of weakness; instead, he was given to a third party in the West. Aetius didn't want the dwarf any more than Attila did, and so he sent him back to Aspar in Constantinople. Forget about following the money. If you want to know who's in charge in *this* story, you have to follow the dwarf.

EXHIBIT SIX

Edecon's relationship with Zerko
suggests that Edecon once served Bleda
before Bleda was murdered by Attila.

A few years later, Edecon was in Constantinople on a diplomatic mission. While he was there, he persuaded Zerko to come back with him to Pannonia. Edecon promised to use his influence with Attila to have Zerko reunited with his wife. But Attila was not amused when Zerko returned home. Edecon's request was denied, though Attila did spare the dwarf's life. Zerko's punishment, it seems, was to be perpetually separated from the wife Bleda had given him.

Why did Edecon put his own prestige on the line and take such a personal interest in Zerko's fate? Could it be that Edecon, too, once served Bleda before he served Attila and therefore felt an obligation to look after his late chieftain's "property"?

A possible clue is found in an ancient source, Prosper of Aquitaine, who tells us that after Attila killed his brother, "he compelled Bleda's followers to follow him."[72] Edecon's reputation as a warrior would make him a prime addition to Attila's inner circle. If Edecon had in fact once served Bleda (which is suggested by his close relationship with Zerko), then Edecon suddenly emerges as a more complex figure and a more intriguing suspect, one whose motives for wanting Attila dead had more to do with personal revenge than financial gain. The phrase we encountered earlier, "by the balance of justice," looks a lot less cryptic when you can wrap it up in flesh and blood and put a name behind it. Edecon did thwart the first assassination attempt (after agreeing to it)—but only because he feared it would not succeed. A few years later Edecon would be persuaded once again, when the conditions were right, to pursue his vengeance against the man who had murdered his chieftain, Bleda.

Priscus would remember the odd tensions of that night when he dined with Attila—the hostilities and unspoken grievances that were held in check by the powerful presence of one man. But it was the faces, more than anything else, that lingered in his memory. There was the face of that Moorish dwarf, a face crushed by humiliation and loss. There was the face of Attila, who "remained unmoved," Priscus wrote. "His expression never changed. Nor did he reveal in word or deed that he had any laughter in him at all." Priscus would also remember how that stony expression gave way to a smile when Attila's youngest son, Ernach, came to the table. Attila patted the boy's cheeks and looked at him tenderly. The affection surprised Priscus, since Attila had completely ignored his other sons all night. A barbarian seated near Priscus leaned over and filled him in: Attila's behavior had everything to do with an important prophecy. The Huns would be defeated, an oracle had said, but their empire would be restored by Ernach. Attila's youngest son was a child of destiny and the apple of his eye. Centuries later, German poets relished the tale of what actually happened to the favorite son. This human touch, the paternal stroking of Ernach's cheek, would undergo a perverse twist as the story of Attila's death grew to legendary proportions in the northern lands of the Goths.

FOUR

INCIDENT IN BURGUNDY

DESPITE the entertainment, the dinner party wasn't nearly as bad as the German poets later recorded it. The hall wasn't torched and Attila didn't end up devouring the hearts of his own sons before the evening was over. Still, that's how the poets remembered Attila, not so much at *this* feast but at the one that culminated in his death. The barbarian king soberly depicted by Priscus underwent centuries of fantastic, mythic re-creations as his legend became the common property of the Middle Ages. Far from the plains and rivers of Hungary, the name of Attila lived on in the mouths of poets. Over time, as we have seen, he became Ætla in England, Etzel in Germany, and Atli in Scandinavia, the form of his name keeping pace with the phonetic changes occurring within the various Germanic dialects. This man who had controlled the lives of so many people (half the world once trembled at the mention of his name) was now at the mercy of a handful of poets.

Why did the story of Attila's death spawn more legends than the fall of Troy?

And how can these spurious accounts help solve the mystery of his death?

The memories of the Germanic tribes may have been faulty (Homer's was, too), but there remains a trace of historical truth even in the most fantastic stories they told.[73] Attila wasn't killed by his young German bride; but their stories do provide evidence that murder was in fact suspected from the very beginning.

Attila's death occurred within a distinct political and religious climate, and this is what we must reconstruct if we're to make any headway in cracking the case. Attila died at a most advantageous time for his enemies, when he was strategically the weakest. A confluence of interests—German insiders, Western and Eastern Romans—would have had to come together in a plot that spanned the Empire. It is time to focus on the German part of the puzzle. The evidence we'll examine is as wide-ranging as the Germanic tribes themselves, from ecclesiastical histories written in Constantinople to lurid stories told about Attila on the snow-swept farms of medieval Greenland. Everything will bring us back to this question, "What did the Germans know and when did they know it?"

WHO'S YOUR DADDY?

We left Priscus and Maximin at a feast somewhere in Attila's territory, watching as Attila tenderly stroked the face of his young son. Up to this point we've approached the truth behind his death as a story about Huns and Romans. But it's also a story about Germans, those loosely confederated tribes who were under Attila's control: the Ostrogoths, Gepids, Herulians, Rugians, Scirians, Thuringians, Lombards, Alemanni, and Burgundians.[74] When the Huns thundered into Europe in the fourth century, the balance of power that had held for centuries between Rome and the northern barbarians was violently disrupted. The Huns built no great cities and authored no great ideas, but they still managed to influence the course of Western civilization in a profound way. How? By setting off a continental shoving match from east to west. Nineteenth-century historians used a more technical term to describe this chaotic period—the *Völkerwanderung* (the "folk wandering"), though nowadays, it's simply referred to as the Great Migrations.[75] All across Europe people were dislodged from their native homelands, including the Angles and Saxons who packed up for England in the fifth century. The turmoil didn't come to an end until the Vikings said so, after settling first Iceland, then Greenland, and even exploring the eastern coastline of North America around the year 1000.

If you were German and really didn't want to move, you could pick sides and become either Hunnish vassals or Roman *foederati* (federated allies). The Huns were very persuasive, and their ranks soon swelled with German warriors; but there were some notable holdouts as well. Never under Attila's "big tent" were the Franks, the Vandals, and the Visigoths, although the Huns maintained relations with them—sometimes hostile and sometimes friendly. More often than not, the Franks were a thorn in Attila's side and one of the excuses he used to invade the Western Empire in 451. With their headquarters in Gaul, the Franks were in a good position to benefit strategically when Rome finally collapsed. In time, they would become the most powerful force in Europe under Charlemagne's rule, and would give their name to the nation of France.

The Vandals—who gave their name not to a nation but to an antisocial behavior—were one of the most fiercely independent of the Germanic tribes. They migrated south from the Carpathian Basin as early as the third century A.D. as the Huns began pressing in from the east. Eventually, the Vandals settled in the Roman provinces of Spain and North Africa, where they controlled vital shipping lanes and pursued a policy of blockades, embargoes, and general piracy. For nearly fifty years the Vandals were ruled by Gaiseric, an indomitable man who is generally acknowledged as the greatest barbarian leader of his time. The reputation of the Vandals was assured in 455 when Gaiseric sacked Rome, the Eternal City, looting it at will and carrying back treasures and hostages to their capital at Carthage.

The Goths played an ambivalent role in the Roman drama, at times contributing to the Empire's collapse, and at other times helping to prop it up. From a purely philological standpoint the Goths were the most important of the Germanic tribes, hands down. Migrating south from Sweden in the first century B.C., the Goths began a long, southerly trek toward the Black Sea. Along the way they divided into two main branches, probably in the fourth century A.D. From this point on they would be known as the eastern Goths (Ostrogoths) and the western Goths (Visigoths).[76] The Visigoths dealt the Romans a major defeat at Adrianopolis in 378, an event that deeply shook the Empire and that must be seen, in retrospect, as a preview of coming attractions. Thirty years later the Visigothic king, Alaric, surrounded Rome but spared the city intact. Only weeks after withdrawing his forces from Rome, Alaric suddenly took ill and died in 410. Another harbinger of things to come? Attila, too, would threaten Rome, withdraw his troops, and die (so they say) of natural causes. Either history just keeps repeating itself or historians just keep repeating themselves. We'll soon see that the historians, not the events, seem to be caught in a loop.

There would be more conflict in the decades to come as the Visigoths settled in Gaul. Two decades of war with Rome ensued, during which the Huns were often used as Roman proxies; but eventually, the Visigoths, too, would join the Roman cause and form the backbone of Rome's defense when Attila invaded the West in 451. Later on, after the Western Empire collapsed, the Visigoths would maintain an independent kingdom in Spain until the Muslims arrived in the eighth century. Very few traces remain from their centuries in Iberia—some place-names and a few loan words in Spanish. Long before they ever migrated into Spain, however, the Visigoths had already produced their most enduring cultural legacy: the translation of the Bible into the Gothic language by a fourth-century Visigothic priest named Wulfila (Little Wolf). A large portion of Wulfila's translation has survived, making this text the Rosetta Stone of Germanic philology—the oldest surviving specimen of any written Germanic dialect.

Here's how Wulfila rendered the familiar opening phrase of the Lord's Prayer into Gothic: *Atta unsar thu in himinam*, "Our Father which art in heaven." If that first word, *Atta*, looks familiar to you, it's because most scholars believe that *this* is the root word forming Attila's name. Hard to believe, I know, but the subjugated Germanic tribes referred to Attila by the nickname "Father." They even went one step further by adding the diminutive -*ila* to make the word more familiar, more intimate—"Daddy." Among the Germanic tribes of the fifth century, then, the question "Who's your daddy?" was the most important political question you could ask.

Some scholars (mostly Hungarians) have found it hard to swallow that a Hun would have a Germanic name, but this is rather easily explained. For several decades there had been considerable intermingling between the Huns and Goths.[77] We can imagine how the nickname might have arisen by recalling that nineteenth-century Native Americans referred to the U.S. president as the Great White Father. Russian peasants, too, used to call the czar *batyushka*, the diminutive form of "father" and roughly equivalent to "daddy." But the question seems also to have been asked and answered for us in ancient times. Jordanes anticipated this very objection when he wrote: "Don't let some ignorant person quibble over the fact that the tribes of men use many names, the Sarmatians from the Germans and the Goths frequently from the Huns."[78] Even today, we don't necessarily assume that a boy is Irish just because he's named Sean or Patrick.

If we can grant that Attila's name means "Daddy," and is not taken from the Turkish name for the Volga River, Ätil, as some scholars have asserted, then suddenly—hold on!—we have a pronunciation problem on our hands. You've probably been mispronouncing Attila's name, I'm guessing, for the first three chapters of this book, accenting the second syllable: a-TIL-la. But if the name is really Germanic, then the accent is completely wrong. When Proto-Germanic split off from its parent language, Indo-European, sometime before 500 B.C., the new dialect distinguished itself (in part) by a regular shift of the word accent to the first syllable. Curiously, this ancient tendency to lean a little harder on the first syllable of a word explains some of the quirks of American dialectal speech. Take, for instance, how some speakers in the southern United States pronounce *Detroit* and *police* (two words of French origin where the accent would normally fall on the second syllable) as DEE-troit and POH-lice. Cultural snobs may regard this as a mark of unsophistication; the linguist, however, hears an ancient pedigree behind these pronunciations, a linguistic force that's over three thousand years old. This accent shift also accounts for the loss of grammatical word endings as you read your way from *Beowulf* to Chaucer to Shakespeare. It also accounts for how Attila's name *must* be pronounced, with the accent on the first syllable: AT-til-a. Does it matter how his name was pronounced? Not really. But there's an important reminder here. We can only understand his name—its meaning and pronunciation—as the product of living historical forces. So, too, with Attila's life and death.

Attila's name holds other secrets, too, and these are somewhat more relevant to our story. In the Latin and Greek histories, Attila's name retained a stable written form: *Attila*. But the oral form of Attila's name shows a different history as poets continued to sing about him centuries after his death. The Germanic languages were changing—becoming Old English, Old High German, and Old Icelandic—and Attila's name changed, too, like every other word. These phonetic developments are like linguistic fingerprints, enabling us to reconstruct and even date the history of the legends. For example, the medieval German form of Attila's name, *Etzel*, clearly shows the effects of what's called umlaut in the Germanic languages, whereby a front vowel (an *i* or *e*) in a second, unstressed syllable affects the quality of the vowel in the first, stressed syllable.[79]

It sounds technical, but it's really pretty simple to illustrate. (For your sake as well as mine, I'll keep this excursion into linguistic reconstruction as brief as possible.) Linguists classify vowels according to where the sound is formed within the speaker's mouth. There are front vowels and back vowels, high vowels and low vowels. When you go to the doctor and he sticks a tongue depressor in your mouth, he asks you to emit a low back vowel: *Aaaaah*, written phonetically as [a]. When we try to imitate the squeaking of a mouse—*Eeeeeh*—we form the vowel high and toward the front of the mouth, which is written phonetically as [i]. What kind of vowel you make depends on the place in your mouth where you're forming the sound. From the front to the back of your mouth, you form the following vowels: i-e-u-o-a, which (when read phonetically, in English anyway) sounds something like *"ee-ay-oo-oh-ah."* (Notice how your jaw drops to its lowest position, the tongue-depressor position, as you go from *ee* to *ah*.) Umlaut is the tendency of a back vowel in the stressed first syllable to imitate the position of the front vowel in the unstressed second syllable. There's a very simple reason why this change occurs: *It makes the word easier to pronounce.* When both vowels in both syllables are produced in the same part of the mouth, then you don't have to work as hard to articulate the sound.

Everything's clearer with an illustration, so here goes. Umlaut is what turned the *Angles* into the *English*. When the suffix -*ish* was added to the unstressed second syllable to form an adjective, the process was kicked into gear. Here's how it looks:

ANGL-*ish* ➜ ENGL-*ish*

The [i] in the second unstressed syllable exerts an influence on the [a] in the first stressed syllable. Rather than laboring one's mouth to go from a back vowel [a] to the front vowel [i], the speaker anticipates the second vowel— meets it halfway, as it were—and thereby simplifies the articulation of the word.

Many pairs of words in English preserve this ancient vowel shift, even where the original endings of the word that brought about the change in the first place have been lost. Go back far enough in the history of English (even before the Old English we have in *Beowulf*), and the plural form of *man* would have looked something like *manniz*. The old plural ending -*iz* has long since been sloughed off, but the vowel change that it produced remains like a fossil: *men*. The back vowel [a] has shifted to a front vowel [e] to make it closer to the articulation of the back vowel in the ending [iz]. Incidentally, Wulfila's Gothic New Testament gives us the data we need—the earliest, most "primitive" Germanic forms—to reconstruct these lost words.

Just as the Angles became the English through umlaut, so also Attila became Etzel. I don't want to belabor the phonetics of it, and I'm sure you don't want me to either, but you shouldn't just have to take my word for it. So, apologies aside, here's how a philologist would describe the changes from Attila to Etzel. Attila became Ezzilo in Old High German, where he makes a brief appearance as a "ring-giving" king. Phonetically, the name demonstrates both umlaut, which turned the initial [a] into [e], and the High

German consonant shift, which turned the intervocalic -tt- into -zz-. Later on, the final vowel was lost in Middle High German (a process known as apocopation), which yielded Etzel as the final result.

And here's where all this ceases to be a pedantic excursion into linguistic laws and becomes instead a crucial piece of historical evidence. The vowel shift known as umlaut occurred around the sixth century, which means that Attila's name has been a continuous part of Germanic vocabulary ever since his life and death. The High German consonant shift, too, occurred between the sixth and eighth centuries. Attila's name and character were therefore not arbitrarily reintroduced into Germanic poetry at a later date. If this had happened, then we'd encounter the form of the name found in the historical sources (Attila).[80] Instead, we see the name changing like every other word in the native languages of the Germanic poets—since they never stopped talking about him. The stories told about Attila were produced within an unbroken chain of tradition that goes back to the fifth century. We cannot simply dismiss these accounts because they're so obviously fictionalized. As Heinrich Schliemann demonstrated about Homer and Troy, there is almost always a dimly recalled memory lying at the heart of a legend.

If this weren't so, philologists would have nothing to do.

BUSBECQ'S LEXICON

Unlike their western cousins, the Ostrogoths cast their lots with the Huns and formed the leading edge of Attila's army. After the last of the Caesars was deposed in 476, the Ostrogoths established a kingdom centered in Italy that stretched as far east as the Black Sea. The Ostrogothic Kingdom reached its zenith in the sixth century under Theodoric the Great, who would be remembered for centuries to come as the Dietrich of medieval German poetry. It was during Theodoric's reign, perhaps around 525, that a well-educated Roman named Cassiodorus wrote an extensive history of the Goths, the purpose being to provide the new overlords of Italy with a history every bit as glorious as Rome's. Cassiodorus relied on many earlier authors, among whom was Priscus the rhetorician. The history that Cassiodorus penned lasted no longer (unfortunately) than the Ostrogothic Kingdom did. By the middle of the sixth century, the Eastern Roman Empire under Justinian the Great had broken the Gothic stranglehold on Italy.

An Ostrogoth in Justinian's court named Jordanes took the several volume *Gothic History* that Cassiodorus had written forty years earlier for his patron Theodoric and produced his own condensed version. After the cutting and pasting was done, Jordanes had produced a very different *Gothic History*, a tendentious piece of propaganda that peddled the Byzantine line. The message to his fellow Goths was clear. *Yes, we have a glorious history— kings such as Ermanaric and Theodoric testify to that. And yes, our greatness has at times been overshadowed, most notably by that parenthesis in history represented by Attila and the Huns. But now there is nothing to be gained by defying the divine right of Justinian. We are ennobled by our association with the Empire, just as we were once degraded by our subservience to the Huns.* The account of Attila's death that Jordanes preserved—the so-called "historical" account—is couched within this larger ideological framework. Attila's death is *not* a fact, neutrally observed. It is, rather, woven into the fabric of Jordanes's propaganda.

The Ostrogoths were destined thereafter to be absorbed into the other Germanic tribes. Their stories may have survived, but their national identity had been lost. Amazingly, though, one small group of Ostrogoths seems to have outlasted the Middle Ages intact, along the shores of the Black Sea in the region of southern Ukraine known as the Crimea. As early as the ninth century, travelers to the Crimean Peninsula began noticing that a people lived there who spoke a language that sounded like German, even though they dressed like Turks. The Crimea had been the ancient center of Ostrogothic culture; it was here that one of their greatest kings, Ermanaric, had ruled in the fourth century, before they were subjugated to the Huns and before their subsequent rise to power in Italy. Was it possible that the Goths survived the destruction of their kingdom and maintained their ancient language and traditions? It's not only possible, it's likely.

Off and on over the centuries, travelers continued to mention this unusual people who seemed so out of place. Everyone noticed how different their language was, how much like German it sounded. But this was long before the rise of modern linguistics, so nobody bothered to write any words down and *study* them—nobody, that is, until the sixteenth century. The Austrian ambassador to Istanbul from 1555 to 1562, a Flemish diplomat with an imposing name, Ogier Ghislain de Busbecq, was intrigued enough by the reports he'd heard to explore whether or not these were indeed the "last of the Goths." He was a well-educated man, an accomplished polyglot, and he had cultivated the humanistic curiosity so typical of the Renaissance. Under the reign of Suleiman the Magnificent, this city at the heart of the Ottoman Empire was a feast of discovery for Busbecq. For all his brilliance and curiosity, however, the Flemish ambassador is best remembered as a footnote in the exotic history of the tulip. Busbecq collected bulbs from the gardens of Suleiman and brought them back to Vienna, where they were cultivated and subsequently distributed to Holland and the rest of Western Europe. "The Turks call them *tulipam*," Busbecq wrote in his botanical survey of Suleiman's garden, though it's widely held that Busbecq misunderstood the translator's description of how the flower resembled a *turban*. This is our "linguist" in action and these are his "methods," but we're stuck with him, since Busbecq is our only link back to the mystery of the Crimean Goths.

Ancient culture interested him just as much as horticulture did. He was, after all, a Renaissance man. The persistent reports of a German enclave within the Ottoman Empire had to be checked out, and so he asked his interpreters to track down any "German-speaking people" who might come into the Grand Bazaar at Istanbul. It wasn't long before two merchants had been located. Busbecq invited them to dinner and for several hours he interviewed them and carefully recorded their pronunciation of 101 words. Each word was transcribed and its meaning was recorded. The story of this dinner, and the little lexicon of "Crimean Gothic" as it is now called, was written down by Busbecq in a letter he sent to a friend back in Europe. In a little more than two centuries the language would be extinct. A traveler in 1780 was still able to describe a handful of people in the Crimea who looked like Turks but sounded like Germans. Fourteen years later another traveler to the region could find no evidence at all of the people or their language.

Were these strange Crimeans truly descended from the Ostrogoths who once served under Attila? A consensus has slowly formed that, yes, these were Gothic people, not German immigrants from a later period. This conclusion has been arrived at with great difficulty. To start with, Busbecq was no linguist. His instincts were good, but his method left much to be desired. It turns out that neither man whom he interviewed was a fluent speaker of Crimean Gothic. The first had almost completely forgotten his native tongue. The second was a Greek who had learned Crimean Gothic as a second language while living in the region; since Busbecq himself spoke a little Greek (one of nine languages he was conversant in), this non-native speaker was the one he primarily interviewed. It might be assumed, then, that Busbecq was hearing the Gothic words pronounced with a Greek accent.

The raw material that philologists have to work with is the end product of a chaotic line of transmission. To start with, a subject who spoke Crimean Gothic as a second language pronounced the Gothic words with an accent and then translated them into Greek. Busbecq wasn't quite fluent in Greek, so he asked his assistant to translate the Greek explanations into Italian. Then Busbecq translated the Italian renderings of the Greek definitions of the Gothic words into the lingua franca of Renaissance Europe, Latin, when he drafted the letter to his friend. In writing down the Gothic words, Busbecq had to improvise his own crude method of phonetic transcription based on either German or Dutch spelling conventions. Busbecq's letter was eventually printed in France. The printer couldn't read Busbecq's handwriting very well, but that didn't stop him from typesetting and printing it anyway, presumably with numerous errors. The original letter is lost, so this printed version is all that remains of Crimean Gothic.

We start with what should be the best evidence of all—an eyewitness account—but look at how unreliable that evidence has become through the faulty transmission of the form and meaning of these hundred words. The phonetic forms of the words have been filtered down to us as follows:

Crimean Gothic → Greek accent → Dutch or German spelling → French typesetter

Similarly, we can approach the *meaning* of these hundred words only once we've navigated through a bewildering set of barriers:

Crimean Gothic → Greek translation → Italian translation → Latin translation

The story of the Crimean Goths is more than an obscure detective story in the annals of modern linguistics. Busbecq's lexicon is a sobering reminder that our knowledge has discrete limits. All that we know of these ancient Germanic tribes—as indeed all that we know of the death of Attila the Hun—is no more stable or certain than this imperfectly transmitted list of words.

We can imagine a couple of Gothic merchants appearing in the marketplace of Constantinople in 453, just as they did in Busbecq's day. We can imagine Priscus interviewing them through interpreters and writing down the rumors and conflicting accounts of Attila's death. Twenty years later he revised his notes and composed the final version of his history in Greek. In the generation after Priscus died, Cassiodorus took the published Greek account and translated it into Latin, making it a part of his own *Gothic History*. Another generation passed and Jordanes abridged the history of Cassiodorus, making whatever changes were necessary to satisfy his political patron. This is the version that has come down to us even while the original has been lost.

Eyewitnesses (c. 453) → Priscus (c. 470) → Cassiodorus (c. 525) → Jordanes (c. 550)

The historical account of Attila's death might as well have been typeset by a French printer who couldn't read the handwriting.

Bits and pieces of evidence are all we've got, fragments and scattered references that have survived against all odds like the Ostrogoths along the Black Sea. So, we make the best of what is left. With a little luck and a lot of patience, scholars can often break through these formidable obstacles, peeling away layer upon layer of transmitted error and arriving at a fair estimation of the truth. Philologists have been able to demonstrate that the hundred words in Busbecq's lexicon—mishandled and corrupted though they were—are indeed the only surviving specimens of a living Crimean Gothic language.[81] The words Busbecq wrote down at that dinner four centuries ago are more closely related to Wulfila's Gothic translation of the Bible than to modern dialects of German. Amazingly, the language had survived until the eighteenth century.

It's unlikely that any more groups of Germans disguised in Turkish clothes are awaiting discovery. So we're left with nothing but a tribal name for some of these other shadowy groups—"minor" tribes by the blunt reckoning of history. The Alemanni, the Thuringians, the Rugians, the Herulians, and the Scirians appear in the registry of nations that Jordanes gives us in his *Gothic History*. The Alemanni inhabited the Alsace region of France, but no trace of them survives except in one of those strangely accidental ways. Their tribal name became the generalized term in the Romance languages for the German nation: Allemagne in French, Alemannia in Italian, and Alemania in Spanish. Of the Thuringians and the Rugians we know next to nothing. Nor do we know much about the Herulians—not much that's reliable, anyway. A few scattered references here and there imply that they were a tribe of homosexual pirates who later participated in the settling of Iceland, but we're probably wise to be skeptical of these accounts.[82]

The Scirians are likewise obscure, though (too bad for them) they seem to have been federated with the Herulians. The Scirians merit another footnote, however, in that Jordanes identifies Edecon as hailing from this tribe.[83] Priscus calls Edecon a Scythian—that is, a Hun—but ever since the time of Herodotus this word had been a catch-all term for "savages who live beyond the borders." The evidence does suggest that Attila's lieutenant was a German. Later on, we'll take up the question of whether or not we can link Edecon with Odovacer, the German chieftain who deposed Rome's last emperor in 476. If so, then we can conclude that the Scirians did quite well for themselves after all.

The Gepids are somewhat better known to us, once again largely through what Jordanes has written. Their domain was farther to the north, in modern Poland, though their alliance with the Huns gave them the opportunity to travel widely in Europe. If Jordanes is to be believed, and by now his credibility is stretching thin, the tribal name of the Gepids means the "Slow Ones."[84] Of course, this is an example of the folk etymologies we find everywhere in ancient literature. It's hard to imagine Attila, whose signature military technique was devastating speed, shouting orders to the Slow Ones to outflank the Romans on the right. Indeed, history itself has called this pejorative name into doubt. One year after Attila died, the Gepids declared their independence from the Huns and dealt them a decisive defeat at the Battle of Nedao. The sons of Attila never recovered from this astonishingly quick payback, and Attila's Empire would never be reconstituted.

Attila's death exposed the fragility of the barbarian alliance: it had held together only through intimidation and brute force. Among the many tribes to emerge from Hunnish subjugation were the Lombards. Unlike the Gepids, the Lombards had the good sense to name themselves before somebody else did. They were the "Long Beards," as they explained it to anyone willing to listen, because their long beards were uniquely favored by Wotan, the Teutonic Zeus. With divine favor resting upon their facial hair, the Lombards invaded Italy in 568 under Alboin's leadership, supplanted the Ostrogoths, and were themselves later supplanted by the Franks in the eighth century. The cultural remains of their sojourn in Italy include their laws and their legends. The Lombard Laws have been described by an English historian as showing "something that is like a genius for law."[85] Decide for yourself:

> Concerning big toes. He who cuts off the big toe of another man's field slave shall pay two gold coins as compensation.

Whether this is genius or not, I don't know, but the laws are certainly quite comprehensive. (Separate laws govern the second, third, fourth, and fifth toes.)

The legends of the Lombards make for spicier reading, especially the tragic story of King Alboin and his wife, Rosimund. Writing in the eighth century, Paul the Deacon relates how Alboin killed his wife's father (he was a Gepid), fashioned a drinking vessel from his skull, and was poisoned by his wife out of revenge. Some scholars have held that this delightful story lies at the heart of the revenge plot that German poets told about Attila.[86] But this is surely wrong. As we'll soon see, the revenge plot must have circulated from the very moment that Attila died, some two centuries before Alboin and Rosimund began having their difficulties.

EXHIBIT SEVEN

The murder allegation existed from the
very beginning and was not concocted later in the
poetic imagination of the Germanic tribes.

The revenge plot has everything to do with another minor tribe, the Burgundians. Sandwiched between the Romans and the Huns, the Burgundians could never make their mind up which way they wanted to lean. In the end their indecision became their undoing. When push came to shove—as it must with the Romans on one side and the Huns on the other—the Burgundians found they had no friends at all and they were nearly wiped out by the Huns in 437. What happened to the Burgundians is the central problem we need to follow in this chapter. The story of this little nation that flourished for a generation on the western side of the Rhine might have become an insignificant footnote in the early history of Europe if not for the poets. But the poets just couldn't get enough of this tragedy—and centuries later, neither could Wagner.

MICHAEL A. BABCOCK

THE FALL OF THE BURGUNDIANS

How did a minor event in history, the "fall of the Burgundians," become the centerpiece of a nation's mythology? In order to answer this question, we must examine another kind of reconstruction philologists do: the reconstruction of legendary history.

The Burgundians were among those tribes who suddenly found themselves crowded when the Huns moved in from the East. Led by their king Gundahar, the Burgundians crossed over the Rhine in 406.[87] Some remained on the eastern side of the river, refusing to knuckle under to the Huns and converting to Christianity as a safeguard. In 430 these eastern Burgundians even managed to chalk up a victory against Octar, one of Attila's uncles. We'll come back to this obscure battle shortly, and especially to the manner of Octar's death, the details of which correspond closely to what historians would later write about Attila.

By 413 the Burgundians under King Gundahar had established a kingdom in Worms and entered into an alliance with the Empire as Roman *foederati*. But the political tranquility was shattered in the early 430s when the Burgundians began agitating for more land. They invaded the area around modern Trier and Metz but were soundly defeated in a counterattack led by the Roman general Aetius in 435–36. Among the best troops under Roman command were the crack units of Hunnish cavalry. As a young man, Aetius had been a diplomatic hostage in the Hunnish camp, where he learned their language, established personal relationships with their leaders, and assimilated their military techniques. Later, as a Roman general, Aetius would rely on his extensive personal contacts among the Huns to deploy them as Roman proxies. He even used them as leverage in his own political battles back in Italy, threatening at one time to invade Italy with his army of Huns if he didn't get his way.

A short peace was followed by another conflict in 437, this time fought only between the Burgundians and the Huns. Once again, we are so limited by our sources that we don't have a clue what precipitated this new round of fighting. Aetius didn't take part in the final campaign himself, though the Huns may have been unleashed on the little kingdom at his command. The results were devastating. Thousands of Burgundians were slaughtered in the bloodbath, including Gundahar and the entire royal family. The short but shining moment of Burgundian independence—a kind of German Camelot—had come to an end. The catastrophe would forever be remembered as "the fall of the Burgundians."

That's the history of it, as far as we understand the threadbare details that have survived. The critical element that has *not* survived, however, is what started the fighting in the first place. Here's where the poets found their opening—and ran with it. The historical figure of Gundahar survived in the poetic accounts as Gunther in the southern German epics and Gunnar in the northern Scandinavian poems. Attila, who had played no historical role at all in the fall of the Burgundians, was brought into the narrative nonetheless. This is significant (as we shall see), especially since the poets dovetailed the Burgundian disaster with Attila's death, events that were separated in history by at least sixteen years.[88] Before long the story acquired an epic scale; new characters were added to the cast and new plot-lines were developed. The story of Gundahar and Attila would become the great national epic of medieval Germany; it would fall into obscurity only to be revived by Richard Wagner and the Brothers Grimm during the nationalistic frenzy of the nineteenth century.

At some point in the early development of the epic, two separate stories were fused together. This bipartite structure is seen most clearly in the fullest expression of the story, the thirteenth-century German poem known as the *Nibelungenlied*, or the "Poem of the Nibelungs."[89] The two halves of the poem reflect how the epic evolved from historical events to oral legends to a finished literary epic. It will be necessary to sketch the plot briefly— very briefly—so that this process of development can be understood more fully. The main point we want to keep our eye on, and ultimately come back to, is the philological assumption that these fabulous tales actually contain some trace memories of ancient times.[90]

Who were the Nibelungs? Not another obscure Germanic tribe but the legendary keepers of the gold of the Rhine—greedy dwarfs. In the poem, the peerless Germanic hero Siegfried acquired the golden horde of the Nibelungs, earning him the right to court Kriemhild, sister of Gunther (who is based upon the historical Burgundian king Gundahar). Krie*mhild*'s name may also conceal a remote historical reference to Attila's last bride, (H)*ildi*co—a possibility that will become more significant as the plot unfolds. Like Siegfried, Gunther is looking for a wife, and he casts his eyes westward toward Brunhild, the queen of Iceland. The problem for Gunther is that Brunhild has the strength and will of an Amazon. No ordinary man could best her in battle or in bed.

The first half of the *Nibelungenlied* is a self-contained tale that follows the ill-fated love affairs of Siegfried, a warrior, and Gunther, the king. Little or no historical content is to be found in this tale of a dragon-slayer, a magic cloak, a dwarf, and an Amazon. The two heroes vow to help each other in their separate courtships. If Siegfried can secure Brunhild's hand for Gunther, then King Gunther will allow Siegfried to marry his sister, Kriemhild. Siegfried is pretty confident of the outcome; after all, he has a magic cloak. He uses it to defeat Brunhild in competition and deceive her into thinking he's actually Gunther. Siegfried takes a ring and girdle from Brunhild as a token of his victory. Weddings follow and it appears that everyone is living happily ever after.

That is, until the queens quarrel.

The plot turns on a cat fight between Brunhild and Kriemhild. Years have gone by and Siegfried and Kriemhild are visiting Gunther and Brunhild at Worms. Brunhild has been harboring an intense jealousy over how much power and influence Siegfried has been acquiring at the expense of her husband, Gunther. She rips into Kriemhild without warning and Kriemhild dishes it right back. "You were tricked into marrying Gunther!" Kriemhild taunts. But Brunhild doesn't believe a word of it, until Kriemhild produces the ring and girdle Siegfried had taken the night he deflowered her. Brunhild responds by setting in motion a plot that draws in her husband and his right-hand man, Hagen. Siegfried is treacherously murdered. This is roughly where the first of the two stories originally ended, as reconstructed by philologists over the past two hundred years. It's a fanciful tale of love, deception, and revenge involving an ensemble of five main characters—two couples, with the highly complex figure of Hagen right in the middle of the action.

Gunther	Siegfried
Hagen	
Brunhild	Kriemhild

Keep your eye on Hagen. Later on, we'll ask (though only in passing) if he might really be Aetius, who occupied an equally ambiguous position in the historical account of the Burgundian disaster.

The second half of the *Nibelungenlied* is more "historical" in the sense that it is based loosely on the fall of the Burgundians and the death of Attila. Now it's Kriemhild's turn to nurse her hatred and plot her revenge. She had trusted Hagen; she had even confided in him, wrongly believing he was Siegfried's friend. Hagen had acquired the golden horde of the Nibelungs, Siegfried's rightful possession, and sank it in the Rhine just to spite her. There was nothing left for her to do as a dispossessed widow but give her hand in marriage to Etzel, the king of the Huns. If she were patient, perhaps she could someday wreak a fitting vengeance on her husband's murderers. This second revenge plot unfolds with another ensemble of five characters, this time with Etzel replacing Siegfried as Kriemhild's husband.

Gunther	Etzel
Hagen	
Brunhild	Kriemhild

By the time the *Nibelungenlied* achieved its final literary form in the thirteenth century in southern Germany, Attila had undergone an extreme literary makeover. He had become generous, wise, loyal, domestic. He had become, in a phrase, great husband material. The literary tastes of the times made these changes necessary. The raw, edgy style of heroic poetry was "out"; the refined, elegant, and verbose medieval romance was "in"—the style made popular by the French courts. Two details capture the essential shift in outlook: The nobles now drink wine at the table, not beer, and there are *ladies* at the feasts who are constantly fussing over their clothes and accessories. Etzel is pictured as the docile figurehead in a splendid court—a court that could rival King Arthur's. When we read of courtly ladies in magnificent attire and knights who embodied the chivalry of a later age, we are tempted to think that nothing "historical" could possibly remain in such an elaborate fiction. But a careful reading, a kind of literary archaeology, can excavate some strange and unexpected echoes of the past, reminding us once again of how much history may lie hidden beneath the layers of legend.

Etzel dotes on his wife, but Kriemhild hardly notices. She is consumed with thoughts of revenge. It takes several years, but her opportunity finally comes when the Burgundians accept an invitation and pay them a visit in Hungary. Gunther and Hagen bring thousands of their knights and walk into the trap Kriemhild has meticulously laid for them. "Kriemhild's old grief was embedded deep in her heart," the poet sings. But then, as the story is nearing its awful climax, we read something very puzzling: "Since there was no beginning the fighting in any other way, Kriemhild had Etzel's son carried to the table." The poet then interjects as a parenthesis: "How could a woman ever do a more dreadful thing in pursuit of her revenge?" By now we're expecting something terrible to happen, especially since the poet has told us in effect to brace ourselves. The tension increases even more when we read: "Four of Etzel's followers went immediately and returned with the young Prince Ortlieb to the king's table. Hagen, too, was seated there, and because of his murderous hate the boy was soon to die."

Hagen remarks that the boy has an "ill-fated look" on his face as if to foreshadow his imminent death. But nothing happens at the table; the curious little episode is unresolved and the tension fizzles out. It's not until a later chapter that Ortlieb is beheaded by Hagen, after the fighting had already begun. The problem with this is that the poet introduced the episode by suggesting that bringing Ortlieb to the table would *cause* the fighting to start, and bring the revenge to its conclusion. But that doesn't happen. What we read instead is what one critic has called a "strange non sequitur,"[91] something unmotivated and unfulfilled, completely pointless from the standpoint of the plot. We've got another one of those dangling socks here, as I've called them. We *know* something happened at the table in an earlier version of the story—the inconsistencies alone would tell us this. But we can go a step further since we have other versions that tell us what that "something" was. In the Old Icelandic *Thiðrekssaga* (thirteenth century), young Ortlieb is told to strike Hagen in the face and, when Ortlieb does, Hagen immediately beheads him and the fighting begins.

The "boy at the table" may be a historical echo, something of importance that was distantly recalled about Attila's son. Remember where we left Attila at the end of the last chapter? He was sitting at his table in the middle of the dining hall. While everyone else was enjoying the entertainment, Attila presided over the feast impassively, unmoved by all the mirth. And then Priscus noticed Attila's face suddenly light up when his youngest son, Ernach, was brought to his table. It may seem like a trivial parallel—two texts in which Attila's son is brought to the table during a feast—but the motif must be ancient (it appears in different forms in different versions) and it must be meaningful. Something salient was etched into the German memory. (It does seem incredible that a detail this small might actually be preserved over the centuries, disguised within a story that has dragons and magic cloaks; but it's no more incredible than finding a little band of Goths along the shores of the Black Sea, disguised as Turks.) What was the salient feature? Though the table itself is insignificant, what the boy at the table represented was not: a widely known prophecy about Attila's death. Priscus was so intrigued by Attila's change of behavior that he leaned over the banqueting table and asked a barbarian sitting nearby for an explanation. Why did Attila show such affection to his youngest son when he ignored his older ones? Because of the oracle, Priscus was told. The great chieftain would die and his empire would collapse and then be reunited under the rule of his youngest son, Ernach. We can only wonder how many times Ernach was brought to the table so that his father could stroke his cheek. What Priscus witnessed on that one occasion must have happened often—often enough so that everyone knew the prophecy, and often enough for Ernach to wend his way into medieval poetry. The irony, of course, is that the boy at the table was transformed in the Germanic tradition from the object of Attila's hope to the harbinger of his death.[92]

But Etzel doesn't die in the German version, the *Nibelungenlied*.[93] Kriemhild's final vengeance is directed instead against Gunther and Hagen. When we look to the North, however, we uncover the older form of the story, just as we did with the boy at the table. The Scandinavian version tells us Attila was the original object of his wife's revenge; here, Attila certainly dies at the end. We encounter the same cast of characters in the North, though the names are slightly altered: Sigurð, Gunnar, Guðrun (not Kriemhild), Brynhildr, Högni, and Atli. (The eth symbol in Icelandic, ð, is pronounced "th.") We wouldn't even be able to compare these northern tales to the *Nibelungenlied* if the Vikings hadn't loved the sea. They took their stories with them when they settled Iceland and Greenland around the year 1000. Eventually several dozen poems about the early Germanic gods and heroes were written down on vellum parchment, stitched up into a book, and forgotten.

In 1643 a manuscript hunter and cleric named Bishop Brynjólfur discovered a book that consisted of 45 pages of Old Icelandic poetry. We don't know where he found the *Codex Regius*, as it's now called, but paleographic evidence allows us to reconstruct its early history. The style of writing and the type of vellum are among the clues that point to its production in Iceland in the second half of the thirteenth century. The poetic "lays" (short dramatic poems in epic style) had been copied from older manuscripts, which themselves were dependent on oral traditions reaching all the way back to the Great Migrations. The several dozen poems in this collection are known as *The Poetic Edda*, and they're recognized as the greatest surviving repository of old Germanic culture. When these poems were rediscovered, the stark world of the pre-Christian North came to life once again—the world of Oðin (Wotan in Old English) and Thor, Sigurð and Atli. Philologists were now able to reconstruct the lost world of the tribes who had served both Attila and Aetius, the tribes who ushered out the ancient world and fashioned the Middle Ages from what remained. Just as Wulfila's Gothic translation is the Rosetta Stone for the reconstruction of Germanic languages, and the *Nibelungenlied* for texts and legends, so also *The Poetic Edda* is the foundation for reconstructing pre-Christian Germanic myth, religion, and cultural lore.

Attila's appearance in this pantheon of heroes and villains is short and definitely not sweet. He's called Atli, and he's a bloodthirsty tyrant, greedy for gold, and willing to further his ends (as Attila was) by murdering his own brother. Two poems in the *Edda* are devoted to his story.[94] The first is known as the *Atlakviða* (at-la-KVEE-thuh), the "Lay of Atli." It's a masterpiece of economy, told with dramatic intensity in little more than 150 lines. The language is stark and vivid, punctuated by "screeching geese" and clanging mugs of ale; the characters are fierce and the plot is luridly violent. The second poem, *Atlamál* (at-la-MOWL), the "Ballad of Atli," is considered a later production. By common consensus, it's the inferior of the two, marred by digressions and overblown dialogue, though it preserves the same basic story line.

The single manuscript in which these poems survive, the *Codex Regius*, tells us in a heading that the two Atli poems come from Greenland, the furthest outpost of medieval European civilization. This claim is probably true, at least about the second poem, *Atlamál*. Whoever wrote down these poems certainly knew more than we do about where they came from. There's ample internal evidence to back up the claim that these stories were preserved in the little farms clustered along the coast of southern Greenland. The *Atlamál* poet seems quite ignorant of life in Iceland or Norway. Details of flora and fauna also give him away: for instance, a minor character has a prophetic dream about a white bear, generally identified as a polar bear. Even Attila has adapted to his new surroundings. His innumerable throngs have been reduced to a mere thirty warriors—an embarrassing number, but all that the imagination could scrounge up in the bleak landscape of that cold and barren island at the end of the world where the geese are always screeching.

The conclusion of both poems shows how the ancient poetic imagination drew together two historical events that were completely unrelated: the death of Attila in 453 and the fall of the Burgundians in 436–37. Attila's death was thus explained as payback for an old offense. Let's look at the climactic scene of *Atlakviða*. It's one of the most gruesome moments in medieval literature, a moment of revenge that is breathtaking in its violence. As we join the action, Atli is lifting a large mug of ale with his Hunnish warriors.[95]

> *Atli's ale-cups rang*
> *heavy with drink,*
> *as in the hall together*
> *the Huns assembled their host,*
> *long-moustached men.*
> *Brisk warriors entered.*

We continue reading with horror, knowing already what Guðrun has done. It wasn't enough to kill the man who killed her brothers, Gunnar and Högni. She had to eliminate Atli's children—who were, of course, *her* children as well. With cold determination, she ordered her two sons to be killed. Their hearts were cut from their chests, basted with honey, roasted over the open fire, and served to Attila on a plate.

> *With gleaming face she darted*
> *to bring drink,*
> *daemonic woman, for the warriors—*
> *picked out morsels to eat with the ale,*
> *with repulsion, for the blanched faces—*
> *and then told Atli his shame:*
> *"You have your own sons"*
> *—giver of swords—*
> *bleeding hearts from their bodies*
> *chewed with honey.*
> *You are digesting, proud one,*

We get a further sense of this in what follows. Socrates relates with satisfaction how the bishop Proclus preached a sermon that interpreted these amazing events in light of Ezekiel's prophecies against the princes of the North, Gog and Magog. "For I will judge him with death, and with blood, and with overflowing rain, and with hail-stones," Proclus thundered from the pulpit. "I will also rain fire and brimstone upon him, and upon all his bands, and upon many nations that are with him. And I will be magnified, and glorified, and I will be known in the eyes of many nations: and they shall know that I am the Lord." The sermon was received with great applause, and Socrates notes in particular that the "application" of this Old Testament prophecy to current events "enhanced the estimation in which Proclus was held."

I'm being too hard on Socrates. His history is an invaluable source of information for this period, and we can't hold him accountable for a standard of accuracy that has only evolved in modern times. In his defense, we should remember that the nineteenth-century fantasy about reconstructing the past *wie es eigentlich war* ("as it actually was") is no more credible than Socrates's uncritical compilation of portents and miracles.[99] The historian working under the nineteenth-century delusion of an absolute historical truth would sift out the specific facts which were believable. This usually meant separating out the miracles and discarding them without further comment. Philologists have always had a leg up on the traditional historian in one important way: philologists don't care all that much whether a story is "true" or not, at least not as the first order of business. The philologist cares only that people actually *told* that story in some form or other. Paradoxically, this disinterested view of factuality often leads us closer to the truth. In reading Socrates the Scholar, the philologist is not primarily concerned with separating out the myth from the fact. (Good luck trying to do that.) Rather, the philologist wants to understand how the story turned out in its current form and what that form tells us about the culture that produced it.

---

slaughtered human meat,
eating it as ale-morsels,
sending it to the high seats.

"You will not again call
to your knee
Erpr or Eitill,
both merry with feasting—
you will not see again
at the centre of the dais
the bounteous princes
fitting shafts to their spears,
clipping manes,
or cantering their horses."

The boy, or rather *boys*, have been brought to the table once again, though in a very different manner from Ortlieb or Ernach. Guðrun's final taunt—"You will not again call your sons to your knee"—recalls the old prophecy that Priscus heard on his diplomatic trip in 449. The ultimate payback in the poetic imagination of the Germanic tribes was not just that Attila died for all the grief he caused them but that his children and his empire had been utterly destroyed. Guðrun's revenge is complete when she kills the unarmed Atli: "With her sword she gave blood for the bed to drink." And then she torches the hall.

The geese are still screeching in Greenland, though now they screech where no one hears them, around the ruined foundations of the farms and churches of those early Norse settlers. In 1408 a young couple was married in the stone church at Hvalsey. This is the last record we have of a dying settlement. It's believed that by 1480 the farms in Greenland had fallen quiet. What ultimately became of these descendants of Vikings, who themselves were descendants of the Goths who had served a thousand years earlier under Attila's command? The mystery has never been solved. Island colonies tend to be deeply conservative, tenaciously preserving the traditions and lore of the mother country. We can be sure that right up to the end, whatever that end was, the horrible tale of Atli helped them pass the longest winter nights when the wind was howling and the snow was blowing in drifts so tall they nearly covered the farmhouse roofs.

SOCRATES THE SCHOLAR

What catalyst brought the death of Attila and the fall of the Burgundians together into one narrative? The "boy at the table" suggests these two stories must have been connected very early on; but the question of *why* still remains. One possible answer lies deep within the ecclesiastical archives of Constantinople, in a history of the Church written by an early contemporary of Priscus, a certain Socrates Scholasticus. We know Socrates "the Scholar" only from what he tells us in the seven books of his *Ecclesiastical History*.[96] And that's not much. We can guess that he was born around 380 and died no later than 450. Priscus may have known the elderly Socrates, but even if their paths never crossed, there can be little doubt that Priscus would have been familiar with his work.

In reporting the events of his time, Socrates never misses an opportunity to praise the emperor, who was also his benefactor, Theodosius II. He compares the emperor to Moses—the "meekest man on the face of the earth"— which was a clever way to account for the indecisiveness, vacillation, capitulation, and overall incompetence that most other historians, ancient and modern, have tended to see in Theodosius. After enumerating the emperor's virtues, Socrates assures us that he's not writing these things "from adulation" but is "truthfully narrating facts such as everybody can attest." The facts, however, are not so easily attested, and they are certainly not universally conceded. Writing in the seventh century, John of Antioch painted a radically different picture, which he derived no doubt from authentic early sources, Priscus among them. His judgment of Theodosius? "He lived in cowardice and gained peace by money, not arms. He was under the control

of the eunuchs in everything. They contrived to bring affairs to such a pitch of absurdity that, though Theodosius was of a noble nature, they beguiled him, to put it briefly, as children are beguiled with toys, and united in accomplishing nothing worthy of note."[97]

Adulatory praise didn't come easily to Priscus, though every bureaucrat has to stoop to it now and then. Socrates, though, was downright slavish in his assertion of the emperor's divine right and his Mosaic resolve in the face of his enemies. The invasion of the Empire by Attila's uncle Rua is a case in point. Socrates relates how the Huns were dealt a mighty blow when they crossed the border under Rua's command.[98] When Theodosius heard the news, he "immediately committed the management of the matter to God as was his custom" and the bad news quickly turned to good. Rua had barely begun his campaign when he was struck dead by a thunderbolt. Plague soon followed, destroying most of the barbarian troops. And then, "as if this was not sufficient, fire came down from heaven, and consumed many of the survivors." This is not history as we normally expect it; it's ecclesiastical legend. But there's still history here—a few facts that can be skimmed off the top (the death of Rua, for example). All the rest is sanctimonious posturing.

But even in *that*—the posturing—we can extract some real historical information. The fact that Socrates is carrying water for the Church tells us something about how Church and State were becoming codependent in the Eastern Roman Empire. The story of Rua's death offers one more opportunity to endorse this alliance—an alliance that would define the politics of the Byzantine Empire for centuries to come. We are told that the Huns clearly understood what the heavenly portents meant. God was on the side of the Romans. This tidy interpretation fails to explain why the Huns were later so successful. But none of this is offered by Socrates as a carefully weighed historical assessment; the subsequent history of the Balkan campaigns would prove such an assessment to be insupportable. Rather, the story about Rua conforms to a broader calculus—one that is ideological, one that is completely untethered by facts.

EXHIBIT EIGHT

The official account of Attila's death has been modeled in part on the ecclesiastical story told of the death of his uncle Octar.

In this case, the culture that produced a lightning-struck Rua also produced a tale about his brother, Octar, another one of Attila's uncles.[100] Here's where the Burgundians reenter the scene. As we noted earlier, when Gundahar led his tribe over the Rhine in 406, some of the Burgundians stayed behind. These transrhenanian Burgundians, as they're awkwardly called, thus found themselves sandwiched between hostile forces. Socrates tells us their story, how this small tribe of "peaceful carpenters" turned to the "Roman god" Christ in 430 for protection against the Huns. Shortly thereafter Octar died one night in his camp while besieging the new converts. According to Socrates, Octar died "from the effects of a surfeit" (an overindulgence in food and drink), and three thousand Burgundians were then able to rout ten thousand leaderless Huns. The story is improbable on several counts, neatly summarized by one scholar: "the existence of a Germanic tribe of peaceful carpenters, their conversion within a week, and the victory of three thousand artisans over ten thousand of the most formidable warriors of the century."[101] Nevertheless, there is history here. The Burgundians were converted, there was a conflict, and a Hunnish leader died. It's the *manner* of his death, however, that should raise eyebrows.

So, as was asked before: Does history keep repeating itself, or do the historians?

Socrates is writing an *ecclesiastical* history, so he's pressing these events into a theological mold. There's little daylight between the history of the Church and the history of the Empire; both are the instruments God uses to unfold his plan in human affairs. Emperor Theodosius is a Mosaic figure because he is God's representative on earth. Infidels who challenge the progress of God's will, such as Rua and Octar, face divine judgment. God has many ways to accomplish his judgment, but a particular favorite seems to have been the gluttonous feast. What better way for Octar and Attila to die than flat on their backs? The Germans might have wanted vengeance—their legends tell us this—but the churchmen of the Eastern Empire were satisfied with Attila's humiliation.

The orthodox account of Attila's death has just taken another major hit. It's looking more and more like an ecclesiastical cover story, a morality tale about the drunken and prideful enemies of God. Of course, it's still possible that the stories about Octar and Attila are true. When two witnesses tell identical stories on the witness stand, they might indeed be telling the truth. But they might also have been comparing notes out in the hallway. That's what a good prosecutor has to determine. We'll do that in Chapter Six when we bring a surprise witness to the stand, St. John Chrysostom, the "Golden-Voiced Preacher" of Constantinople. In the homilies that John delivered in the early fifth century, we'll find the archetypal story pattern of the gluttonous and godless strongman—the very pattern that Socrates and Priscus would later apply to Octar and Attila.

BLOOD ON THE FLOOR

We've found that the official account of Attila's death by natural causes is related unexpectedly to the incident in Burgundy nearly a quarter century earlier. But what about the allegations of murder? Are these nothing more than the wild concoctions of a later poetic imagination? Several converging lines of evidence say no. In the previous chapter we saw that Jordanes is not telling us the whole truth; he edited his text and removed another account in which Attila was said to have died "by the balance of justice." While he earlier suggested an explicit connection between Attila's death and the treachery and violence of Bleda's death, Jordanes in the end fails to deliver on his promise several pages later. Attila doesn't die so tragically and so heroically.

He goes out with a whimper. We can't escape the fact that the two passages in Jordanes cannot be reconciled. There's something missing—an eighteen-minute gap, as it were—something Priscus knew and that was ultimately suppressed as his words were transmitted, like Busbecq's lexicon, through layer after layer of editing. Though Jordanes tried to clean up after himself when he revised the text, the blood is still on the floor.

We first became suspicious of the historical account by listening closely to what Jordanes was saying. The German poets have fueled our suspicions all the more by reminding us how old the murder story is. It turns out that the Germans aren't the only ones who believed that Attila died violently. The oldest reference to murder is found in the *Chronicle* of a Byzantine historian, Marcellinus Comes, which was compiled around 518. Under the entry for the year 454, Marcellinus recorded the following stark summary: *"Attila rex Hunnorum Europae orbator provinciae noctu mulieris manu cultroque confoditur."* "Attila, king of the Huns and ravager of the provinces of Europe, was stabbed with a dagger one night by his wife." What are we to make of this? Idle gossip, the historians all say. Rumors borrowed from the Goths. Perhaps. But for all the obvious errors in his *Chronicle*—Attila's death occurred in 453, not 454—Marcellinus was in a position to know things. He was a court insider in Constantinople in the early decades of the sixth century. He was writing a mere generation after Priscus had completed his *History*. Even though Marcellinus must have read the history by Priscus, scholars have been very reluctant to suggest that Priscus was the source for what Marcellinus wrote. Marcellinus makes inexcusable blunders in his history—he gets the year wrong for Attila's death!—and that makes him easy to dismiss. But more importantly, his account has been deemed irrelevant because it corresponds too closely to what the Icelandic and Greenlandish poems would later claim. Since we know that *those* accounts are fictional, Marcellinus is discredited by association. Of course, the logic here is circular, but that doesn't prevent it from appearing under the most impressive scholarly bylines.

There was one scholar, however, who seemed to break ranks. Years ago when I first began wrestling with this problem, I came across a passing reference that intrigued me but that I was never able to track down and follow up on—my own "grassy knoll" witness. I had found an obscure reference, tucked away in a footnote in Julius Moravcsik's essay "Attila's Death in History and Legend" (1932). The footnote referred to a certain Karl Bierbach, who had published a doctoral dissertation in philology in Berlin in 1906 called *Die letzten Jahre Attilas* ("Attila's Last Years"). Bierbach was cited for his belief that Marcellinus had derived his account of Attila's death from Priscus. That was all there was to it, a mere reference with no details and no supporting evidence. But it leaped out at me because it was a rare deviation from the orthodox line. What did Bierbach know that had been overlooked by everyone else? Unfortunately, I could never get my hands on this obscure text. No more than a few hundred copies had been printed and it was practically unavailable (as far as I could determine) anywhere in the United States.

Years later, in the age of the Internet, I went looking for Karl Bierbach all over again. And this time I found him—in a used bookstore, a virtual bookstore, in Berlin. My copy, which had once belonged to a certain Professor Hofmeister, took about six weeks to arrive. I opened the little package, took out the seventy-eight-page book, sat down in a lawn chair in the fading light of a summer day, and prepared (at last!) to solve the mystery. I went immediately to the section on Attila's death and read the summary. "We can never penetrate to the truth," Bierbach concluded somberly. "The death of the powerful and terrifying Hunnish lord remains clouded in darkness."[102] So much for my grassy knoll!

But in spite of Bierbach's agnosticism, there really *are* some gems in his work that scholars have overlooked. He was deeply skeptical of the orthodox account Jordanes has given us, and he offered some finely nuanced reflections. He noted, for example, that "one might readily believe that Attila had died of a hemorrhage if not for the foolish drunkenness he's credited with." Bierbach doesn't follow through on his instincts here, but he's right on target. As we've already noted, Attila's drunkenness doesn't square with the sobriety pictured by Priscus at the feast. It's a simple observation, but it's bolstered by the evidence from Socrates Scholasticus. The story of Attila's uncle Octar should make us suspicious about what Jordanes wrote about Attila. Later on we'll add one more source that will nail down the cover-up, but for now we've reached the point of reasonable doubt. Bierbach helps point us in that direction, even if he doesn't "solve" the mystery.

Bierbach also wondered if the ancient chroniclers were hinting at murder through their choice of words. For example, the Spanish chronicler Hydatius (c. 400–69) is one of our earliest independent sources, even though he relates the events of his day (such as the death of Attila) from the position of a distant observer: "*Repetunt sedes, ad quas rex eorum Attila mox reversus interiit.*" That is, after the Italian campaign of 452, "the Huns went back to their home (Pannonia), where their king Attila died soon after returning." The word *mox* (soon) is interesting here as evidence that helps us date Attila's death to the first part of 453. But the pivotal word is *"interiit,"* which suggests, to Bierbach anyway, a violent death. We derive our verb "to inter" from this Latin word which conveys a sense of perishing, dying, coming to ruin, ceasing to exist. There's a fairly wide range of meanings here—some neutral, some not—and these meanings would ultimately be fixed by the context in which the word was used. Unfortunately, we don't have much context to work with in the little that Hydatius has reported, and Bierbach's hunch is not too convincing by itself.

Our suspicions are on firmer ground, however, with another Spanish chronicler, Isidore of Seville (c. 560–636). Though Isidore wrote over a century after Hydatius, he may have been better positioned to pass on information that had circulated in oral form. Spain had become the center of the Visigothic Kingdom after the Fall of Rome, and Isidore was deeply engaged in the project of teasing the Goths away from their Arian roots. The *Chronicle* he wrote shows how embedded he was within the language and traditions of the Germanic culture that pervaded Spain in the early medieval period. Here's what Isidore recorded: *"Ad quas rex eorum Attila mox ut remeavit, occobuit."* "When their king Attila returned, he died." The word *"occobuit"* ("went to rest," "lay down in the grave") doesn't allow much room for a conspiracy, but Bierbach once again senses that something is amiss. Virgil had used the word to describe how Hector and Paris are "lying" or "resting" in their graves. Of course, they arrived at that position through violence, but this doesn't require us to infer the same for Attila.

Among the whole range of Latin words describing death—and the Romans had plenty of synonyms to choose from—these words fall pretty close to the middle of the connotative spectrum. There's no bombshell lurking within the etymologies; Bierbach may be on to something, but unfortunately he can offer no more than a "feeling" that violent connotations are hanging in the air. Feelings don't rate very high as evidence, either in a courtroom or in a philological analysis. Ultimately, Bierbach's "method" is no more reliable than reading tea leaves. In the end you see what you want to see.

Even if we construe *occobuit* so as to suggest a violent death (and I'm not convinced we should), we're given no wiggle room at all in other ancient references. Prosper of Aquitaine, a mid-fifth-century historian, wrote simply that *"Attila in sedibus suis mortuo,"* "Attila died in his home country." Most of the references to Attila's death in early sources are like this: bland statements that convey no hint of a scandal. A typical example comes from the biography of a fifth-century Roman saint, which was written by his disciple Eugippius. The opening line of the *Life of St. Severinus* reads, *"Tempore, quo Attila, rex Hunnorum, defunctus est,"* "At the time when Attila, king of the Huns, had died" (or, "became defunct" in the sense of his life running out). Death doesn't get any more neutral than that. There's so much more we'd like to know, which Eugippius might have been in a position to tell us. He lived in Pannonia, as did his hero, St. Severinus, who worked among refugees from the Hunnish campaigns. Eugippius tells us that the old saint predicted the time of his own death and gave up the ghost while singing Psalm 150. How can he be *that* specific about a saint nobody even remembers, and yet be so tight-lipped—so *boring*—in what he says about Attila? Of course he's not writing a biography of Attila and so we would be wrong to say that Eugippius referred to Attila's death in a flat tone because he had nothing else to report. Overall, our ancient sources give us information about the Huns very grudgingly; what we end up relying on are peripheral references—afterthoughts culled from ecclesiastical histories, lives of saints, homilies, and chronicles of world history. As always, we've got to do the best we can with what we've got.

I closed Bierbach's little book, disappointed to find no smoking gun— or, rather, no dripping dagger. But I did find an open mind that was willing to question (if not prepared to answer) whether or not we've got the story all wrong. Bierbach's suspicions also prompted me to go back and look more closely at what Marcellinus had written—to read it the way Bierbach would. Marcellinus (and Priscus before him) would have had better sources of information available to them than Hydatius or Isidore: the Ostrogoths, former allies of Attila and regional neighbors in the Black Sea. Marcellinus gives us not one but two different accounts and intentionally sets them against each other. He qualifies his story of the bloody dagger with this curious statement: *"Quidam vero sanguinis rejectione necatum perhibent."* "Some, however, maintain that the death came from choking on blood." These six Latin words are teeming with problems and possibilities. Was it a bloody nose or a bloody dagger? The transcription of two accounts side by side in 518 can mean only one thing: Sixty-five years after Attila died it was considered an open question as to what had happened. Marcellinus gives us the bloody dagger first, which has the effect of elevating its authority. The bloody nose is presented only as an alternative view, and not, certainly, as a more credible one. If there's a rumor behind what Marcellinus wrote (as historians believe), then the rumor seems to lie not behind the first story but behind the second. At least this is what Marcellinus is asking us to accept. For *this* historian, anyway, death by hemorrhage doesn't rise beyond an account that "some maintain." And even then, Marcellinus undercuts this second version when he uses the word *necatum*, which, in the Latin, is certainly not a neutral word for dying, but which most obviously refers to a violent demise. It's like saying, "Others maintain, however, that Attila was *slain* by choking on blood." The word can also mean "to quench" (as in putting out a fire) or "to drown," and these meanings would seem literal and appropriate for describing a natural death by asphyxiation. Still, the word *necatum* is so closely associated with violent death that we can easily infer that someone is behind the "putting out" of Attila's fire.

These textual problems cannot be dismissed. They are clues that point to Attila's murder. But the evidence is more significant yet when we remember that Marcellinus is not some marginal figure toiling away in a distant province. He is a court insider, an advisor to the future emperor Justinian the Great. Marcellinus is suggesting (if we'll only listen) that a widespread knowledge of Attila's murder existed within the court at Constantinople. It's not surprising that Spaniards and Gauls don't know much about what had happened. And it's not surprising that Eugippius doesn't care about the specifics when he uses Attila's death as a historical marker. But Marcellinus must have approached this subject with a different degree of interest. And his equivocation between two accounts doesn't have to imply ignorance or gullibility. He might be suggesting the broad outlines of a cover-up. In another generation, the "others" who "maintained" the alternate view of natural causes—propagandists such as Jordanes—would win the historical argument. That argument would be "won," however, not by evidence but by the *suppression* of evidence.

There's more blood on the floor, however, which Jordanes couldn't wipe up, such as the *Chronographia* ("world history") of John Malalas, "the most stupid of the Byzantine historians" in one scholar's view.[103] Malalas gives us three—count them—*three* accounts of Attila's death preserved in the fragmentary remains of the original Greek. The first account we know well: Attila died of a hemorrhage. The second one we've already encountered in Germanic poetry and the *Chronicle* of Marcellinus Comes: Attila was murdered by a woman. Between these two accounts Malalas invokes the name of Priscus as his authority. Our options are to dismiss out of hand this reference to Priscus as historians have always done. The sober reasoning that informs this judgment? "Malalas is stupid." On the other hand, we can keep an open mind as to whether or not any ancient material is truly preserved in the reports that Malalas, with all his faults, has transcribed.

Something new breaks through in the third account. Malalas relates that Attila was murdered by a bodyguard who had been bribed by Aetius, the great Western general who defeated Attila at the Battle of Châlons. Where does *this* allegation come from? Could there be anything to it? An ingenious

answer to these questions comes in the form of a classic philological reconstruction, and it would seem to slam the door shut on this line of inquiry.[104]
In the manuscript tradition of the *Chronicle* of Marcellinus Comes a misun-
derstanding led eventually to a corruption of the text. Being a chronicle,
each of the entries that Marcellinus recorded is found under a rubric that begins "In the year of the consulship of so-and-so." Marcellinus has inaccu-
rately placed the event of Attila's death in the year 454, during the
consulship of Aetius and Studius. As the manuscript was passed down, the
heading became confused with the text itself, so that the name of the obscure consul Studius was transformed into a noun meaning, roughly, "by
studiousness"—that is, diligently, zealously. Or, as the passage came to be understood, "Attila was stabbed *at the instigation* of Aetius."

It's a brilliant reconstruction—and it's probably true. Still, we can tease
out possibilities. Perhaps we can even reconstruct the passage from the opposite angle, finding the error not in the textual transmission but rather in
its original composition. We know that there's an error in the text, because
Marcellinus has wrongly dated Attila's death to 454. But what if Marcellinus
misfiled Attila's death under this year because he was familiar with the allegations that Aetius was involved? Aetius began his fourth consulship in 454,
the same year he was assassinated by Emperor Valentinian III. Allegations
that Aetius was involved in Attila's death may have thus corrupted the text
of Marcellinus Comes. These allegations may also have spilled over into
Germanic legend; as a political figure well known among the Germanic
tribes (recall that he had been a hostage among the Huns and Goths), Aetius
may have been remembered as the well-connected and manipulative character we know as Hagen.[105] All this speculation is a different way, at least, of
looking at evidence that at first seemed to be exculpatory for Aetius. But, of
course, we're reading tea leaves once again.

When I first began working on this problem years ago, I remember how
I'd leave the research library at the University of Minnesota in the dead of
winter after searching for answers in the dusty shelves and puzzling over
these sources without really getting anywhere. I would trudge back to my
car bundled in coat and gloves and scarf, the wheels still turning in my

head, and navigate home in the snow. In my head—and on the road—there was a lot of spinning, but not much traction. That's how I began to feel about Attila's death. Gradually, though, I became convinced that the key to this mystery was to be found in bringing to life the social, political, and religious climate that produced the textual traditions in Constantinople. The unexpected parallel between the deaths of Octar and Attila marked the first significant shift in my thinking. The second would come many years later when I would uncover in the homiletic literature of Constantinople a close parallel to what Jordanes wrote about Attila's gluttonous feast and death. Suddenly I had reached a tipping point. No longer was I looking at tea leaves; I was now seeing the evidence of a conspiracy, a murder, and a cover-up.

Bierbach's suspicions looked more credible now. Marcellinus Comes struck me as a far more trustworthy source of information, once I became convinced that the official version was dead wrong. Even "stupid Malalas" might have known a thing or two, I reasoned. Perhaps the Germanic accounts, so lurid and perverse, contained a grain of truth. Our digression into Germanic lore has shown that the Gothic tribes were talking murder and revenge from the moment Attila's body was found. We've also seen how long their memories were and how a few small details, such as the boy at the table, took on a life of their own. Of course, we have to look past dragons and superheroes to see the truth—but then, so did Heinrich Schliemann at Troy.

The next challenge was to draw all these suspicions together into a coherent theory that answered more questions than it raised. Marcian was an obvious "person of interest" in the investigation, as the Eastern Empire stood to benefit most directly from Attila's death. But Aetius, too, would be central to this task. He knew Attila both as friend and foe. He had many well-placed contacts within Attila's retinue. The textual record clearly shows that someone at some point began to suspect Aetius, even if that someone was a clueless scribe who couldn't figure out what Marcellinus had written. Malalas (who is always ready to share a story, or two, or three), too, points the finger at Aetius. But could we connect the Roman general more directly to Attila's death without having to rely on the notoriously inept Malalas? The answer, I believe, is yes—if we are open to the possibility that Aetius lived on in Germanic legend, transformed into the villainous figure of Hagen. Attila and Gundahar both had an afterlife, so why not Aetius, too?

The whole purpose of an unimpeachable account—a "historical version" that no one doubts—is to avoid finding yourself in a mess where nothing seems very certain, and where every piece of evidence can be countered by another. But the more we probe, the less truthful "history" appears to be. We find ourselves constantly surprised by the improbable—by German-speaking Turks who happen to turn up if you'll only scour the countryside.

When we last saw Priscus at Attila's feast, he was as confident as the *Encyclopedia Britannica*. The world looked certain to him; the purpose of his diplomatic mission was clear. But it was all a farce. Not until he returned home to Constantinople would he learn the shocking truth: He and Maximin had been useful idiots in the emperor's plot to assassinate Attila. Priscus would never again be so naive.

Nor should we be.

FIVE

THE CHRYSAPHIUS AFFAIR

AFTER the feast with Attila, and somewhere between Philippopolis and Constantinople, Maximin and Priscus came across Bigilas on the road, arranging his gear and repacking his bags. He was probably making sure the gold was well hidden. They saluted their fellow Roman, even though they weren't too happy to see him, judging from the terseness of what Priscus records. In fact, Priscus doesn't say much at all about the return trip. There were a few crucifixions along the way—those always grab your attention—two unfortunate Huns had been dragged into a village and ended up with their heads posted on stakes and decorated with horns. But nothing else was memorable about the journey back to Constantinople, except for the persistently grouchy mood of their new traveling companion, Berica, the Goth who was seated next to Attila at the feast. Berica was one of the multinational *logades*, as Priscus called them—the "chosen men" who surrounded Attila almost like cabinet secretaries. Five are mentioned by Priscus in his narrative: Edecon, Orestes, Onegesh, Scottas, and Berica.[106] No doubt Berica was sent along to keep an eye on the ambassadors. Things had been fine until they crossed the Danube; but then he was all attitude, brusquely demanding that Maximin return the horse he'd been given and refusing to converse with them any further.

Running into Bigilas and his son (for his son was traveling with him this time) was a small thing. It wouldn't have been mentioned at all if there hadn't been a nasty surprise waiting for the translator at the end of his journey. When he reached the outskirts of Attila's camp, Bigilas and his son were surrounded, arrested, and taken to Attila. "You worthless beast," Attila said. It wasn't the first time Bigilas had been berated this way with what must have been Attila's favorite epithet. "What is all this gold you're carrying?" Bigilas feebly declared that the gold was for buying provisions on the journey and ransoming Roman hostages. "Nonsense," Attila replied. "It's much more gold than you need. Not to mention, I expressly told Maximin that no hostages would be ransomed until I gave the word." Attila then pointed to the young man standing next to Bigilas. "Strike down the lad," he said, "if I don't hear a full confession."

The swords were raised, and that's all it took for Bigilas to blurt out the story. He told them everything—everything about that day in the palace when Edecon and the emperor's top advisor, Chrysaphius, had concocted the plan. "Put me to death," he said, weeping, "but spare my son." Attila was satisfied that he now had the truth, since Bigilas was confirming the story Edecon had already told him. Bigilas was placed in chains, and was to remain bound until his son could return to Constantinople, secure another fifty pounds of gold, and bring it back as a ransom. One can only imagine how long the nights must have been as Bigilas waited. What if the emperor were to cut his losses and abandon him to his fate? Like every traveler north of the capital, Bigilas had seen the grisly evidence of Attila's vengeance, the beheaded corpses of deserters impaled on stakes. There could be little doubt he'd end up like that, too.

THE MIDDLE WAY

The court was thrown into sudden disarray when the son of Bigilas returned without Bigilas. The little traveling party, which included Orestes and another senior Hunnish diplomat named Eslas, made their way through the streets of Constantinople toward the palace. Theodosius was quickly informed that an embassy had arrived in the city. "The son of Bigilas—but not Bigilas?" he must have asked. "Orestes and Eslas? But what of Edecon?" He readied himself for the news, which he still hoped would be good, despite the curious makeup of the party now approaching the palace. Leading the entourage were Orestes and Eslas, an elderly Hunnish diplomat who had been around since Rua's day. Theodosius never expected the devastating message they delivered. The plan had not just failed, it had been *botched*.

Attila was alive and well.

And now he was *very* angry.

The son's instructions were clear. If he wanted to see his father again, he would have to bring back more gold. Orestes was to provide an object lesson. At Attila's command he wore the same money bag around his neck that Bigilas had used. He was to present himself at the court and confront Emperor Theodosius and the eunuch Chrysaphius with the taunting question, "Do you remember this bag?" Eslas, the senior diplomat, would follow this up with the usual defiant speech:[107]

> Theodosius is the son of a nobly born father. Attila, too, is of noble birth, the son of Mundiuch. But Attila, unlike Theodosius, has brought honor to his ancestors. Theodosius has squandered his nobility by paying tribute and acting like a backstabbing houseslave. Attila is not used to being disrespected and won't let Theodosius off the hook unless he hands over the eunuch for punishment.

Chrysaphius knew he had nothing to fear from Theodosius. *Him* he could manipulate like a puppet on strings. But there were others in the court

Marble bust of Theodosius II, Eastern Roman Emperor
(A.D. 408–50). Theodosius tried, and failed, to have
Attila killed in 449. (Louvre: Paris, France)
Erich Lessing / Art Resource, NY

who might be willing to surrender him to the Hun. The emperor's sister, Pulcheria, for example. She was (in the eunuch's view) the most dangerous foe imaginable—a religious fanatic. Chrysaphius understood killing out of self-interest, but Pulcheria would kill you over a doctrinal dispute.

How did Priscus react when the news filtered out into the imperial bureaucracy? He doesn't tell us, unfortunately, but he must have felt confusion, betrayal, and anger. Who wouldn't? After he calmed down, he did what came naturally to him: he tried to make sense out of it, and ultimately he didn't feel too bad at all.[108] All the little irregularities he had noticed on the journey now fit into place. Irregularities such as the dinner quarrel at Sardica and the swaggering self-confidence of Bigilas; the peevish complaining of Orestes about his treatment at the palace; Attila's hostility toward Bigilas and the contempt shown toward Maximin. All these "dangling socks" revealed an underlying structure, a conspiracy Priscus had been very close to, but was unable to see. You don't shake off a jolt like that very easily; it had to shape his view of the world, how he wrote his history, and how he narrated the death of Attila. Recall that he would be far from the action, far away in Egypt, when he got the news that Attila had died. *If you can't know what's going on right under your nose, then how can you possibly know what's going on across the Mediterannean?* Priscus channeled that skepticism into a method. The very qualities that have endeared him to modern historians—his realism, his sense of character and motive, his quirky personal observations—are ways of handling a world where the truth is often concealed within the intricately plotted details of life. He never stopped being a court historian and an imperial mouthpiece; he just became cleverer at his job.

The interview would become a critical part of his method. We know Priscus debriefed Bigilas extensively after the hapless interpreter returned from captivity (just as he must have interviewed witnesses after Attila's death).[109] The story Bigilas told him began with Edecon and Orestes in Constantinople in 448, pursuing gold and fugitives on Attila's behalf. The devastating Balkan campaigns of 447 had led to a significant upswing in diplomatic activity on both sides. Most of the negotiations skirted the central issue that divided them—namely, that Attila would have to annihilate the Romans, or vice versa, since they were fundamentally unable to coexist. The on-again-off-again negotiations were inconclusive interludes between times of war. In lieu of laying waste to provincial cities, the Huns would dispute trading rights, quibble over how much back tribute was owed, and complain bitterly about the fugitives. As best we can tell, the Huns viewed these discussions of "controversial points" (Attila's phrase!)[110] as opportunities for peaceful scavenging—just another way, that is, to plunder the enemy. It didn't really matter if nothing much was agreed to as long as the horses were loaded down with treasure for the return trip. Perhaps the Romans were slow to figure this out about the Huns, and so they kept playing the game, kept drafting letters that never quite satisfied Attila.

One Roman, though, finally caught on to the futility of it all, a powerful eunuch named Chrysaphius Zstommas. Chrysaphius had risen through the ranks to become the emperor's chief advisor, his grand chamberlain, in 442 or 443. His predecessor, Cyrus, had been a man of "incorruptible" character, the prefect of Constantinople and a popular politician among the masses. It is particularly interesting that Priscus calls the prefect "completely incorruptible," as Cyrus was both a poet (which Priscus could identify with) and a pagan. It's a curious commentary on the age that when men of character were required, Christian emperors turned to pagan poets. Though incorruptible, Cyrus did seem to suffer from a swollen head. Priscus pictures him riding to and from the chariot races, arriving in the official carriage of one of the offices he held, only to depart later in the carriage of the *second* office he held, as if to underscore how truly indispensable he was to the Empire. At the races, the crowd would chant "Constantine founded, but Cyrus restored," until the emperor couldn't take it anymore, fired him, and forced him to retire from politics and become a priest in a city far from the capital. It had been a roller-coaster career—from pagan prefect to provincial bishop![111]

Someone must have convinced the cowardly Theodosius to do this to Cyrus, and Chrysaphius might as well be suspected since he filled the political vacuum very quickly.[112] Before long Chrysaphius "controlled everything, plundered the possessions of everyone, and was hated by all."[113] If anyone could understand the mind of Attila, *this* would be the man. Never popular with the people (no one chanted for him in the Hippodrome), Chrysaphius survived by making himself indispensable to the emperor. The eunuch's rise to power coincided with the upsurge of violence in the Balkans, and Theodosius relied more and more on his counsel as the bleak news bulletins were received. Through the 440s Theodosius pursued a policy that charted a middle way between containment and engagement. He liked to think of the tribute money paid out each year to the Huns as "foreign aid" to potential *foederati* instead of the shakedown money it actually was. The smoldering ruins of Sardica finally convinced Chrysaphius that their policy wasn't working.

And that's where things stood when Edecon and Orestes arrived in Constantinople in 448. Edecon was a barbarian (either a Hun or a German) and Orestes was a Roman by birth;[114] they had little in common except their allegiance to Attila. Sparks were always guaranteed when they traveled together as a team. Attila knew this, of course—one of his great skills as a leader was his ability to read character—and so he balanced them against each other as a security precaution. Edecon was among the most trusted of Attila's inner circle and was known among the Huns for his uncommon bravery in battle. Orestes was a literate man who could advise Attila knowingly about the Romans and their ways. Both were essential members of Attila's cabinet. And both hated each other's guts.

This was not Edecon's first trip to the Eastern capital, but he was still awestruck by the sheer scale of the city, its monuments and wealth.[115] Edecon and the rest of the diplomatic team would have entered the city through the Golden Gate in the Theodosian Walls. A mile into the city and he crossed the Walls of Constantine—the original boundaries that the emperor had set for his new capital in 324.[116] The main road taking him into the heart of Constantinople was a grand boulevard known as the Mese (or "Middle Way"); it remains the main artery in old Istanbul today, though it is now called the Divan Yolu. Fifteen hundred years ago the Mese was lined with imperial monuments—statues of gods and goddesses, emperors, philosophers, and athletes. Marble porticoes along the sides of the Mese housed shopkeepers who were busy selling their wares. As he walked down the Mese toward the ancient acropolis of Byzantium, by the Aqueduct of Valens and through the bustling throngs of the city's half million inhabitants, Edecon passed by the Forum of Theodosius. The centerpiece of this largest of the several public squares in Constantinople was a huge triumphal arch and an ornately sculpted column—all now in ruins—which commemorated the victories of Theodosius the Great.

A little ways farther and he passed the oval-shaped Forum of Constantinople. Today, it's not a very impressive set of ruins, but back then it was a colossal witness to the power and wealth and history of Rome. You couldn't walk by it casually. The forum's focal point was the column, some 120 feet high, where a spectacular dedication ceremony was held for the new city in 330. Beneath the base of the column, pagan and Christian relics, artifacts collected from Troy and Jerusalem, had been buried. At the top of the column stood a massive bronze statue of Constantine styling himself as Apollo. A violent gale brought the statue down in 1106; it was never restored and was ultimately lost. Also in the Oval Forum was the priceless bronze Athena sculpted by Phidias in the fifth century B.C. and taken from the Acropolis overlooking Athens. Around the open square, fur traders sold goods from as far away as Russia.

Only a few paces farther down the Mese were the walls of Emperor Septimius Severus, who destroyed the city in A.D. 196 and then thought twice about what he'd done. These walls defined the ancient acropolis of the Greek city-state, and once you passed this line, you were entering into the administrative heart of the city. The famous churches of Constantinople were built here on the acropolis. The Great Palace was also here, the official residence of the Roman and later the Byzantine emperors. Surrounding the Great Palace was a community square, the Augustaeum, the hub of civic life in ancient Constantinople. Here is where the perfumers sold their scents, since the sweet aromas rising up around the palace were considered a fitting tribute to the sacred person of the emperor and his household.

At one corner of the Augustaeum the official starting point of the Mese was marked by a triumphal archway, known as the Golden Milestone, and usually referred to as the Milion. Named for a similar milestone in the Roman Forum, the Milion marked the beginning point of all roads leading out of the city. The various milestones you encountered along the highways of the Eastern Empire were measured from this one spot in the heart of the capital. Modern tour guides in Istanbul will take you to the spot and point out an unimpressive stone shaft and tell you it's the Milion. It's not. The Milion disappeared after the Fall of Constantinople in 1453. What you'd be looking at is the remnant of an Ottoman water-control tower, though it stands (archaeologists believe) on the very spot that functioned as the geographical reference point of the Eastern Empire.

If Edecon had a little time to kill before his audience with the emperor, he could stroll over to the western side of the Augustaeum, where the enormous Hippodrome rose several stories high. Begun in A.D. 203 by Septimius Severus, the Hippodrome could accommodate a hundred thousand spectators, who cheered on their favorite teams in the chariot races—the Blues, Greens, Reds, or Whites. Sadly, very little of this structure has survived after centuries of plundering and rebuilding. Several extraordinary monuments, however, may still be seen in what was once the center of the action. The most intriguing of these is the Egyptian Obelisk. First erected along the banks of the Nile by Pharaoh Thutmose III around 1500 B.C., the obelisk was hauled off to Constantinople sometime in the fourth century, where it lay for years along the seashore—a big unwieldy slab that no one could budge. Finally, Theodosius the Great got tired of seeing it there and commanded his engineers to find a way to move it to the Hippodrome, where it has stood since 390.

The Serpent Column was another monument displayed in the center of the stadium, also transplanted from its original location. This bronze statue depicting three intertwined serpents had been removed by Constantine from Greece, where it had adorned the Temple of Apollo at Delphi since the mid-fifth century B.C. It stood unmolested in its new home for centuries until a drunken Polish diplomat (so one story goes) lopped off the serpents' heads in 1700. Fortunately, one of the heads resurfaced in 1847; apart from this, we would have little idea what the magnificent object had once looked like.

There was plenty for Edecon to see and admire as he worked his way along the Mese from the Golden Gate to the Great Palace. All the buildings, all the monuments, all the artifacts uprooted from their original homes in Egypt and Greece testified to Roman superiority. All these objects had been lifted right out from under the noses of the Greek and Egyptian gods. Divine favor must, therefore, rest with the Romans, allowing them to exercise their will over the world, all the way from the Golden Milestone to the farthest provinces. The Mese was never intended to be just another efficient civil-engineering project, a wide avenue that funneled thousands of people into the city. Constantine had planned it as a brilliant piece of propaganda that advertised the central position of the Romans and their incredible staying power among the civilizations of the world.

GIFTED BY FATE

Edecon arrived at the gate and was admitted into the beautifully terraced gardens of the palace grounds. The palace itself was a series of buildings, a sprawling complex of pavilions that covered 120,000 square yards. The ruins of the palace now lie beneath the Blue Mosque in Istanbul, making excavation nearly impossible. Some idea of its original splendor has been suggested by a few mosaics that have recently been unearthed; they are extraordinary, and still richly colored in reds and blues. Multiply these mosaics many times over, cover the inlaid ceilings with gold, position marble and bronze statues at every turn, cover the floors and walls with exquisite rugs and tapestries, and it's easy to see why Edecon was impressed. For all his power, Attila had nothing to compare with this. His traveling tent villages and his wooden palace suffered badly by comparison to the scale and opulence of the imperial residence, not to mention everything Edecon had seen on the avenue leading in.

The emperors of Rome were no longer considered gods, as they had been in pagan times, but they were still considered divine. It was a subtle difference. A Christian emperor was God's true representative on earth, an equal of the apostles. His person was sacred; his palace was sacred; his family and advisors were sacred. When he signed an official document, he did so with his Sacred Hand. It was a rare thing to be admitted for an audience, called (appropriately) a Silence, as that was the only disposition allowed in his Sacred Presence. You could kiss the purple hem of his Sacred Robe, or his big Sacred Ring, but you couldn't speak. Diplomatic visits were the only times when the elaborate protocol was relaxed.

Once he was standing before the emperor, Edecon took out Attila's letters and unrolled them. He read, and Bigilas translated, but it was pure Attila, word for word, railing about the fugitives, redefining the borders by fiat, and demanding that none but outstanding ambassadors of consular rank should hereafter be sent to him. "If there's the slightest hesitation in sending these men," the letter concluded, "then I myself will come down to Sardica to receive them." This reference to the city recently destroyed just north of Constantinople must have been intended (and understood) as a threat. Chrysaphius could see, even if the emperor couldn't, that a change in policy was long overdue.

Edecon was formally excused and made his way along with Bigilas to another part of the palace for a previously scheduled meeting with Chrysaphius. As he entered the eunuch's chambers, Edecon gawked at the gilded interiors and ornate mosaics and must have made some comment to Bigilas about their splendor. If you've ever tried to carry on a conversation through a third-party translator, then you can recognize the dynamics of what was going on. Edecon had said something that was not necessarily directed at Chrysaphius; but the awkward moment was quickly smoothed over. "He's admiring your room," Bigilas said, and this must have caused the eunuch to raise his eyebrows.

"Well, then," Chrysaphius said. "Tell our honored guest that he, too, might live in a house with a golden roof. Of course, if he wants to live like a Roman, then he must first abandon Scythian ways." Edecon's initial response was guarded and almost funny. "I couldn't do that without my master's permission." Chrysaphius probed a little further, as Priscus describes it:

> Then the eunuch inquired whether admission to Attila's presence was easy for him and whether he had any authority among the Scythians. In reply Edecon said that he was an intimate friend of Attila and that he was entrusted with his bodyguard along with men chosen for this duty. On specified days, he said, each of them in turn guarded Attila with arms.

Neither the question nor the answer are self-explanatory. This whole account is being remembered by Bigilas (after he was double-crossed by Edecon) and transcribed by Priscus (after he was deceived by Bigilas), which simply means that it's not a neutral transcription but an interpretation made later in light of new information, not to mention bruised egos. The question could not have been put as directly as Bigilas remembers it—at least not right off the bat—since it's a nakedly suspicious inquiry into Attila's security arrangements. Chrysaphius was far too subtle to do this. Being a clever judge of character (which was a basic survival skill for Byzantine eunuchs), Chrysaphius would have probed Edecon's vanity a little more thoroughly. Priscus had done the same thing when he convinced Scottas to secure an audience with Attila, and Priscus wasn't even a eunuch. The conversation must have gone something like this:

Chrysaphius:	So, I understand you are a man of high standing among the Huns.
Edecon:	I'm the chieftain's right hand.
Chrysaphius:	As an important man, then, I would suppose you have access to the king?
Edecon:	I'm his close friend and have free access into his presence.

One way or another, the dialogue has got to be "reconstructed," since it's clearly a précis of what happened, filtered through memory and recorded many years later. As with Busbecq's lexicon, there's a lot standing between us and what happened in the eunuch's chambers. How we ultimately reconstruct the event depends upon our presuppositions. The biggest presupposition of all concerns Edecon's motivation: was he genuinely conspiring against Attila or was he only pretending to do so?

If you believe that Edecon was deceiving Chrysaphius from the start— that the embassy to Constantinople was a sting operation—then you have no problem with Edecon's talkative manner. He entered the eunuch's room talking about the wealth he saw and he casually divulged, with little prompting, the security protocol at Attila's court. All this makes sense if he came to the palace with a conspiracy of his own: to feign avarice, ensnare the emperor in a plot, and then turn the tables on him. The plan would have had Attila's full knowledge and consent. Edecon's talkativeness, then, was part of the setup, a way to broadcast that his considerable assets were for sale. If this was the plan, then it worked brilliantly. There are many problems with this view, not the least of which is that strategems like this were the modus operandi of Byzantine eunuchs, not barbarian warriors. Edecon would have been out of his league trying to outsmart Chrysaphius face-to-face.

On the other hand, if you believe, as I do, that Edecon was truly corrupted, then you've got to unpack the dialogue—stretch out the seduction and make it more plausible. In all likelihood, their first conversation was general and cautious. Later on that day as the plot was formulated over dinner, Edecon would have provided specific operational details, but only after he had agreed to betray Attila. When Bigilas recounted the events to Priscus, however, he collapsed the events and the conversations together. This is how memory works—as a highly efficient, built-in storytelling mechanism. We may think we're recalling "what happened," but more often than not we're interpreting the events, pressing them into some pattern of meaning. The more often we recall an event, the more like a *story* it becomes. The edges become smoother as the lines of causation are clarified. Some details are judged to be incidental and get edited out. Other details are resequenced and embellished in light of what is later known. Even when we're dealing with a reliable eyewitness account, facts remain elusive creatures, lost in the thicket of a story that's being formed within a human mind.

Chrysaphius may have been intending to recruit Edecon all along; or he may have been nimble enough to adjust to Edecon's unguarded expressions of greed. When the doors opened and Edecon stood there slack-jawed, his eyes tracking from the brightly painted walls to the gilded ceiling to the richly embroidered curtains, Chrysaphius knew he had found his opening. The eunuch knew better than to press too much during that first conversation. "I want to talk with you more," he said to Edecon. "But this time, let's get together informally over dinner. I've got some important ideas to run by you." And then he emphasized, "*Just you*, and no one else." Edecon was flattered—the exclusion of Orestes must have especially pleased him—and so he accepted without hesitation. That evening before they sat down to dinner, the two men took each other's right hands and swore oaths of secrecy. Chrysaphius promised that he would advance the interests of Edecon; and Edecon promised that he would not reveal the proposal to anyone, whatever that proposal turned out to be, even if he decided in the end to walk away from it.

Chrysaphius got right to the point. "Here's the deal. Head back home, kill Attila, return to us, and I'll personally see to it that you're a very happy man." The next thing Priscus records is that "Edecon promised." Was it really that easy? Once again, the events are being compressed and edited. Historians have long wondered if Edecon was successfully recruited by Chrysaphius or if he was playing the role of a double agent from the start, an *agent provocateur*.[117] Priscus has answered the question by his silence. Both Bigilas and Priscus were intimately involved with Edecon. Both had lived through the same events, though they witnessed them from different perspectives. At no point does either man doubt that Edecon had been recruited, only to get cold feet later on. If either Bigilas or Priscus thought that Edecon was dissembling, then Priscus would have told us here. We would have read something like, "Edecon promised to do this, but only so as to entrap Chrysaphius in his own plot."[118] Instead, we read only that "Edecon promised." We should opt for the simplest explanation and stop trying to be cleverer than Priscus. If our man on the scene had no doubts about Edecon, then neither should we.

After agreeing to the proposal, Edecon said that he'd need some money—"not a great deal, but fifty pounds of gold to be given to the force under my command so that they might perfectly cooperate with me in the attack."[119] This is the time when Edecon most logically would have laid out the security arrangements at Attila's court—not, as Bigilas had remembered it, in response to the first question Chrysaphius asked him earlier that day. Why did Edecon ask for so little? If he were truly deceiving Chrysaphius from the start, then why didn't he milk the eunuch for all he could get, knowing that he was going to keep the money anyway? The Hunnish method was always to extract the maximum cash allowance from every encounter as quickly as possible. Once again, Edecon's behavior here is consistent with the view that he was, in fact, recruited and was already looking ahead to the riches promised to him once he returned.

We can't get into Edecon's mind, of course, but we can always speculate. Perhaps he thought he was just acting out his name—a Germanic name (perhaps), related to the Gothic word *audagjan* and meaning something like "favored by fate" or "gifted by fate."[120] The sense of "blessed" and "rich" is still conveyed at a later period by Old English *eadig* and Old High German *otac*. By casting his lot with the Romans, whose wealth and power he admired, Edecon could finally live up to his name. Twenty years later, his son Odovacer would demonstrate that he, too, was gifted by fate when he became the first barbarian king of Italy. As suggested by Jakob Grimm, the name *Odovacer* may be a compound word of the root for "wealthy" and the root for "watcher" or "protector." Thus, the name might mean something like "wealthy and vigilant one." In the names of both father and son we can discern a royal family, a proud heritage that had become subordinated to the will of an alien people.

Of course, these etymologies are nonsense if Edecon wasn't Germanic. Priscus calls him a Scythian, but that hasn't stopped a host of scholars (mostly Germans) from claiming that Priscus didn't really mean *Hun*. British scholar E. A. Thompson begs to differ, however. "If Edecon was a German," he asked, "why had Chrysaphius to speak to him through Bigilas, the interpreter of the Hunnic language?" This is easily answered. Aetius himself was probably trilingual, fluent in Latin, Gothic, and Hunnic. Bigilas, too, was probably able to translate into both Gothic and Hunnic as well. In any event, Edecon would have spoken Attila's language regardless of his nationality. It is generally accepted that the so-called *logades*, or "chosen men," who surrounded Attila were drawn from many nations; it would not be at all surprising, then, for Edecon to be a German. By calling him a Scythian, Priscus may have meant only that Edecon was a vassal of the Huns, not that he was a Hun himself. Edecon's treachery is much easier to understand if he was a German. The Huns loved gold, to be sure, but they were positively immune to the temptations of luxury.

The planning began in earnest as Edecon, the one gifted by fate, made some specific suggestions. "Bigilas should be sent with a message about the fugitives," he said, "and I will communicate through him how to send the gold." Edecon argued that the payoff should not be sent immediately. Attila always inventoried the gifts when diplomats arrived home, and it would not be possible to conceal the gold from those traveling with him. Oddly, Edecon never seems to have thought that the gifts that Chrysaphius lavished on him would pose the same problem he anticipated with the gold. In the end, Edecon couldn't hide the presents; Orestes knew he'd been slighted and he resented it deeply. Even a eunuch who thinks of everything could not have thought of this. If Chrysaphius had only invited Orestes in for refreshments before they left, if he had just evened the tally by giving Orestes the same number of gifts, then the plot would never have come undone in Sardica.

Let's return to the question of motive one last time. No consensus has emerged among the historians one way or the other.[121] Some wonder if Edecon ever did go over to the other side. Gibbon expresses some uncertainty when he writes that "the perfidious conspiracy was defeated by the dissimulation, *or the repentance,* of Edecon."[122] Hodgkin believes that Edecon "had only *feigned* compliance from the first." There are many problems with this view, which we've already noted, such as the silence of Priscus; in order to sustain the view that Edecon acted duplicitously with Chrysaphius, many improbabilities must be brushed aside. For example, if Edecon were executing a plot hatched by Attila, then wouldn't Orestes have known about it, too? Edecon might as well have taken the gold with him and saved Bigilas the return trip. Instead, these details are consistent with what Edecon told Chrysaphius, namely, that he did not want to be found out. He was so concerned about this that he backed off the plan when the first questions began to surface. The dispute in Sardica about gifts and equal treatment marks the point when the plan began to unravel. Orestes was asking too many questions. At some point between Sardica and Pannonia, Edecon abandoned the plan and resolved to tell Attila all about it, presenting it as a rare opportunity to extract more concessions from Theodosius. After the plot was exposed, Attila sent Orestes, not Edecon, to Constantinople. This may have been because Edecon broke his oath with Chrysaphius and couldn't show his face in the capital again; but it might also have been because Attila did not view him as entirely above suspicion. Orestes, however, had never been party to the plan.

EXHIBIT NINE

The failed assassination plot of 449 provides the blueprint for understanding what would happen four years later when Attila died.

Does it even matter what Edecon's true motives were? Yes, since Edecon's journey from loyalty to treason and back to loyalty has a direct bearing on Attila's death and the subsequent collapse of the Hun Empire. If Edecon could agree once to assassinate Attila, then he could agree twice. The Chrysaphius Affair was a dry run for the plot that would eventually claim Attila's life. From his comfortable seat in the Senate, Marcian had watched the whole thing unfold. He had witnessed everything—the vacillations of Theodosius, Attila's terrifying ability to survive, the possibility of "turning" Attila's lieutenants against him if the price were right. Marcian must have scrutinized why the plot had failed; he understood the strategic blunder of attacking the enemy at his greatest strength. The plot had suffered from rotten timing. But that was about to change when a strange message arrived from Rome.

A MESSAGE FROM ROME

John of Antioch tells us in his (seventh century) chronicle that a messenger arrived in Constantinople in June 450 with disturbing news from Rome. A member of the royal family, Justa Grata Honoria, was stirring up trouble.

The crisis had started, as many do, in a moment of passion. The sister of Emperor Valentinian III had been caught in bed with her personal assistant, a man named Eugenius, who was promptly put to death. There must be more to the story than this, since lasciviousness was hardly a capital offense in the Roman world.[123] The severity with which the emperor handled his sister's indiscretion suggests that a political union, and not just a physical one, was in the works. This is doubly suggested by Valentinian's next move. He betrothed his sister to a stodgy old senator named Flavius Bassus Herculanus, a man of impeccable character who, John of Antioch tells us, "did not aspire to royalty or revolution."

It was a garden-variety scandal, and the affair by itself would hardly have turned heads. But Honoria wouldn't fade into the oblivion of a respectable marriage quite so easily, hence the urgency of the message received in the Eastern capital. The revenge she sought was intended for her brother, but it resulted in a geopolitical crisis. You could call it the Doomsday option: she deployed the ultimate fifth-century weapon of mass destruction, Attila the Hun, in a family squabble. Honoria sent another one of her unlucky assistants, a eunuch named Hyacinthus, on a secret mission to the barbarian court.[124] The eunuch carried a ring and a message from Honoria: "Be my defender!" The ring might have been sent to confirm the authenticity of the message, but Attila understood it as a proposal of marriage. What else could it be? From that point on, he would harass the Western Empire—out of greed, not chivalry—in the relentless pursuit of his bride. What had begun in bed would end up in a battlefield.

When Hyacinthus returned, he was immediately arrested, tortured for his information, and beheaded. Valentinian would have gladly done the same to his sister, but Mother intervened before he got the chance. This would be the last time Galla Placidia would exert her influence; she died before the year was out, leaving Honoria with no ally but Attila. Even he was unable to save her. Circumstantial evidence and the witness of silence is all we have to go on when reconstructing her unhappy fate. Whether she ever married Herculanus or not we don't know; but she remained in a precarious position for months, possibly for several years, before slipping

**Marble bust of Valentinian III, Western Roman emperor
(A.D. 425–455). Photo by Ch. Larrieu. (Louvre: Paris, France)**
Réunion des Musées Nationaux / Art Resource, NY

altogether off the historical radar screen. It is generally believed (for reasons we'll examine later) that she was executed at some point between 452 and 455.

Who sent the message from Rome to Constantinople?[125] John of Antioch doesn't tell us. Perhaps Aetius felt it was necessary to give a heads-up to Theodosius that "Attila was involved with the royal family at Rome." Perhaps the message came from Attila—his way of informing Theodosius that the emperor's worst nightmare was now engaged to one of his relatives and that he had every intention of joining the family. No matter what the crisis, the emperor's instincts were always the same: *Cave in, always cave in.*

Theodosius sent his own message to Valentinian urging the Western emperor to surrender his sister to Attila at once, though it's difficult to see what the strategic value of this would be to Constantinople. Perhaps Theodosius believed that the Empire could forge an alliance with Attila through marriage. In the long run, though, it proved far better that Valentinian flatly refused to comply. Attila would pursue this dead-end, long-distance relationship for the rest of his life, and his obsession with Rome turned out to be the salvation of Constantinople.

These events unfolded in the immediate wake of the Chrysaphius Affair. Theodosius had refused to hand over the powerful eunuch who was steering the Empire toward ruin, but suddenly he had no qualms about surrendering his own blood relative, Honoria, to Attila's embrace. It makes you wonder what the history was between these cousins. Honoria may have spent some time at the Eastern court, where she would have found herself in the company of her female cousins—Pulcheria, Arcadia, and Marina. They were considerably older than she and considerably more devout. A typical day began with sustained prayer in the chapel followed by a reflective walk through the palace gardens.[126] The afternoon was rounded out by long sessions of weaving and embroidering as well as visits to hospitals where they waited on the poor. After dinner (meals were always taken together) there was plenty of time for singing hymns and psalms before retiring to bed. It was a dreary place for a young woman who dreamed of power and money and sex. We don't know that Honoria lived in Constantinople as a young woman (some scholars claim she did); for whatever reasons, though, it's apparent that Theodosius did not retain fond memories of her. Nor did Pulcheria, the emperor's sister—the saint and perpetual virgin. Theodosius and his sister must have talked it over and decided that since virginity didn't suit Honoria, they might as well translate her carnality into political gain.

After the Chrysaphius Affair was exposed, probably in the winter of 449–50, Theodosius sent an embassy to Attila, trying to smooth things over after the assassination attempt. The diplomatic overture met with unexpected success. Attila was flattered by the consular rank of the ambassadors,

Nomus and Anatolius, and magnanimously declared that he no longer had any interest in pursuing the villainous eunuch. (Attila was already looking westward.) Chrysaphius must have sighed in relief, but in a matter of weeks a hunting trip would reverse his fortunes once again. In July 450 Theodosius went out riding or hunting, his favorite activity. But on this day he was thrown from his horse and sustained a fatal injury to his spine.[127] He died on July 28. It had been the longest reign of any emperor in the nearly five hundred years since Caesar Augustus defeated Mark Antony at Actium. The death of Theodosius meant one thing for the eunuch: his political capital had finally run out.

As no male heir had been produced in the forty-three years of his reign, Theodosius gathered a few senators around his deathbed and designated a successor. "It has been revealed to me," Theodosius said, looking straight at Marcian, "that you will reign after my death." But before that could happen, the emperor's sister was to have a brief go at it. When Theodosius drew his last breath, Pulcheria was proclaimed empress—the first time this had happened in Roman history. The saintly woman wasn't grasping for power; she simply had a debt to settle before relinquishing power to Marcian. Chrysaphius was dragged before the city gates and publicly executed without trial. The specific charges aren't spelled out in the historical record, but take your pick. Chrysaphius had embezzled and extorted his way to wealth. He had brought the Empire to its knees through his policies of appeasement. He was also a heretic—a Monophysite, who believed that Jesus had but one nature, his divine nature. The political environment in Constantinople seems so strange to our modern sensibility in part because everyone then was a theologian. Or so it seems from our remote vantage point. Theological disputes had become pressing matters of state. Even the imperial family was divided over the nature of Christ: Theodosius was sympathetic to the Monophysites, while Pulcheria staunchly defended the orthodox position of "two distinct natures held together in one form."[128]

With conspiracies and banishments and executions, theological disputation had evolved into a blood sport in fifth-century Constantinople. Doctrine provoked a passionate intensity that could only be matched at the chariot races. In fact, what happened in the Hippodrome was politics and religion on wheels, with a hundred thousand screaming partisans thrown in for good measure. The chariot teams were designated by color—the Blues, Greens, Whites, and Reds—and who you supported said much about your political and theological views and your social and economic status. Here, too, Chrysaphius found himself on the wrong side. He supported the Greens, while Marcian supported the Blues. But then Pulcheria was the one who had the eunuch killed, and we don't know how closely she followed the races. The eunuch's doctrinal position is what mattered most to her, and ridding the city of this odious man would be the singular achievement of her one-month reign. Why not surrender Chrysaphius to the Hun and kill two birds with one stone? Chrysaphius would be gone and Attila would be happy. Pulcheria, though, was seeking a purer vengeance, not for political reasons but for theological ones. Once Chrysaphius had been dealt with, she married Marcian and legitimized his accession to the throne on August 25, 450.

The coronation was celebrated at the Hebdomon, a coastal plain lying along one of the main roads leading out of Constantinople.[129] Located at the seventh milestone from the city's center, the Hebdomon was ideally suited for ceremonies requiring large numbers of people. The ceremony was presided over by the patriarch of Constantinople, Anatolius, and involved the formal declarations of the new emperor and his new subjects. Everyone spoke in unison: "Hear, O God, we call upon thee. Marcian will be emperor. The public weal demands Marcian. The palace expects Marcian. This is the wish of the palace, the army, and the Senate." Marcian then stepped up on the dais and a chain was placed around his head. "Marcian Augustus, thou conquerest!" they shouted. "God gave thee and God will keep thee. A long reign! God will protect the Christian Empire." This was followed by the coronation and Marcian's investiture with the imperial purple. Pulcheria herself placed the crown on his head. That crown may have been the first time the characteristic Byzantine crown with *pendilia* was used—jeweled pendants hanging down on either side of the crown. It would continue to characterize Byzantine coronations for a thousand years.

EXHIBIT TEN

Marcian was a resolute, battle-hardened soldier who had the motive, means, and opportunity to mastermind Attila's death.

Change—drastic change—was felt immediately, and not just in the style of crown. A contemporary inscription found in Thrace describes Marcian as "applying prompt remedies to restore a falling world."[130] Every branch of the government was shaken up and restaffed. Maximin, for example, was promoted to the office of chamberlain, occupying one of the top four ministerial positions in Marcian's administration.[131] (As Maximin's sidekick, Priscus, too, would see his own career take off.) Marcian moved quickly to pursue "all enemies foreign and domestic" with a renewed boldness. The emperor and empress targeted heresy as the greatest danger inside the Empire. The religious allies of Chrysaphius were deposed and within a year the Council of Chalcedon was convened. Marcian inaugurated a robust new foreign policy as well to deal with the persistent threat of Hunnish blackmail and invasion. "It was the opinion of Marcian," wrote Gibbon, "that war should be avoided as long as it is possible to preserve a secure and honourable peace; but it was likewise his opinion that peace cannot be honourable or secure, if the sovereign betrays a pusillanimous aversion to war."[132] With typical adroitness, Gibbon has captured both the abruptness of the change and the mettle of the man who was driving it.

THE LAD WITH A LITTLE GOLD

Marcian's rise to the throne is somewhat obscure. He was a sixty-year-old man at the time of his accession. His life and career had been one of steady advancement, just as his seven-year reign would be noted for its remarkable stability and clear sense of direction.[133] He had been a military man for almost twenty years, serving under powerful Roman generals. In fact, his commanding officer in Libya, Aspar, was one of those around the emperor's deathbed on that July day when Marcian was handpicked for the throne. (There can be little doubt that Aspar was the real kingmaker behind the transition.) When Marcian retired from the military, he served in the Senate and would have observed at close hand the inner workings of the government; no doubt he deplored the vacillations and indecisiveness of Theodosius. But then Marcian was coming to the throne at a different stage in his life—at the end, not the beginning—and he had the very life experiences that Theodosius, who had worn the purple since childhood, had never known. Theodosius had been cocooned within the insular world of the palace eunuchs; but Marcian would not be so easily controlled. The new emperor would approach his duties with the decisiveness of a field commander and the subtlety of a senator. Marcian's high view of his duty is recorded in the second *Novella* ("new law") of his imperial code: "It is our business to provide for the care of the human race."

Not everyone was pleased, certainly not the Monophysites whom Marcian and Pulcheria targeted at the Council of Chalcedon. A late Egyptian source—John of Nikiu (seventh century)—must be recording some authentic objections from an earlier age when he narrates the events that unfolded after the death of the "excellent emperor Theodosius."

> Pulcheria audaciously promulgated an imperial decree without taking the advice of Valentinian, the emperor of Rome, or that of the chief officers and senate, and married Marcian, the commander-in-chief of the army, and placed the imperial crown on his head and made him emperor. And she became his wife and sacrificed her virginity.

That last claim, in particular, concerning Pulcheria's sacrificed virginity, would have come as a surprise to Marcian. Everything here is at odds with the facts as we know them; it's propaganda of the crudest form. Syria and Egypt were strongholds of Monophysitism, and both provinces gave Marcian his biggest foreign policy headaches after the Ecumenical Council of Chalcedon in 451. (This is what Maximin and Priscus were dealing with, back when we first encountered them in Damascus and Egypt in Chapter Two.) Though he's a late source, John, bishop of Nikiu, is recording the sentiment from that turbulent time. "On the day of Marcian's accession," John continues, "there was darkness over all the earth from the first hour of the day till the evening. And that darkness was like that which had been in the land of Egypt in the days of Moses, the chief of the prophets."

We know little of Marcian's life. We don't even know his full given name. The official nomenclature is Imperator Caesar Flavius Marcianus Augustus, but the only word in this long list that's a *name* is Marcianus, or Marcian. Everything else is a title.[134] About his childhood, nothing but a few threadbare accounts of doubtful authority have been preserved. One of our fullest sources of information is the sixth-century *Ecclesiastical History* (another one!) written by Evagrius Scholasticus (c. 536–600), a lawyer and politician in Constantinople. Evagrius describes the emperor's early years in the typical anecdotal style of Byzantine histories:[135]

> Marcian, as has been recorded by many other writers, and in particular by Priscus, the rhetorician, was by birth a Thracian, and the son of a military man. In his desire to follow his father's mode of life, he had set out for Philippopolis, where he could be enrolled in the legions. . . .

Stopping right there we have ample reason for regret. The phrase "many other writers, and in particular by Priscus" points to all that must have once been in the historical record and which is now irretrievably lost. Regardless of who the "other writers" are (they might be the breezy rumormongers we're running into everywhere), we can be sure that the reference to Priscus is significant. Many of the stories that became corrupted through oral transmission and literary copying originated in the history he wrote, including the story of what happened to the young enlistee from Thrace. We can assume this, since Priscus became the de facto court historian of Marcian's reign.

Evagrius continues his story. On the road to Philippopolis, Marcian "came across the body of a person recently slain, lying exposed upon the ground." Marcian stopped for a considerable time, since "he was singularly compassionate, besides the excellence of his other virtues." He was grieved at the sight and decided to give the body a proper burial. Some other travelers came along the road while he was disposing of the body, and they reported his suspicious behavior to the authorities in Philippopolis. Marcian was arrested, interrogated, charged with murder, and would have been executed if not for a "providential interposition" that revealed the real criminal. Following this close scrape with death, Marcian was finally able to make it to the recruitment bureau. The officers were aware of the incredible happenings along the road and judged that he was a man destined for greatness. Rather than enlisting Marcian as a common foot soldier, they transferred to him the military rank of the man found dead along the road. What a happy coincidence that the man's name was Augustus—a neat prefigurement of the office that Marcian would later hold.

All the early stories agree that Marcian was a man of destiny. Theophanes (ninth century) relates how the young soldier went off to fight in the Persian Wars in the early 420s but was delayed by illness.[136] Marcian was given shelter in the home of two brothers, Julius and Tatian, and he soon recuperated sufficiently to go out hunting with them. Tatian witnessed a great eagle descend and overshadow Marcian as he slept in the field. The brothers concluded that this stranger whom they had nursed back to health was destined someday to become emperor. When Marcian awoke, they described and interpreted the omen. Marcian was reluctant to concur, but he did agree to promote them to high positions in their city if he should ever wear the purple. The brothers thanked him for his promise and gave him two hundred pieces of gold as he departed. This story of friendship and reward may have a historical basis. A young Maximin was also serving under Aspar in Persia in the early 420s. No doubt Marcian and Maximin came to know each other during this time. Later on, when Marcian became emperor, he "remembered" his old friend from the Persian campaign and promoted him to a high office within his administration.

Theophanes has mangled the tale we encountered earlier in Procopius (sixth century). It is the same miraculous story first told about Marcian sleeping beneath the hot Libyan sun in the courtyard of Gaiseric the Vandal. The two hundred pieces of gold, however, come from another story altogether. Theophanes seems to bring together two traditions—the overshadowing eagle and the borrowed gold. The first prefigures Marcian's rise to the throne, while the second previews his fiscal policies. It was claimed that Marcian had arrived in Constantinople as a poor youth with two hundred pieces of borrowed gold in his pocket. Even if the story is a legend, it speaks to his reputation for frugality. He kept a firm hand on the budget, and when he died the imperial treasury had a surplus of a hundred thousand pounds of gold.[137] As propaganda, the story tells us that Marcian knew the importance of good stewardship—he had scraped together a living. Why would he throw money away by giving tribute to a barbarian?

Borrowed gold and hovering eagles. There's no mention in these sources of chopping down a cherry tree, but that's the type of story we're dealing with. So why tell them if they're not true? Procopius and Evagrius and Theophanes most likely *did* believe them, but that's really beside the point. Stories are a way of understanding and interpreting the world, of simplifying what is complex, such as the unseen forces of history.[138] The character of the man is reduced to a few concrete images—gold jangling in the pocket, an eagle hovering in the hot sun, a cherry tree lying on its side. Generations of Americans learned to affirm the honesty of George Washington by visualizing a swing of the ax followed by a solemn declaration. Public perception and official propaganda merged in the telling of this legend. Similarly, Marcian's reputation for fiscal responsibility and unshakable steadiness is expressed in a simple but profound way. Who but a supremely self-confident man could catch a few winks in the hot sun while awaiting execution? That's the kind of man you want to follow.

The summer of 450 marked a sudden turning point in the Empire's dealings with Attila. In June the message had arrived from Rome about Honoria. In

July Theodosius died and Pulcheria became empress. In August Chrysaphius was executed and Marcian was proclaimed Augustus. The new emperor moved quickly on all fronts, and we can assume that the planning began pretty early for another shot at Attila. Marcian knew that it was politically destabilizing to allow his enemy to pace back and forth along the borders of the Eastern and Western Empires any longer. The only permanent and cost-effective remedy was assassination.

Attila would not be expecting the Romans to try it again, and this would give Marcian the advantage he needed. Edecon, too, would be above suspicion; he had demonstrated his loyalty by foiling the first plot. What Attila never counted on, though, was a drastic change in his fortune and the weakening of his alliances. Over the next two years, Attila turned his attention first to Gaul and then to Italy and squandered his reputation as the invincible warrior. Marcian had been given some breathing room; now he could wait until Attila was most vulnerable and strike him preemptively. But for now, the emperor's first gambit was to harden the Empire's position. Henceforth, there would be no more handouts. Marcian sent an embassy to Attila informing him that he had been eliminated from the annual budget. The lad with a little gold in his pocket was making good.

We can't know, of course, when Marcian first got the idea to try again what had failed so badly once before. He had witnessed the ineptitude of Theodosius and must have played the policy options out in his mind. We can be sure that Maximin and Priscus told Marcian their story and described in detail their impressions of Attila and the *logades* who surrounded him. For all his disdain of Theodosius, Priscus does seem to have approved of the assassination attempt; it was about the only muscular thing Theodosius ever did. Some historians have expressed surprise that Priscus "utters no word of disgust" in his narrative at the "immorality" of assassinating someone under diplomatic cover and concealing it from Maximin.[139] The obvious explanation, that Priscus was a "strong patriot," does ring true; but there's more to it than that. Looking back twenty years later, why would Priscus criticize something that Marcian ended up doing himself—and doing successfully?

THE PERILS OF PLACIDIA

Attila was faced with a choice. East or West? For the time being, let's leave Attila weighing his options in the North and Marcian plotting his strategies in the East. There's a lot going on in the West that requires our attention. This pivotal year, 450, would see that century's most remarkable woman, Galla Placidia, passing from the scene. It is often pointed out that the daughter of Theodosius the Great had imperial connections unmatched by any other matriarch in the history of Rome. Her impressive family tree was her greatest political tool. She was the real deal, an authentic Theodosian, not just in blood but in character. Throughout her public life (as regent and empress mother) she projected an aura of authority, a legitimacy that could not be challenged. Placidia could claim the two names that were political magic in the late Roman world, Constantine and Theodosius, and she parlayed her heritage into a political career that lasted for twenty-five years.[140] Only general Aetius had accumulated more power in the West, most of which had come early on at Placidia's expense. It's a wonderful irony that these two warhorses, who in their youth had plotted each other's destruction, were now able to come together toward the end of their lives and unite in a common purpose: the deliverance of the wayward princess Honoria from the clutches of Attila and the recriminations of her brother Valentinian. But let's back up and let the story play itself out. It's a great story about a great life.

The public career of Galla Placidia was bookended by a touching scene that she lived through twice, first in Barcelona in 415 and then thirty-five years later in Rome—the burial and reburial of her first child, Theodosius. Through all the turmoil of her life, the memory of this little boy was a fixed point for her, a pole star that set the direction for all her ambitions and desires. She was born in 388 to the second wife of Theodosius the Great.[141] She adored her father, and her father obviously loved the little girl deeply; he gave her the imperial title *nobilissima puella*, "most noble girl," and looked after her welfare by bequeathing her a separate palace in Constantinople. Unfortunately, she had half brothers to deal with. Arcadius, in particular, transferred his hatred of his stepmother to the little girl and exiled her when he came to power in the East. (This hostility seems to have been handed down a generation to the next Eastern emperor, Theodosius II, who displayed no love for his aunt Placidia and even less for her daughter, his cousin Honoria.) Placidia's mother died in 394 and her father in 395. She was seven years old and already life had become unbearable.

They were often separated, but Placidia saw her father one last time before he died. Theodosius was in the West, where he made a triumphal visit to Rome (the first time he'd been there) and was astounded by its magnificence.[142] He journeyed then to Milan, where he took up residence in the imperial palaces and sought the blessing of the city's most important man, its bishop, St. Ambrose. But the emperor was homesick for his children, his youngest ones at least, Honorius and Placidia. (Arcadius had already been established as the Eastern emperor.) At some point in 394, the children were brought by land all the way from Constantinople to Milan. It was time for Theodosius to set his affairs in order. Honorius was proclaimed emperor in the West; Placidia was entrusted to her cousin Serena for safekeeping. Serena gladly accepted the responsibility, though it would be a decision she'd live to regret. Bishop Ambrose was to look after their souls.

Theodosius died in Milan on January 17, 395. He had been a different man in the weeks after his children joined him. Tired but full of life, he was buoyed by a hope, not for himself (he knew he was dying) but for his children, his dynasty, and his Empire. He felt like celebrating, and so he ordered that horse races be staged for the local population. Theodosius had every intention of presiding over the festivities, but he got up that morning feeling ill. Honorius was summoned, but by the time he arrived, the emperor felt good enough to attend the morning session. After lunch he was ill again and Honorius stepped in to represent his father at the races that afternoon. By evening the emperor's condition had worsened greatly. He died in the middle of the night with St. Ambrose at his bedside.

Ambrose no doubt prayed for Placidia's soul, as Theodosius had instructed him to do—but only for two years. He died in 397. The little orphan girl grew up quickly, and by the time we see her fifteen years later, around the time Rome was sacked in 410, she had already learned the Roman art of ruthless power. Placidia had been raised in the intervening years by her cousin Serena, wife of the powerful Western generalissimo Stilicho. A Vandal by birth, Stilicho had been a standout in the army of Theodosius and was promoted to *magister equitum* ("master of the horse") in 383; soon thereafter the emperor's niece, Serena, was given to him in marriage. There were those who thought that Stilicho, a barbarian, had climbed too high in the Roman world and had to be stopped. That happened in 408 when Stilicho was accused of sedition; his army abandoned him and he took refuge in a church in Ravenna. With the knowledge and approval of Emperor Honorius, Stilicho was lured out under a false promise of safe passage and was beheaded by an officer named Heraclian, who was later awarded a plum position in Africa for his crime.

Serena was a gracious woman who had opened her home and her heart to her cousin, the daughter of Theodosius. Now Serena was the widow of an unpopular general. Two years later Alaric's army of Visigoths was advancing against Rome. In the panic that ensued, Serena became a convenient scapegoat. Rumors spread throughout the city that Stilicho's widow was conspiring with Alaric to deliver Rome to the barbarian hordes. It was a baseless charge, but the public was clamoring for her death. The Senate obliged and passed a resolution ordering Serena's execution. Emperor Honorius, however, was in Ravenna at the time, cut off from Rome by the Visigothic army. But Placidia, now a twenty-year-old woman, was in Rome, and so the Senate looked to her for the legitimacy they needed. She consented to the proclamation, shared the responsibility, and Serena was strangled or suffocated. We don't know what Placidia's motives were, but it seems that nothing could justify her betrayal of Serena. It would be the one dark blot on her remarkable life.

The sacrifice of Serena hadn't appeased Alaric in the least; he breached the city's defenses and plundered Rome for three days. From time to time in the modern era, archaeologists have turned up stashes of gold and jewelry that were buried in 410 by patricians who didn't survive to come back and retrieve their riches. Placidia was among the Roman nobility who did survive, only to be carried off into captivity. She wandered with the Visigoths for five years, first to the boot of Italy where Alaric died, and then back northward into Gaul and eventually Spain. Alaric was succeeded by another implacable foe of the Empire, Athaulf, whose life had been dedicated to the destruction of Rome, but who would soon fall under the spell of the young Roman princess in his charge. Thus began one of the great love stories of ancient Rome.

The wedding took place in Narbo, the modern French city of Narbonne along the Mediterranean coast. The bridal chamber had been prepared for Placidia in the Roman manner. Platters of gold and jewels (plundered four years earlier from Rome) were carried in by fifty handsome youths and presented to the bride as a wedding gift. Athaulf, the former enemy of Rome, was dressed in a toga. He had been converted not just to Christianity but to the ideals of Rome as well. Long hours of conversation with the well-educated princess had convinced him of the Empire's superior legacy. The story was later told that Athaulf had once sought Rome's destruction, but he now wished to be remembered by posterity as "the author of Roman restoration."[143]

That desire was most clearly expressed a year later when their child was born, a son whom they named after Placidia's father, Theodosius. It's interesting that the little Theodosius should be born in Spain; his grandfather, too, had come from Spain, back when it was still a Roman province. The grand name points toward a grand aspiration—another Spanish Theodosius reigning over a united Empire, an Empire that would include the Visigothic nation. But that was not to be; the child lived only a few days. His body was placed in a silver coffin and buried in a chapel in Barcelona. It was a severe personal loss for Athaulf and Placidia, and they grieved bitterly for their son. Historians in the West, however, looked beyond the human pathos and saw the fulfillment of a biblical prophecy: the offspring of the King of the North and the daughter of the King of the South would not survive (Daniel 11:6).

Within months, Athaulf, too, was dead. He was inspecting his horses in his private stable when one of his servants pulled out a sword and stabbed the king in the groin. Jordanes tells us that the assassin was tired of being mocked for his short stature; other sources tell us that he was avenging the death of his first master, whom Athaulf had killed. Athaulf was succeeded by Singeric, a cruel man who killed all the children Athaulf had by his first wife. As a final insult to the late king, Singeric forced Placidia to walk in front of his horse for twelve miles like a common prisoner. Singeric's reign as king of the Visigoths lasted but seven days before he, too, was murdered and succeeded by Wallia.

Placidia's wanderings continued for another year before she was transferred back to Roman control in 416, part of a settlement reached between Wallia and the Roman general Constantius. Back in Roman hands, she remained a bargaining chip, and before the year was out, her brother, Emperor Honorius, had promised her as a trophy bride to Constantius for his service to the Empire. Constantius was a remarkable general and a patrician, but he was also an insufferable fool. Placidia, who had consented to marry the civilized barbarian Athaulf, and who seemed genuinely to have loved him, was now compelled to marry this man "with large eyes, long neck, and broad head." Placidia was disgusted by him. This was the man, you'll recall, whom Olympiodorus had described as "glancing here and there out of the corners of his eyes so that he showed to all, as the saying goes, 'an appearance worthy of a tyrant.' "[144] In private, however, he was the life of the party, "so pleasant and witty that he even contended with the clowns who often played before his table." Two children were quickly added to the unhappy household: Justa Grata Honoria in 418 and Placidus Valentinianus in 419, the future emperor.

Now that he had connected himself by marriage to the Theodosian House, Constantius took the next logical step and demanded that Honorius recognize him as coemperor in the West. Honorius had no choice, and in 421 Constantius was crowned Augustus; the two emperors then elevated Galla Placidia to the rank of Augusta. There was no joy in Constantinople when the news arrived that a new emperor had been crowned and that Placidia (whose marriage to Athaulf had been roundly condemned) was now honored as Augusta. Emperor Theodosius II and his sister Pulcheria re-fused to recognize the political changes in Italy. Frosty relations between the two courts would be the norm for the next three decades. This unwilling-ness to nurture a common political culture destroyed the Western Empire from within. Not until it was too late did statesmen emerge on the scene, men like Marcian and Aetius, who were sufficiently detached—not from personal ambition but from the silly family disputes of the Theodosian House—to act in the joint interest of the Roman Empire, East and West.

All that Constantius had ever wanted was to become emperor. Once he achieved his goal, he found that the parties weren't quite as much fun, since it wasn't appropriate for emperors to play with the clowns. The Eastern court had repudiated him. He had a wife who hated him and threatened di-vorce on numerous occasions. One such occasion occurred in 421 when a magician showed up at the court in Ravenna and claimed that he could make the barbarians disappear through magic.[145] He was prepared to demonstrate his art when Placidia stepped in. Black magic was nothing a Christian emperor should be dabbling in, she said, and the man must be ex-ecuted. If Constantius refused, then she wanted a divorce. This woman, Placidia, who had sent her own cousin to a violent death, was now a pious defender of the faith. These instincts are not always inconsistent, but Placidia's piety may reflect her years of wandering among the Goths. She may have seen the humiliations and deprivations of her life as a just penance for her crime. The magician was executed, the royal couple stayed married, and Constantius died a disillusioned man only seven months into his reign.[146]

The relationship between Honorius and his half sister Placidia im-proved considerably after Constantius died, so much in fact that the two were often seen kissing each other on the mouth at public events. Honorius was childless and rumored to be impotent, but the improper displays of af-fection were scandalous even for Romans—certainly for Christian Romans. Nothing like this had been seen in public since Emperor Commodus reigned in the late second century. All of this is quite obscure to us, both in a psychological and a historical sense, but we do know that Honorius and

Placidia went from kissing to fighting all over again. And not just the siblings but also their partisans in the streets of Ravenna. To quell the disturbances, the emperor banished Placidia and her children to Constantinople in 423. Her wanderings continued. Placidia would be returning to the city of her childhood after twenty-eight years, back to a court that was no more friendly to her now than when her half brother Arcadius was alive.

As she sailed east, or perhaps it was on her return trip west, her ship was overtaken by a sudden storm. Placidia prayed to St. John the Evangelist, the ship was saved, and in gratitude she vowed to build him a church when she returned to Ravenna. Her chance came sooner than expected, since Honorius died a few months later. Chaos descended upon the West. When a usurper named John rose to power, Placidia brought her children back to Ravenna to assert once again the claims of the Theodosian House. This time she had Eastern political support, as well as an East Roman army behind her. And this is when Aetius enters the political scene, marching toward Italy with an army of Huns and intending to bolster the claims of John the Usurper against the House of Theodosius. Aetius arrived three days too late; John had already been captured in Ravenna. The usurper's right hand was cut off, he was paraded around the Hippodrome on a donkey, and he was finally beheaded. It was a remarkable change of fortunes for the woman who had wandered all her life. In the year 425 Galla Placidia found herself in charge as the empress mother of the little Valentinian III. The general and the empress reached the first of many accommodations in their long and troubled relationship. Aetius was given the military rank of count and was sent to Gaul. The Huns were sent home. Placidia started building the church she had promised to St. John the Evangelist.

The building in Ravenna that is today known as the Church of St. John the Evangelist is a modern reconstruction.[147] The original mosaics are completely lost, but we do have literary descriptions of the extensive imperial portraits. There were portraits of Theodosius II and his wife, Eudocia, of Arcadius and his wife, Eudoxia. There were also portraits of other late Roman emperors, among whom were Constantine the Great, Theodosius the Great, Honorius, Valentinian I, and Constantius. Among the portraits is a picture

The center medallion portrait in this fifth-century crucifix is widely (though not conclusively) taken to represent Galla Placidia and her two children, Valentinian and Honoria. (Museo Civico dell'Eta Cristiana, Brescia, Italy)

Scala / Art Resource, NY

of "Theodosius Most Noble Boy"—probably the little son born to Athaulf and buried in Barcelona. One could read a hundred years of history in these mosaics—a Who's Who of late Roman royalty. Other mosaics depicted apocalyptic scenes from the Revelation of St. John, and we can be sure that the subject matter (the end of the world) was an unintended irony. God was depicted on his throne with twelve sealed books. Next to God was an inscription stating that Placidia, along with her children, had dedicated this church to St. John as a fulfillment of their vow when they were saved from the peril of the sea. Christ was depicted holding a book that bore the Latin text: "Blessed are the merciful, for God will have mercy on them." (Placidia may have reminded her son of this verse when his wrath was kindled against Honoria.) During the Middle Ages the church was extensively modified; it was remodeled again in the Baroque style of the eighteenth century. As recently as the early twentieth century, a few ancient elements could still be seen. A railroad station was built nearby and when it was bombed in 1944, this priceless remnant of antiquity—the summa of a life, a family, and an empire—was also destroyed.[148]

ANATOMY OF A MODERN LEGEND

Placidia was at last able to settle down in her palace in Ravenna. Indeed, the memory of this woman who wandered from Constantinople to Spain will always be linked primarily to this city of marshes, mosaics, and mausoleums. Ravenna was built on marshy islands and lagoons along the Mediterranean Sea. In Republican times it had been an insignificant provincial town, but Caesar Augustus transformed it into an important naval port. Natural defenses made it attractive to Emperor Honorius, who needed every advantage he could get against the invading Goths. Honorius moved the imperial center of gravity from Milan to Ravenna in 404, where the capital would remain for much of the century. The natural monuments that made Ravenna famous in the ancient world have endured since antiquity—the marshy lands and the celebrated forest of pines stretching along the coast. These pines, first planted centuries ago by the Roman legions, survived even a devastating fire in 1905. The religious monuments in Ravenna have also been well preserved over the centuries; but no traces of the imperial palaces remain. Such is the fate of rulers.

Ravenna is also a city of mausoleums. Dante's bones lie here. Theodoric the Great, the Gothic chieftain who ruled Italy in the early sixth century, was buried here in an ugly little mausoleum in 526. But Galla Placidia's crypt is the oldest and most famous of all. As you pass through narrow streets lined with old homes, you come to an open park surrounded by pines in the middle of Ravenna. Nearby you see the Church of San Vitale and a squat little building that only *looks* squat because it has sunk several feet into the marshy ground. It's called the Mausoleum of Galla Placidia; but despite its definitive name, this building certainly never housed the Augusta's bones. The story of how her embalmed remains were turned to ashes is too good to pass up, even if it's not true.

Placidia died in Rome, on November 27, 450. The months leading up to her death were busy ones, full of personal and public tasks. With the entire imperial family in Rome, and with so many important things to do, this was the last time when the Eternal City would feel like the center of the Roman world. Still, this Rome was very different from the one the early Caesars had known. Four hundred years before, Nero had lit his gardens with the burning bodies of Christians; but now the bishop of Rome, Leo, was able to place a quill in the emperor's hand and urge him to prosecute the Church's business. Valentinian was persuaded—along with his wife, Eudoxia, and his mother, Placidia—to write letters to the Eastern emperor, Theodosius II, urging him to ratify Leo's pronouncements on the nature of Christ. The theological controversy raging throughout the Empire had to be settled once and for all, Leo argued. The three short letters have survived, and scholars have been able to conclude from their stylistic differences that each was separately composed. Theodosius was unmoved by the requests, but it didn't matter in the end as he died that summer from a riding accident. His successor, Marcian, would be far more receptive to Leo's appeals.

Once they had worked through Leo's to-do list, the imperial family had personal business to tackle. There was the scandal with Honoria, who (no surprise here) was not invited to write a theological missive. Placidia lived just long enough to see the beginning, if not the end, of the mess that Honoria was making of the world—one final penance, perhaps, for Placidia's betrayal of Serena.[149] A short, bittersweet respite from these troubles was found in the ceremonial reburial of her first child, baby Theodosius, with full imperial honors. Through all the twists and turns of her life, Placidia never forgot the little boy she had held in her arms for just a few days. The

The so-called Mausoleum of Galla Placidia in Ravenna, Italy (exterior view). Contrary to popular belief, the mausoleum does not contain Placidia's remains, though it certainly dates from the fifth century A.D. and may have been commissioned by her.

Vanni / Art Resource, NY

silver casket was disinterred from Barcelona and brought to Saint Peter's in Rome. Pope Leo officiated, and the entire imperial family, along with the Senate, was gathered for the solemn event.[150] Placidia may have been seeking "closure" at the end of her life, but in so doing she choreographed a beautiful preview of how three cultures would blend to create the early Middle Ages. The Germanic tribes, imperial Rome, and the Christian faith were united that day when the son of a Germanic king was buried among the dead Caesars, next to the traditional resting place of Peter.[151]

We know nothing of Placidia's death; but that her burial occurred in Saint Peter's is suggested by the reburial of her beloved son in the family crypt. She must have intended to rest there herself. The story that places her body in Ravenna is a modern legend, fostered during the Renaissance years when Italian cities vied with one another for the prestige of a glorious history. There is little doubt that the famous mausoleum in Ravenna was commissioned by Placidia; but who (if anyone) was ever buried there remains a mystery. Seen from the outside, the building is not very impressive. All the grandeur is reserved for the inner walls and ceilings, where you see exquisite vaultings of blue sky, interspersed with colorful disks, all constructed of hand-cut colored puzzle pieces of brightly colored glass. Over the inner door of the mausoleum stands Christ the Good Shepherd surrounded by grazing sheep. (Carl Jung was sufficiently impressed by the interior decor to have a famous hallucination here in 1913.) These are the oldest surviving mosaics of the late Roman world. J. B. Bury described what you see on the floor as you enter the mausoleum:[152]

> Galla Placidia's own sarcophagus of alabaster stands behind the altar, and her embalmed body in Imperial robes seated on a chair of cypress wood could be seen through a hole in the back till A.D. 1577, when all the contents of the tomb were accidentally burned through the carelessness of children.

Writing in 1889, Bury carefully documented his source for this delightful anecdote: Thomas Hodgkin, who was a banker by day and a historian by night. This is what Hodgkin had written in 1880:

> At the end of the mausoleum, immediately behind the altar, which is made of semi-transparent alabaster, stands the largest of all the sarcophagi, which contains the ashes of Galla Placidia. There are no bas-reliefs on this tomb, which is said to have been once covered with silver plates, long since removed. For eleven centuries the embalmed body of the Augusta remained undisturbed in this tomb, sitting upright in a chair of cypress-wood, and arrayed in royal robes. It was one of the sights of Ravenna to peep through a little hole in the back and see this changeless queen. But unhappily, three hundred years ago some careless or mischievous children, determined to have a thoroughly good look at the stately lady, thrust a lighted taper through the hole. Crowding and pushing, and each one bent on getting the

best view possible, they at length brought the light too near to the corpse: at once royal robes and royal flesh and cypress-wood chair were all wrapped in flames. In a few minutes the work of cremation was accomplished, and the daughter of Theodosius was reduced to ashes as effectually as any daughter of the pagan Caesars. With this anecdote of the year 1577 ends the story of Galla Placidia.

Hodgkin doesn't document his source, but we can reconstruct where the information came from. An American essayist named Charles Dudley Warner published a book in 1872 called *Saunterings* in which he described his travels through Italy. He relates the following about the mausoleum in Ravenna, if you'll bear with the repetitions:

> Behind the altar is the massive sarcophagus of marble (its cover of silver plates was long ago torn off) in which are literally the ashes of the empress. She was immured in it as a mummy, in a sitting position, clothed in imperial robes; and there the ghostly corpse sat in a cypress-wood chair, to be looked at by anybody who chose to peep through the aperture, for more than eleven hundred years, till one day, in 1577, some children introduced a lighted candle, perhaps out of compassion for her who sat so long in darkness, when her clothes caught fire, and she was burned up—a warning to all children not to play with a dead and dry empress.

Even though Hodgkin has not credited Warner, it's rather plain to see from the sequencing and repetition of words that the one text is dependent upon the other. When Hodgkin writes, for example, that the tomb "is said to have been once covered with silver plates," he's passing on a specific detail Warner had also mentioned parenthetically. Working the source backward, we've gone from a professor at Cambridge, to an amateur historian, to a traveler in Italy. The story spread like an urban legend.

Warner didn't invent the story. We can go back one more step to a German historian named Ferdinand Gregorovius, who wrote his own *Wanderings in Italy* between 1856 and 1877. In his travelogues from 1863,

Gregorovius relates the kernel of the story that was passed down through Warner, Hodgkin, and Bury:

> The local tradition in Ravenna relates that Placidia was placed in this sarcophagus, sitting in royal garments on a throne of cypress-wood. Some of Ravenna's later historians describe how this buried figure came to ashes in 1577. Some inquisitive children stuck a lit candle in the opening of the sarcophagus, whereupon the contents of the tomb went up in flames and the sleeping form of Placidia came to ruin.

With Gregorovius we've reached the end of the line. This respected historian, whose meticulous eight-volume survey of the city of Rome in the Middle Ages remains a standard historical work, merely refers us to local traditions and "later historians" who go unnamed. The process of transmission, then, looks like this:

Local Legends ➡ Gregorovius ➡ Warner ➡ Hodgkin ➡ Bury

The point is not to trace this out any further, something that could be done fairly easily and would make an interesting little story in itself. The point, rather, is to recognize how much this chart looks like the one we drew in Chapter One for the orthodox account of Attila's death. If stories like this can enter the "historical" record so easily in the modern era, then we're really in trouble when trying to extract the truth from ancient sources. Still, Gregorovius lends the weight of his reputation to the anecdote when he writes "there is no doubt that" Placidia's remains are in the tomb.

There is no doubt? The 1911 *Encyclopedia Britannica*, the standard of historical sobriety, would note only that the sarcophagus had been "despoiled of its contents." Stewart Oost, who authored a book-length biography of Placidia in 1968, doesn't even mention the throne, the children, the candle, and the ashes. What a pity! After looking at the evidence and reconstructing the legend's history, I was forced to join the agnostics in concluding that we have no idea whose sarcophagus this was and what, if anything, was ever contained within it. My crestfallen reaction (I love a good story as much as anyone) was, "Oh, darn. It's not true after all." Even so, it's hard to shake loose that image, the ghostly image of an embalmed empress, dressed in purple robes and seated, cramped in darkness, for over a thousand years. We'd like to be those children peeping through the hole; I know *I* would, though of course I'd be more careful with the candle. No, I don't want to lose that picture—it's just too good. But lose it we must. And once it's lost, we "know" a little less about the world than we did before.

We've become less certain of these things than scholars were a hundred years ago. I've learned that a curious axiom governs the progress we make as we explore the past: the more we learn about a problem, the less sure we become in our knowledge. My own mentor in philology, a man whose head was a big set of encyclopedias, once observed in class that we really *know less* as we accumulate more data. "If you have one piece of a puzzle," he said, "then you can reconstruct the other ninety-nine pieces pretty much any way you want." I was struck by the cryptic, offhanded remark that seemed to call into question the very possibility of dogmatic knowledge. Looking back, I see how that paradox has shaped my own thinking, charted my own approach, and tempered my own certainties. As a young grad student, I had been writing ambitious papers that tried to reconstruct, say, the "comic ethos" of *Beowulf*. Anatoly (as we familiarly called him) would scribble terse comments in the margins, things like "I am really embarrassed by this." At the end of one of my papers he wrote the following: "Put this in a drawer, take it out in twenty years, and read it again." It was the pedagogical equivalent of a kick in the butt—and it smarted. Recently, I found the yellowed paper in a dusty stack. It had been almost twenty years, and so I read through it again, trying to give myself every benefit of the doubt. And then I threw it away. Anatoly was right. I know a little more about the world now—a *little* more. But I also know a lot less.

It's hard enough to know something—I mean, *really* know it—when you're living through it. (Just ask Priscus.) How much did these actors know of the larger drama they were starring in? A truly substantive figure like Aetius seems "heroic" and "tragic" to us, by which we mean to imply that he understood more than his own immediate interests. Maybe he did, maybe he didn't. Marcian, too, stands out against the drab background of his contemporaries, a rare man of conviction in a world of unctuous eunuchs. Even Placidia, who had seen just about everything, acquitted herself well against the "forces" of history. She survived the sacking of Rome, two forced marriages, two rotten children, and a handful of exiles and revolutions. Through it all she remained deeply motivated by the memory of her father, the memory of her child, and the legacy of the Theodosian House.

Who knows what motivated Honoria. Her mother's health may have been weakening noticeably. Perhaps this would be her chance to emerge from the domineering shadow of her mother and challenge Valentinian's authority. She, too, had a destiny as an Augusta—or so she thought. She, too, sprang from imperial blood. Was she not a granddaughter of Theodosius? What was to prevent her, too, from wielding the power her mother had long enjoyed in the West and which Pulcheria now held in the East? But what actually happened was one of the most memorable instances in history of overplaying one's hand. In the summer of 450, Honoria played out her hand quickly—and she found that it wasn't a very strong hand after all.

SIX

FROM CHÂLONS TO CHALCEDON

I N a letter dated April 23, 451, "in the consulship of the illustrious Adelfius," the bishop of Rome writes to congratulate Marcian Augustus on his recent accession to the Eastern throne.[153] It would be the beginning of an extensive correspondence. "I found still greater cause for congratulation," Leo writes, "when I heard of your strong eagerness for the Church's peace." It's revealing that Leo writes first of the "Church's peace" when he knew full well what was stirring in his own backyard—an invasion, massive in scale, such as Europe would not see again until the beaches of Normandy were stormed in 1944. Two weeks earlier, on April 7, the siege of Metz had begun, right during the holiest time of the Church's calendar, Easter.[154] Attila's army made short shrift of the city and its priests before continuing their march into Gaul. You might think that Leo would mention this—would plead, perhaps, for military assistance from the East. Instead, the first order of business for Leo was the business of the Church.

But if we read Leo carefully, we see that he was aware and fully engaged in the unfolding crisis. No clear line separated religion from politics in Leo's world. The safety of the Church *was* the safety of the Empire, and vice versa. Doing God's work was simply a matter of putting first things first. Everything else, including the safety of the Empire, was the natural by-product of a pure faith. "Your holy desire," Leo continues, "will secure for your empire the same happy condition which you seek for religion. When the Spirit of God establishes harmony among Christian princes, good things will happen. God is well pleased when there is one confession of faith. Christian love and faith will prove unconquerable in every sphere—religious and political—as they make inroads throughout the world. Most glorious emperor, that's how heretics and barbarians will be defeated simultaneously."

EXHIBIT ELEVEN

The letters between Pope Leo and Emperor Marcian reveal a pattern of thinking in which the defense of the Church is equated with the defense of the Empire.

Leo's goals are clear. He wants the two "Christian princes"—Valentinian and Marcian—to put the combined weight of their offices behind "one confession" about the nature of Christ. Theodosius II had wavered on this point. But now that he was dead, and Chrysaphius with him, there was every reason to be hopeful. Leo is urging Marcian to a task already chosen by the new emperor: to combat simultaneously "the falseness of heretics" and "the enmity of barbarians." Even as Leo was writing these words, the Western Empire was being invaded by a huge barbarian army. Within months Attila would be defeated at a battlefield known as Châlons, somewhere in the Champagne province of France. In the East, Marcian would convene a great council at Chalcedon to address the heresies facing the Church. The twin challenges of Châlons and Chalcedon would define the world of 451 and set the stage for Attila's death. His assassination in 453 was not an isolated political event; it was instead the logical next step, after Chalcedon, in shoring up the Empire for God.

GAISERIC'S REVENGE

What was Attila *thinking* when he led a huge army several hundred miles across Europe to invade Gaul? It couldn't possibly work—and yet it almost did. Historians have never resolved the question of why Attila drove tens of thousands of soldiers, horses, and wagons that far from his home territory. The motivations, geography, and ultimate significance of the decisive conflict fought in France remain open historical problems. What's clear is that the Battle of Châlons would be Attila's Waterloo, and he would never recover from the drubbing he received. That wouldn't stop him from trying again the following year, in 452, when he invaded Italy. Both campaigns were unrelenting disasters; Attila caused a lot of destruction, but he had little to show for it in the end. The account that Jordanes gives in his *Gothic History* is as good as it gets for an ancient source.[155] His uncertainties are still our uncertainties and his understanding of these events has never been improved upon by later historians. We should probably thank Priscus for this, as he's undoubtedly the source underlying much of what Jordanes has written.[156] Let's follow, then, how Jordanes describes the battle, which was still vividly remembered a hundred years later by his Gothic countrymen.

We left Attila in the last chapter pondering his options. East or West? Edward Gibbon imagines that "mankind awaited his decision with awful suspense," but that's unlikely.[157] Most people then, as most people now, were preoccupied with the mundane challenges of life. How many would have looked up from their plows to consider the intricate calculations that spanned a continent? Even Attila probably hadn't calculated much, judging from the outcome. Few scholars nowadays concede what earlier scholars took for granted, namely that "consummate military skill may be traced in his campaigns."[158] The back-to-back invasions of Gaul and Italy seem to have been strategic afterthoughts for Attila, impulsively embarked upon and made up on the fly.

Constantinople, not Rome, had been Attila's source of steady income for the previous decade. He would need some inducement, some pretext, to change his long-standing policy and invade the West. He looked around and found several. There was the solicitation from Honoria, whatever the motivation behind it was. How often does a eunuch walk into your camp with an offer like this? We know from what Priscus has recorded that Attila was a deeply superstitious man. Things like this didn't just happen; they were *fated*. He had found the fabled sword of Mars, after all, and believed that his destiny was to rule the world. Half the Empire would be a fitting dowry—a good place to start. But Valentinian firmly refused to hand over his sister, though the temptation must have been very strong indeed. We can be sure that Aetius played a pivotal role in convincing Valentinian to spare Honoria from a future she hadn't taken the time to contemplate. The master strategist, Aetius, understood that if Honoria married Attila, then Valentinian wouldn't need him anymore to protect the Empire. The proposed marriage would have forged an alliance between Valentinian and his new brother-in-law, Attila—an alliance that would have rendered Aetius obsolete.

Other reasons, too, compelled Attila to look westward. Franco-Roman politics were a mess ever since the Frankish king had died. This shadowy figure is often described as the "semimythical king Merovech," founder of the Merovingians, though it's hard to imagine a semimythical king even dying.[159] But whoever he was, he *did* die and leave two sons vying for his throne. Aetius was actively sponsoring the younger prince, whom Priscus describes as "a lad who didn't yet have peach-fuzz on his cheeks and whose blond hair was so long that it poured down around his shoulders." Priscus was obviously taken with the youth. "I saw him," he writes, "when I was in Rome on an embassy."[160] (This was in 450, less than a year before Attila's invasion. Maximin and Priscus were probably in Rome at Marcian's request; the Eastern ambassadors must have met directly with Aetius, hence the opportunity Priscus had to observe the youth firsthand.) Aetius adopted the young Frank, showered him with gifts, and sent him home as a Roman ally. If we have the chronology right, then the Frankish king died shortly thereafter, leading to a power struggle between the two sons. The older son managed to reel Attila in on his side, which—before Châlons—must have made him look like a sure winner. As always, there's much we don't know, but it's safe to assume that the northern route that Attila took into Gaul was probably determined by the Frankish affair.[161] The teenager whom Priscus saw in Rome did gain the throne. We don't know his name, but some say he was the father of Clovis, the "first king" of France.

The rapidly changing situation in the East, economically and politically, also gave Attila good reason to change directions. Throughout the 440s, Constantinople had been a source of steady income for the Huns, so much so that the Balkans had been stripped clean. It was time to exploit new territory. Marcian's forceful rejection of Attila's demands made it clear that he would be no pushover. Sooner or later Attila would have to deal with him; but for now, the West was beckoning with its open borders and its chaotic political scene. None of these are the answers Jordanes gives us. He suggests instead that the idea first came to Attila from the Vandal king Gaiseric who reigned far away in North Africa.

Only distance and a great body of water prevented Gaiseric from being more of a constant threat to Rome. He didn't take part directly in the campaign in Gaul, but he was an enthusiastic cheerleader on the sidelines. Gaiseric stood to benefit politically from the Hunnish invasion, and so he goaded Attila through diplomatic letters to turn his attention to the West. It wasn't so much the Romans that Gaiseric was worried about but the Visigoths. The king of the Visigoths, Theodoric, had given his daughter in marriage many years before to Gaiseric's son, Huneric.[162] They had been a happy couple for a while, until Huneric began suffering delusions followed by bouts of cruelty toward his wife and children. Huneric accused the woman of trying to poison him, and so he cut off her nose and ears and sent her back to her father in Gaul, "despoiled of her natural charms," as Jordanes put it. The "pitiable aspect" of the girl could even stir strangers to grief, and it kindled the undying hatred of Theodoric and the entire Visigothic host. This was the kind of crime you remembered for a long time, the stuff of legends.[163]

Gaiseric knew that his family would feel the wrath of the Visigoths at the first opportunity, and so he opened up a long-distance dialogue with Attila.[164] The goal was to defeat the Visigoths preemptively, and to do so through a proxy army. Jordanes tells us that Gaiseric came to this plan when he learned of Attila's ruthless reputation; he was particularly impressed by how Attila's "mind was bent on the destruction of the whole world." In other words, Attila was Gaiseric's kind of guy. The Vandal king sent gifts to the Hunnish court; several years passed and nothing had come of the overtures. When Attila was having so much success in the Balkans, there was little incentive to go westward. But all that had changed, and it now seemed to him a good time to take Gaiseric up on the suggestion.

Jordanes presents Gaiseric as a leading figure in the drama that unfolded in Gaul. It is strange that Jordanes places the story of Theodoric's daughter in the foreground, implying that it was a precipitating cause of the battle. Several years had separated the atrocities of Huneric and the invasion of Gaul. Clearly, this is an ancient historical interpretation—a linking of events that is intended to bring clarity to a confusing set of facts. It's impossible to tell conclusively whether this interpretation comes from the pen of Jordanes, or from the earlier history of Cassiodorus (which Jordanes is abbreviating), or from the lost history of Priscus. There's some strong evidence, however, that suggests Priscus first drew this remote connection between Attila and Gaiseric as a casus belli. Though we don't have the full account of the Battle of Châlons in the surviving fragments of Priscus, we do have his prefatory remarks, and they clearly point to Gaiseric as an instigating force:[165]

> Attila was of two minds and at a loss which he should attack first, but finally it seemed better to him to enter on the greater war and to march against the West, since his fight there would be not only against the Italians but also against the Goths and Franks—against the Italians so as to seize

Honoria along with her money, and against the Goths *in order to earn the gratitude of Gaiseric.*

When Priscus completed his history in the early 470s, Gaiseric was still a major problem in North Africa. He may have been nearing the end of his half-century reign, but the Vandal warlord was still very much on Roman minds. Since Gaiseric is the filter through which the Battle of Châlons is narrated, we need to fast-forward to the late 460s and early 470s and look at the world as Priscus saw it when he was publishing his history. As always, he was shaping that history to meet the political needs of his patrons.

In 467 a Vandal raiding party hit southern Greece and violated the territory of the Eastern Empire. Leo (who had succeeded Marcian in 457) formed a hasty alliance with the Western Empire. He nominated an ally in the West, Anthemius, to become the new Western emperor (the West had been going through emperors like hotcakes); the pressing goal was to mount a joint operation against the North African stronghold. Leo committed 65,000 pounds of gold and 700 pounds of silver to the expedition: 1,100 ships and 100,000 soldiers and sailors were equipped. The initial sea battles boded well for the Empire. The Western navy, under the command of a certain admiral named Marcellinus, defeated the Vandals on the island of Sardinia in a furious sea battle in which volleys of arrows and pots full of scorpions were hurled at each other. The Eastern navy was placed under the command of Basiliscus, the brother-in-law of Emperor Leo; they sailed to a position forty-five miles outside Carthage, where they took anchor. A third front was opened up when the Eastern general Heracleius landed his troops on the shores of Tripoli and quickly began advancing. Several Vandal cities were quickly overtaken in the assault. The Vandals fought on horseback and even positioned their Moorish allies in the middle of the phalanx on camels. The Roman army was too strong, however, and kept pushing the Vandals back. It began to look as though Gaiseric, the original desert fox, had been backed into a corner.

The weak link was the Eastern navy, which Emperor Leo had placed under the command of his wife's brother, Basiliscus. Nobody knows why the Eastern navy stayed anchored in port outside Carthage when they could have proceeded all the way to the Vandal capital and stormed it by surprise.[166] The delay gave Gaiseric some breathing room, time that he used to full advantage. Gaiseric rushed ambassadors off to Basiliscus asking for a cease-fire even while he was preparing his own navy for a sneak attack. Under the cover of darkness the Vandals struck the Eastern fleet while the Romans were at anchor. The Western fleet in Sardinia was unable to help, since its commander, Marcellinus, had just been assassinated. With both fleets now immobilized, General Heracleius was forced to withdraw his land troops. It was a devastating defeat for the Romans—the last gasp of the Western Empire as a military power. As Priscus looked back at the Battle of Châlons, it seemed logical to blame Gaiseric for what had happened. Attila had long since passed from the scene; Gaiseric was the villain with staying power.

The invasion of Gaul was motivated by much more than Gaiseric's revenge, and yet the power equation in the West must have factored into Attila's calculations. He sent an embassy to Emperor Valentinian, informing him that the Huns had a problem with the Visigoths that didn't involve the Romans. At the same time, Attila sent a separate message to Theodoric, urging him to break his alliance with Rome. "Beneath his great ferocity," Jordanes writes, "Attila was a subtle man who fought with craft before he made war." Attila was not a very good liar, though, and Valentinian dismissed everything the Hun had said. The emperor immediately drafted a letter to Theodoric so as to shore up their alliance. The letter he composed was remarkably lucid, even eloquent, for a man generally considered to be an idiot:

> Bravest of nations, it is the part of prudence for us to unite against the lord of the earth who wishes to enslave the whole world; who requires no just cause for battle, but supposes whatever he does is right. He measures his ambition by his might. License satisfies his pride. Despising law and right, he shows himself an enemy to Nature herself. And thus he, who clearly is the common foe of each, deserves the hatred of all. Pray remember—what

you surely cannot forget—that the Huns do not overthrow nations by means of war, where there is an equal chance, but assail them by treachery, which is a greater cause for anxiety. To say nothing about ourselves, can you suffer such insolence to go unpunished? Since you are mighty in arms, give heed to your own danger and join hands with us in common. Bear aid also to the Empire, of which you hold a part. If you would learn how such an alliance should be sought and welcomed by us, look into the plans of the foe.

Valentinian (we'll pretend that he actually wrote these words) is putting his finger on the character of Attila. In listing Attila's many character defects, the emperor was not just making a case for an alliance and a war. Though it wasn't his intention, of course, he made a splendid case for assassination. You couldn't read Valentinian's indictment and go on blithely concluding that Attila was someone you could do business with. In Valentinian's caricature, Attila was an impulsive, narcissistic megalomaniac—a freak of nature. It's unlikely that Valentinian ever thought these thoughts, or that he ever expressed them in so many words; but the fact that they're recorded so prominently in the record of this war suggests that we've reached a watershed. No more bandaging up of the problem; Attila would have to be dealt with decisively.

The letter did its job. If Theodoric had ever wavered in his support of Rome, you wouldn't know it from how he replied to Valentinian:

Romans, you have attained your desire; you have made Attila our foe also. We will pursue him wherever he summons us, and though he is puffed up by his victories over divers races, yet the Goths know how to fight this haughty foe. I call no war dangerous save one whose cause is weak; for he fears no ill on whom Majesty has smiled.

The Visigoths would form the bulk of the allied army. Filling out the ranks were Franks, Burgundians, and Saxons, as well as Roman troops. They assembled under the joint command of Aetius, "on whom at that time the whole Empire of the West depended." And then with solemn simplicity, Jordanes states: "So they met in the Catalaunian Plains." The location of this battle is hotly disputed and need not concern us.[167] (I am using the traditional name, the Battle of Châlons, though it is also called the Battle of the Catalaunian Plains and the Battle of the Mauriac Plain.) Generations of French colonels have supposedly spent their retirement tooling around the countryside of Champagne looking for evidence of this enormous battle that was fought somewhere in a field, or a plain—"that portion of the earth," Jordanes wrote, "that became the threshing-floor of countless races."

Once the causes of the battle were sketched (Gaiseric's revenge), as well as the broad outline of who met whom and where, Jordanes pauses and sighs, as it were, and offers this philosophical observation:

> What just cause can be found for the encounter of so many nations, or what hatred inspired them all to take arms against each other? It is proof that the human race lives for its kings, for it is at the mad impulse of one mind a slaughter of nations takes place, and at the whim of a haughty ruler that which nature has taken ages to produce perishes in a moment.

This could be a description of Verdun in 1916. These two battles, Châlons and Verdun, were fought less than fifty miles from each other, and both can be described as among the bloodiest in the history of man. Neither battle ended with a clear-cut victory. They were savage exercises in bloodletting, and both were seen as "proof that the human race lives for its kings."

Who is the author of this compelling denunciation of the madness of war? Beneath the Latin of Jordanes we almost certainly have the Greek rhetorician once again—"authentic Priscus," as the German scholars used to put it.[168] And like those scholars, who relied a lot on their ear while claiming that their methods and judgments were objective, I, too, am relying on my ear, *listening* to the passage and hearing Priscus. But I'm not claiming objectivity: all I have is a hunch. After reading these authors for a while, you begin to think you *know* them. Scholars can only acknowledge the constant temptation to substitute instinct for rational inquiry; the temptation can never be avoided. I *do* feel as though I can hear Priscus, the rhetorician and the cynic, a man who witnessed the fifth century from the inside out. Surely by the end of his life, Priscus had earned the right to indulge in a sweeping indictment of human history. Surely the elegiac tone gives him away (I think); the regret seems real, not formulaic, as he laments all that "perishes in a moment"—not just the lives lost but "that which nature has taken ages to produce." Priscus might be thinking back to his time in Egypt, where he saw temples burned to the ground and ancient languages and religions that were lost forever. Or he might be thinking of contemporary events—the colossal failure against Gaiseric and the slow death of the Western Empire. These words sound as if they were drawn from the well of *his* experience.

Priscus gives us a purely secular interpretation of these events, not because he was a pagan (he may have been) but because he was writing history within a pagan classical tradition that found causes in human motivations. All that happened that June in the rolling fields of Champagne was put in play "at the whim of a haughty ruler," a view starkly at odds with the Western chroniclers who would view this battle for centuries to come as God's judgment upon his Church. The western memory would be filled with saints and bishops who stood before the onrushing army, bravely defying the hordes city by city. Attila was the whip in God's hand. He was the *flagellum Dei*, the Scourge of God. Many scholars (especially French) believe that a residue of truth, an ancient itinerary, can be salvaged from these legends. The idea is very simple: though we can be sure that eleven thousand virgins under the leadership of St. Ursula never perished in Cologne, the fact that this story was told at all suggests that Attila passed this way. Trier, Metz, Reims, Paris—these cities and more had their own run-in with the Scourge of God. The outcome in each city depended on how the sins of the people were balanced by the prayers of the saints.

Where was Attila leading his army? Perhaps he was heading south to Toulouse, near the Spanish border in Aquitaine, where the Visigothic kings had held court since the days of Athaulf and Wallia. Nobody knows what the final destination was, since the battle was joined prematurely. As they ransacked their way through the French countryside, Attila's army came to a standstill at the walls of Orléans. Gibbon relates the thrilling story of how battering rams shook the walls while the people trembled and prayed. The city's bishop, Anianus, walked among the people and encouraged them to keep praying and hoping. Twice he sent a messenger to the highest point of the ramparts to scout the horizon for any sign of help. Nothing could be seen but the swarming hordes of barbarians below. "Go and check again," the bishop said, and this time the messenger spotted a small cloud on the horizon. Hope at last! The dust cloud grew bigger and soon the Roman ensign could be seen. Aetius and Theodoric were driving their armies to the defense of Orléans!

But wait!—none of this happened. Gibbon's account is completely wrong.[169] The story he relates comes from the *Life of St. Anianus*, which was written to enhance the reputation of a local hero. The story of the little cloud on the horizon is adapted from the Old Testament story of the prophet Elijah as related in I Kings 18. Jordanes tells us that Attila had prearranged the surrender of the city with Sangiban, the king of the Alans. Aetius found out about the treachery, though, and thwarted Attila's plans by fortifying the city's defenses. As for Sangiban, Aetius and Theodoric placed him and his troops in the center column of the allied armies, right where they could keep an eye on him. When Attila arrived, he was surprised by the stiff resistance and he quickly withdrew his forces back into the open fields. The two armies would take several more days to position themselves for the decisive showdown.

THE LAST OF THE ROMANS

How did it come about that Flavius Aetius, born far away in modern Bulgaria, arrived at this battlefield in Gaul? Gibbon called him a "haughty and perfidious soul." The sixth-century historian Procopius called him "the last of the Romans." The truth is that he was both. Aetius stands out as the great tragic figure of Rome's final century, a century chock-full of idiots and traitors. Upon his shoulders fell the task of saving Rome, and he brought to this task an intimate knowledge of the barbarian world. He was a realist who worked with what life gave him; but he had also nurtured (perhaps) a strain of idealism about Rome's past and destiny. In this man we see something tragic—a greatness of character that was wasted on his time, a touch of nobility rendered insignificant by the accident of when he lived. His actions and character *as a Roman* could only derive meaning from the idea of an imperial Rome, an idea that no longer corresponded to the material world of men and cities and armies. His army was Roman in name only, having become a patchwork of tribal allegiances. The great army that defended Gaul in 451 was an army of convenience—Franks and Visigoths and a few Romans—cobbled together for this one task and then disbanded.

The rise of Flavius Aetius from obscurity to greatness is a story of achievement and survival, courage and villainy, self-sacrifice and self-assertion, which can only partially be reconstructed. We do know the basic facts. He was born far from the centers of political power in Durostorum in the province of Lower Moesia. The ancient ruins of this Roman city lie beneath the modern Bulgarian city of Silistra on the Danube River separating Bulgaria from Rumania. Durostorum was typical of the great provincial cities that projected and maintained Roman civilization in the outlying regions. Though it had large public buildings and shrines, basilicas and baths, Durostorum remained very much a city on the frontier. This was a region teeming with Goths, and from his youth Aetius would have seen the world through the multicultural prism of his boyhood home.

As a young man, probably no more than a teenager, Aetius was sent as a hostage to Alaric, the Visigothic king. In the ancient world "hostages" from prominent families were swapped between warring cultures like diplomatic pawns—kind of like trip-wire troops in the cold war, staking out their positions near Checkpoint Charlie. The theory was very simple: you were less likely to wage war on each other if the sons of your noblest families were eating at your enemy's table. Hostages also ensured a steady flow of information back and forth between rival cultures; relationships were formed at the highest levels of each nation that would last for years. The downside, of course, was that your trade secrets were very quickly learned by the other side. A military mind held hostage in the enemy's camp, studying the enemy up close year after year, could be a very dangerous weapon to hand back across the border. That was Aetius. He flourished among the Visigoths and was a favorite of the Visigothic king, who reportedly admired the awesome beauty of the boy, his eyes that so foretold his destiny:

> Alaric gave Aetius his first bow and arrows, and praised the swing of his arm as he bore his weapons—forgetting that he was a Roman. . . . He called him "son," and preferred to say that he was nature's pledge to him, rather than a pledge of peace. It was with Alaric looking on that Aetius first felt and enjoyed his youth flaming up in the fierce pursuits of war.

(The doting father figure, by the way, is the same Alaric who sacked Rome in 410.) These lofty lines come from a panegyric written by a Spanish poet named Merobaudes who hung around the courts of Rome and Ravenna. We should take what he wrote with a grain of salt. Imperial poets are notoriously unreliable, singing as they do for their pay. How we know what we do of Merobaudes—and through him, how we know a little more about Aetius—is one of those minor detective stories that make up the history of philology.

For fifteen hundred years Merobaudes, poet laureate for Emperor Valentinian III, was known to us through a single reference in the *Chronicle* of Hydatius, a contemporary and fellow Spaniard. Hydatius briefly mentions Merobaudes under the year 443, describing him as a poet and orator who had been honored with a statue. Our knowledge of the Spaniard increased sharply in 1813 when the base of his statue was discovered in the ruins of Trajan's Forum in Rome. The lengthy inscription dates itself to 435 and praises Merobaudes as a warrior and a poet. Ten years after the marble fragment was discovered, a scholar named Niebuhr found a palimpsest manuscript in the St. Gall Monastery in Switzerland and identified the text (based on linguistic similarities to the inscription) as a work by Merobaudes. It was a celebratory poem about Aetius. Nothing expresses the sorry state of our knowledge of the fifth century better than the image of a palimpsest, those "recycled" manuscripts of the Middle Ages. Picture a scribe scraping away the ink from an earlier text and then overwriting the vellum parchment with something new. The scholar's challenge is to recover the text that was scraped away and written over. Today, new imaging technologies can bring lost texts to light; but in 1823, Niebuhr was on his own.

After all the effort one might have hoped for something more earth-shattering than a badly written poem. And yet it does give us information, through the fog of its propaganda. The poetic picture of young Aetius, so comfortable in the presence of Alaric that the barbarian "forgot that he was a Roman," meshes nicely with the historical accounts of the general's life. How else could Aetius have commanded the respect of German legions if he was not viewed (in some measure at least) as being German himself? A man so admired would not easily be forgotten. In fact, it would be surprising if Aetius were *not* remembered in the oral poems of the Germans who fought under his command, just as he was remembered in the official poems of the Romans. Some scholars believe he was indeed remembered; some have gone so far as to suggest that the historical figure of Aetius lies behind the manipulative figure of Hagen in the epic of the Nibelungs. It can't be proven, but it wouldn't surprise me.

When his apprenticeship with Alaric was over, the young Roman returned home only to find himself shipped off once again. This time the assignment would take him to the court of Attila's uncle Rua, where he would live as a guest and serve as an honorary Hun. His position was probably very much like that of Orestes, the Roman officer who became one of Attila's most trusted lieutenants. But unlike Orestes, Aetius returned home again to his fatherland after a few years, having learned the language, customs, and military techniques of Rome's greatest enemy. Aetius was about the same age as Attila and Bleda. We can imagine Aetius taking the measure of each man: the older brother who was always joking, always having fun, and the younger brother, Attila, who was serious and resolute. Later on when Attila ruled the Huns and Aetius commanded the armies of the West, we see the grudging respect—perhaps it was friendship—that must have developed early on between the two young men. The story of their confrontation in Gaul, for all its world-historical implications, is also a richly human drama of a mutual respect that had turned to bitter hostility.

In the first glimpse of Aetius the historical record gives us, we see an impetuous young man making a dreadfully wrong decision. His first political maneuver was to cast his lots behind a loser, a usurper named John. The Western emperor Honorius, son of Theodosius the Great, had died in 423. He left behind a power vacuum in Rome and an ambitious sister, Galla Placidia, who was very keen to fill that vacuum herself. The problem? Galla Placidia and her two children were nowhere near the scene of the action. They had been exiled earlier that year to Constantinople. Even so, her son Valentinian III was too young to assume the reins of power all by himself. That's when the political machinery of the Theodosian House began to swing into full combat mode. Placidia gathered up her children and caught the first boat to Italy. During a layover in Thessalonica, little Valentinian was proclaimed Caesar in 424.

Meanwhile, Aetius was also moving west toward Italy with an army of sixty thousand Huns under his command. He was intending to support the pretensions of John, a civil servant, against the claims of the Theodosian House. It was a bad choice. A young general named Aspar (whom we've already encountered several times, most notably as Marcian's patron) was leading his own forces from the east toward Italy for a showdown at Ravenna. John was defeated, captured, and sentenced to death by Placidia. Aetius was fortunate to have survived the debacle. We don't know the ins and outs of what happened, but it's likely that sixty thousand Huns standing at his back made it much easier for Galla Placidia to pardon him and restore him to favor. In his first botched foray into the political arena, Aetius showed that he had learned well what Alaric had taught him: a large force threatening Rome creates many opportunities to negotiate. Not only did he survive, he flourished. His army of Huns led him to victories in Gaul, which soon became his base of power. His years with Alaric and Rua were paying off as he was able to leverage his influence with the barbarians to enhance his position and authority. By 429 he was suspected in the death of a rival patrician, Felix.

How did such a devious and ambitious man become known as "the last of the Romans"? He's always gotten good press, Edward Gibbon notwithstanding, but this is due more to the rotten company he kept than to his own innate qualities. Who wouldn't look good compared to Attila the Hun, the "Scourge of God," and Valentinian III, a "weak and worthless" man?[170] Aetius, though, was cast from the great mold of Roman despots; he was as ruthless, self-serving, arrogant, petty, and *great* as Julius Caesar had been. He may not have deserved a sword in the gut, but he wasn't altogether without guile.

The Latin phrase *ultimus Romanorum,* "last of the Romans," comes from the tearful eulogy that Brutus spoke over the body of Cassius in 42 B.C.[171] The hint of tragedy and nobility implicit in that phrase always resonated deeply throughout Roman history. Originally used by Brutus when the Roman Republic was collapsing into civil war, the phrase experienced a revival of usage in the fourth and fifth centuries when Rome once again was undergoing a tectonic shift. The phrase must have been on the lips of every patrician when the pagan symbol of Rome, the Altar of Victory, was removed from the Senate floor in the fourth century—the clearest indication yet that the classical world had given way to the Christian. Pagan and Christian alike could see that Rome was on its way out.

It was, in fact, not a Roman but a Goth—Stilicho—who was first honored with this title in the fifth century. Stilicho was the German-born strongman of the Western Empire, and the very fact that the poet Claudian would eulogize him with this ancient phrase suggests the complex ambiguities that were now shaping Rome's destiny. Stilicho represented something completely new, and dangerous, in Roman history: the barbarian "master of soldiers." Though he strove to be even more Roman than the Romans, Stilicho was suspected of treason and executed in 408, after which Alaric marched the Visigoths toward Rome and sacked it in 410. It's a curious irony that Aetius would later be given the same title as Stilicho, *ultimus*

Romanorum. Like Stilicho, Aetius would be accused of treason and assassinated in 454. And once again the Germans would come calling, sacking the city in 455.

There were others who were given the ultimate distinction of this title, last of the Romans—Boethius, Cassiodorus, Justinian. But the title was especially fitting for Aetius. Writing in the sixth century, Procopius called both Aetius and Boniface the last of the Romans, noting that each had "attained to such a degree of high-mindedness and excellence in every respect that if one should call either of them 'the last of the Romans' he would not err, so true was it that all the excellent qualities of the Romans were summed up in these two men." How "excellent" these two Roman generals were is fully on display in the conflict that divided them.

With Felix out of the way in 429, Aetius turned his attention to the governor of North Africa, Count Boniface. A favorite of Placidia, Boniface was the only man remaining who could thwart his rise to power. The struggle between them would last for several years, culminating in a pitched battle in 432 in which Aetius was defeated. Boniface, though victorious, would die soon thereafter from wounds suffered in the conflict. Gibbon summarized the tragedy: "Their union might have supported a sinking empire; their discord was the fatal and immediate cause of the loss of Africa."[172] What happened between Aetius and Boniface is pure Machiavelli. It's worth looking at more closely since this story affords us the one insight we have into the machinations of the noble patrician Aetius, a man fully capable of helping to engineer the death of Attila.

The conflict between Aetius and Boniface began around 428 and accelerated after the death (by assassination?) of Placidia's master of soldiers, Felix. Aetius retraced Julius Caesar's ancient steps and brought his army back from Gaul. Placidia had no choice but to recognize him as her new master of soldiers. But Aetius wasn't done yet. He next persuaded Placidia that Boniface was plotting a coup from Africa. She could test his loyalty, Aetius argued, by recalling him immediately to Italy. At the same time, however, Aetius was sending a private message to Boniface, advising him to ignore Placidia's command altogether and claiming that she was plotting to assassinate him as soon as he disembarked from Africa. The final element in this brilliant and devious choreography was to convince Placidia that the general's refusal to return was prima facie evidence of his treachery.

If the test of statesmanship is one's ability to subjugate personal ambition to the greater good, both Flavius Aetius and Count Boniface flunked miserably. Boniface remained in Africa at the duplicitous urging of his rival and forged an ill-advised alliance with the young king of the Vandals, Gaiseric. The Vandals were invited to migrate to North Africa, where the province would be divided equally between the Germans and the Romans. But sharing was not something that the Vandal king had ever learned to do, and Boniface soon regretted his gambit. Far from shoring up his power base, Boniface would now have to defend Roman interests against the new German immigrants. The ubiquitous general Aspar was sent from the East to bolster the Roman defenses, but Africa had already become a lost cause. Boniface and Aspar were driven back by Gaiseric in 432, and Roman captives were executed—though not, happily, a man named Marcian who had an eagle hovering over his head. Aspar, Marcian, and a dwarf named Zerko made their way back to Constantinople. Boniface, too, abandoned Africa. Another chapter in Rome's collapse had been written.

By now the truth had come out (we don't know how) that Aetius had tricked Boniface into rebellion. The count was restored to favor by Placidia, and this set the stage for the final face-to-face showdown with Aetius, which was fought in 432. Boniface won the battle but lost the war. Most of what we know about the protracted struggle between these two titans of the Western Empire comes from the pen of Procopius. There's no question that he could spin a good yarn, which is partly why historians read him with such suspicion. Some details in the story fit together with too much poetic precision. For example, Procopius relates that Boniface was struck in battle by a javelin thrown by Aetius himself. It probably didn't happen that way, but we don't have to read it literally to recognize that there's a kind of truth behind the poetic license.

After the conflict with Boniface, Aetius fled back to the Huns and renewed his old friendship with Rua. Once again with the Huns at his back, Aetius persuaded Placidia to receive him again into the service of the Western Empire; he was reinstated in his former office in 434. In 436–37 he unleashed the Huns upon the restless Burgundians, destroying their kingdom, killing the royal family of Gundahar, and laying the groundwork for the rise of medieval German legend. Our knowledge of the next decade, the 440s, is severely restricted by sources that are paltry and bare. We do know that Aetius was spending more and more time in Italy (his son Gaudentius was born in Rome in 440). We know as well that there was constant tension with the Visigoths and the Franks, and that relations with the Huns had changed drastically. For reasons that are obscure to us, the alliance between Aetius and the Huns was severed. Did the murder of Bleda in 445 lead to these changes? We don't know; but from this point on, Aetius became the Hun's chief nemesis whose destruction Attila would seek at Châlons.

On another front, we can be sure that Aetius was busy cultivating his relationship with the court of Valentinian. In 437 the teenaged emperor, who was now nearing the end of his regency, traveled to Constantinople to wed his second cousin, Eudoxia, the daughter of Emperor Theodosius II. He returned to Italy as emperor in his own right. We are told that Eudoxia was exceedingly beautiful, but this didn't stop the young emperor from pursuing other men's wives throughout his reign. Add to this defect his fascination with sorcerers and astrologers, and Placidia must have been quite disappointed with how her son turned out. Though she herself had stepped into public life with blood on her hands, Placidia managed to atone for the crime against Serena and even achieved by the end of her life a genuine reputation for piety. When she wrote the letter in 450 to Theodosius II, urging him toward orthodox doctrine, she really meant it. That Valentinian and Eudoxia wrote letters, too, speaks of her continuing influence over the court. Placidia's successful appeal for Honoria's life also suggests that she had not, in the end, become a figurehead.

EXHIBIT TWELVE

Aetius no longer needed Attila as a political wedge once he'd allied himself with Marcian and betrothed his son to Valentinian's daughter.

Was Valentinian savvy enough to acknowledge how much he needed Aetius? Or had Placidia counseled him to bury the family hatchet?[173] (Aetius had never been forgiven for supporting John the Usurper back in 425.) Some clues may be found in the political betrothals of Valentinian's daughters. His first daughter, Eudocia, was betrothed as an infant to the son of Gaiseric, the Vandal king of North Africa. His second daughter was significantly named Placidia, and was (just as significantly) betrothed to Gaudentius, the son of Aetius. If we only knew the politics behind all this! Aetius must have been threatened by the apparent alliance between Valentinian and Gaiseric and managed to arrange his own alliance through marriage. He could not have done this without some support from within the imperial house. Could Placidia actually have encouraged the betrothal of her namesake to the son of Aetius? Though it seems improbable given the old animosities, it must have happened nonetheless.

Both Aetius and Placidia had grown old gracefully (for Roman warhorses anyway), and they had learned how to accommodate each other's ambitions. True, they would never be pinochle partners at family gatherings, but they no longer plotted each other's death. A remarkable convergence of interests had brought them together at last.[174] Aetius had never once attempted to seize the throne for himself—a stunning fact, indeed, as he could have taken power at any point in his career. He did nurture imperial ambitions for his son, however. Placidia, too, was looking ahead. Her miserable son had produced no male heir. What was to become of the Theodosian line? If things had worked out the way Placidia and Aetius intended, there can be no doubt that Gaudentius would have become emperor and the Augustan rule might have extended beyond 476. These well-laid plans began to fall apart after Placidia died in 450. Aetius had always viewed the Huns as a political insurance policy; as long as they were a threat, the imperial family needed him. Attila was no longer useful to Aetius once the betrothal of his son had secured his position at court. We know, in hindsight, that Aetius had made the biggest miscalculation of his life by trusting the emperor. But there can be little doubt about his view of the world as Aetius surveyed the battlefield in June 451. He looked out across the thousands of soldiers—Visigoths, Franks, Burgundians. The very tribes that he had confronted over the past decade were now assembled to defend Rome. Perhaps he also looked up at the sky the night before the battle and found reason there to be hopeful. The great general, the last of the Romans, had one simple goal in mind: the vigorous defense of the Empire that his son would inherit.

OF COMETS AND ANIMAL ENTRAILS

The bright heavenly body we now call Halley's Comet streaked across the sky in June 451. This would be one of the most amazing conjunctions of history and astronomy ever recorded, perhaps even more remarkable than when Halley's Comet showed up at the Battle of Hastings in 1066. The appearance of a comet always meant that something was in the works, but it remained for the wise men to figure out what that "something" was. When you have timing this precise, the job is much easier. During the very week when Attila was withdrawing his troops from Orléans, the comet had just appeared in the constellation Taurus; it would disappear from Virgo by the middle of August, not to be seen again for seventy-nine years. Oddly, there is no contemporary record of the occurrence—we know of its appearance only through mathematical calculation. But perhaps the record is not so silent. Two years later Attila lay dead and the portent was fully realized. Marcian's dream of the broken bow in the sky may be a stylized recollection, a post hoc adaptation, of the comet that appeared like a terrifying herald in the sky.

There may be another allusion to the comet in what Attila did next. As he withdrew from Orléans, he called his soothsayers together and commanded them to read his future from the entrails of sacrificed animals and the scrapings on bones. What was it that made him uncertain and fearful? Jordanes says he was troubled by the unexpected resistance at Orléans. But could it be more than that? Attila had seen the omen in the sky and he prepared himself for the worst. "There's good news and bad news," the soothsayers told him after scrutinizing the animal guts.

"Give me the bad news first."

"You're going to be defeated—but your enemy will lose his life." The soothsayers didn't identify the "chief commander of the foe" who would die, but Attila immediately thought of the Roman general, "since Aetius stood in the way of his plans." This leads us to another one of those many problems of interpretation that keep turning up, since it wasn't Aetius who ended up dying in the battle but Theodoric, king of the Visigoths. So who was wrong: Attila or the soothsayers? After Theodoric was thrown from his horse and trampled underfoot, Jordanes notes that "this was what the soothsayers had told to Attila in prophecy, though he understood it of Aetius."

The Visigoths were probably the main targets of Attila's force. Though the Huns were taking the scenic route through the Rhine Valley and into northern Gaul, Toulouse in the South was the ultimate destination. The soothsayers knew this. But Attila was fixated on Aetius. Why? In answering this we've got to start from the assumption that there's nothing historical here, since there's no plausible way that Jordanes (Priscus actually) could have acquired this information in the first place. It's doubtful that a transcript of Attila's conversation with the soothsayers was taken down verbatim, preserved through the battle, stored in an archive, and recovered years later by Priscus through a Freedom of Information request. "History" wasn't written that way. Perhaps an eyewitness related something to Priscus about soothsayers in Attila's camp (an unlikely possibility); but even so, the story as we have it is a *story*, a fictionalization constructed out of real historical circumstances. Attila's fixation on Aetius is how Priscus gets us ready for the rest of the story—a story in which Attila would be doggedly pursuing Aetius through Italy, only to be hoodwinked *by Aetius* into leaving Italy and then being assassinated in his home territory. As Attila rightly believed, "Aetius stood in the way of his plans."[175]

"It was not only a famous battle," Jordanes writes, "but one that was complicated and confused." Still thinking about the prophecy, Attila decided to begin the fighting around three in the afternoon, so that darkness could come to his defense. The battlefield was "a plain rising by a sharp slope to a ridge, which both armies sought to gain." The Huns took control of the right side of the hill, and the Romans and Visigoths took the left; and "then began a struggle for the yet untaken crest." Jordanes carefully notes how the opposing armies were arrayed. As you faced the allied side, the Visigoths were positioned on the left flank and the Romans on the right. The Alan king, Sangiban, who was suspected of collaborating with Attila, was placed in the middle of the army, since "one who has difficulties placed in the way of his flight readily submits to the necessity of fighting." On the other side, the strongest Hunnish troops were placed in the middle of the ranks, so that Attila would receive the maximum protection in the midst of battle.

Attila directed his men to take the ridge, but when they got there, they found that Aetius had beaten them to the punch. The allied forces were thus able to beat back the attack. The Huns weren't used to being outmaneuvered on the battlefield; surprise, speed of attack, and positional advantage were the key elements of the Hunnish military doctrine. But then Aetius knew that. He had been trained as a Hun warrior, side by side with Attila, when he lived as a young hostage in the court of Rua. He understood exactly what Attila would try to do, and he did it quicker. The Huns were "thrown into confusion by this event." The tide of the battle was already turning against Attila, and so he stood up and rallied his troops with a speech.

The speech was a passionate call to arms, but like so many of the details that flesh out the battle narrative, it cannot be treated as historical. The ancient Greek historians whom Priscus so admired, Thucydides and Herodotus, made up speeches all the time. Far from being records of what

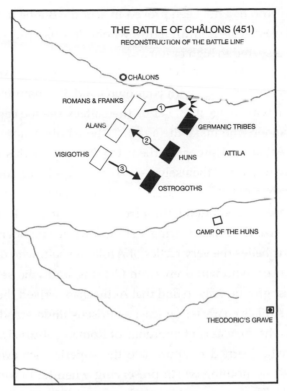

A reconstruction of the battle lines at Châlons (A.D. 451).
For the first and only time, Attila the Hun was defeated
in battle by forces led by the Western Roman general
Aetius. (1) Roman forces seized the high ground on
Attila's right. (2) Attila responds by driving back the
Alans in the center. (3) Attila tries to hit the Visigoths in
their flank, but Theodoric counterattacks while the
Romans press from the right. Theodoric was killed, but
Attila was forced to withdraw in defeat.
Map by Matthew Pamer

happened, these speeches are valuable records of what ancient historians *believed*. Jordanes will only claim that the speech was delivered "on this wise," and it should thus be understood as an exposition of character. "Here you stand," Attila began, "after conquering mighty nations and subduing the world. I therefore think it foolish for me to goad you with words, as though you were men who had not been proved in action." But he has a few choice words nonetheless. This taciturn figure whom Priscus observed at the banqueting table is stirred to high oratory.

"War is your usual custom," the chieftain declares. "And nothing is sweeter than to seek revenge with your own hand. It is nature's right for one to glut the soul with vengeance. Let us then attack the foe eagerly; for they are ever the bolder who make the attack." The whole history of the Huns, according to Attila, had prepared them for "the joy of this conflict." The Huns can only rely upon themselves—no one else—since "defending oneself by alliance is proof of cowardice." The Romans, who must rely on others for their defense, "are smitten with terror before our attack. They seek the heights, they seize the hills," fearing a showdown in the open fields below. All this rhetoric belies the very tactics of Attila himself, who defended himself with alliances, who withdrew from Orléans, and who sent his men to take the highest ground only to find that Aetius had arrived there first. What is clear about Attila's character (at least as Priscus understood it from close observation) is that he was contemptuous of Roman culture. Unlike the Germanic tribes who learned to appreciate the superior achievements of the Empire, Attila saw nothing worth preserving when he looked at Rome or Constantinople. They were, in his mind, a cowardly and effeminate lot, as evident by their manner of warfare: "You know how unimpressive and ineffective the Roman attack is," he says. "While they are still gathering in order and forming in one line with locked shields, they are checked, I will not say by the first wound, but even by the dust of battle!" You would think that Attila knew better; Aetius was no wimp. But Attila's speech is directed not against one brave man (an unusual man, to be sure, who was as much a Goth and Hun as a Roman) but against a whole civilization.

Once again we can discern Priscus behind this speech that Jordanes records, since its rhetoric is patterned upon ancient Greek models. The words are made up, since it's inconceivable that such a speech could be delivered in the heat of battle; but the sense we get of Attila's character is genuine. What's not to admire in his courage?

Then on to the fray with stout hearts, as is your wont. Despise their battle line! Seek swift victory in that spot where the battle rages. For when the sinews are cut the limbs soon relax, nor can a body stand when you have taken away the bones. Let your courage rise and your own fury burst forth! Now show your cunning, Huns, now your deeds of arms! Let the wounded exact in return the death of his foe; let the unwounded revel in the slaughter of the enemy.

There's much to admire, but also much to fear. Attila would smash the whole imperial world and not shed a tear for all that was lost, all that "took ages for nature to produce." The tension is very real; the admiration that Priscus felt for a heroic figure (though an enemy) is mingled with the terror of what hangs in the balance. This brings real power to the portrait of Attila. It's as though Priscus *wants* to like him, even though he knows he's bad for Civilization. Heroism like this is Greek, and Priscus ennobles himself by ennobling his subject matter: he recasts Attila within the heroic ideals of the ancients.[176] Thucydides and Herodotus weren't the only ones privileged to describe great men who moved the world. Like the heroes of old, Attila embraces Fate with ready abandon. "No spear shall harm those who are sure to live," he declares. "And those who are sure to die Fate overtakes even in peace." When he speaks of dying "in peace," Attila has no idea that he would survive this battle and another year of fierce campaigning, only to die in his wedding bed. But Priscus knows that it wouldn't be the unseen hand of Fate but the machinations of men that would finally overtake him.

MONSIEUR BONHOMME'S DISCOVERY

Near the little French village of Pouan, along the bank of the Aube River, a laborer named Jacques Bonhomme was digging for gravel one day in 1842.[177] Some three feet below the surface his pickax turned up human remains and some artifacts, which, upon inspection, proved to be of considerable antiquity: a rusted two-edged sword; various golden ornaments, including a serpentine necklace, an armlet, fibulae, and buckles; and a golden ring with the word HEVA inscribed in Roman capitals. The style of the artifacts clearly marked them out as Visigothic—the Germanic tribe allied with Aetius against Attila's forces. And though not an especially rich treasure trove, the artifacts suggested that this was the grave of someone important. The find was purchased by Emperor Napoleon III and subsequently given to the city of Troyes to be displayed in the local museum.

Was this the grave of the Visigothic chieftain Theodoric who fell in that fierce battle against Attila in 451? Jordanes writes that Theodoric was riding by his troops, shouting words of encouragement, when he was thrown from his horse and trampled underfoot. The next day his body was recovered from among the *innumera cadavera*, "innumerable corpses." With the Huns looking on as witnesses, Theodoric was "honored with songs and carried away for burial." It's entirely possible that this place along the Aube River is where they carried him—and where he lay undisturbed for 1,391 years until Monsieur Bonhomme planted his pickax.

Other artifacts have since been found in the fields, riverbanks, and mounds of Champagne: Visigothic belt buckles, swords with gold-plated handles, and animal bones.[178] Napoleon III was fascinated by the history of the region and actively encouraged digging for artifacts. He even visited the little hamlets around Châlons several times, inspecting where "the ground is indented and heaped up in ranges of grassy mounds and trenches," as Edward Creasy described it in the nineteenth century. Creasy believed, as did the emperor, that these features "attest the work of man's hands in ages past" and that "this quiet spot has once been the fortified position of a huge military host." Actually, these mounds may have predated the campaign of 451 by many centuries; archaeologists now believe they go back to the time of the earliest Celtic settlements, though they might well have been used by the combatants at Châlons as well.

* * *

June 20, 451, was the night Attila *should* have died.[179] The first skirmish of the battle had turned out badly for Attila. Aetius took the high ground and beat back the Huns. Defeat was something that Attila was not used to. Ever since a shepherd found the fabled Sword of Mars, Attila had seen himself as the invincible conqueror of the world. His greatest weapon, however, was not a legendary sword but bands of archers who roamed the battlefield on horseback. Highly mobile, they would quickly find a weak spot, attack ferociously, and then disperse and regroup. Like Germany's Panzer divisions in 1939, these "rapid attack forces" conducted a type of warfare never seen before, one that struck terror in the heart of the enemy. But Attila took his greatest asset and threw it away. It is commonly understood by military historians that the singular advantage of mobility and speed is exactly what Attila gave up when he opted to face the allied forces in pitched battle.

After Attila's rousing speech to his troops, the armies clashed "hand to hand and the fight grew fierce, confused, monstrous, unrelenting—a fight whose like no ancient time has ever recorded." The battle grew to an apocalyptic scale in the memory of the Germans. Jordanes (or Cassiodorus before him) may have added some of the details to the account of Priscus, details drawn no doubt from eyewitnesses—the kind of teary-eyed old veterans Priscus had seen at Attila's banquet. The enthusiasm for blood and guts seems to spring from the same kind of heart that gave us *Beowulf*; it's an enthusiasm better suited to the purposes of the *Gothic History* of Jordanes or Cassiodorus than to the imperial history of Priscus. "Such deeds were done in that battle," we read, "that a brave man who missed this marvelous spectacle could not hope to see anything so wonderful all his life long." The ethos here is very different from the earlier denunciation of the madness and raw destructive power of war. It may seem that we've chucked the science altogether by now, as though philology is just an elaborate way to channel voices. ("This sounds like Priscus, and this sounds like Jordanes.") We do have to listen to our ears—a good reading habit to develop, as long as we don't claim infallibility for what we hear. Fortunately, though, the text helps us to sort this out and clarify our instincts:

For, *if we may believe our elders,* a brook flowing between low banks through the plain was greatly increased by blood from the wounds of the slain. It was not flooded by showers, as brooks usually rise, but was swollen by a strange stream and turned into a torrent by the increase of blood. Those whose wounds drove them to slake their parching thirst drank water mingled with gore. In their wretched plight they were forced to drink what they thought was the blood they had poured from their own wounds.

The phrase "if we may believe our elders" is a clear reference backward, either by Jordanes around 550 or, more probably, by Cassiodorus around 525 to eyewitness accounts preserved orally among the Germanic people. Even an account this well preserved, with its wealth of convincing details, has been shaped through many filters—immediate political needs, literary models, and cultural memory.

Night was falling. Attila would be saved by the late start to the battle. As the Visigoths struck hard "and nearly slew Attila," he erected a barricade of wagons and prepared to make his last stand. "He was like a lion pierced by hunting spears," Jordanes writes, "who paces to and fro before the mouth of his den and dares not spring, but ceases not to terrify the neighborhood by his roaring." At no point does Jordanes call Attila's courage into doubt. On the contrary, Jordanes writes that "*it was said* that the king remained supremely brave even in this extremity." It's impossible to know who the phrase "it was said" refers to, though this phrase captures in a nutshell what philologists are always trying to figure out: *Who said what?* Priscus, Cassiodorus, Gothic eyewitnesses, or poets—any of these could lie behind the grudging admiration for the warlord's bravery. Surrounded by wagons and apparently out of options, Attila ordered a funeral pyre to be prepared with horse saddles and other supplies. If the enemy attacked and broke through the line, he would throw himself on the fire to deny them the satisfaction of slaying him in battle.

What happened that night remains a mystery.

Jordanes claims that Thorismud, the son of Theodoric, fought bravely right up to the Hun encampment and was wounded in the head. Dragged from his horse and disoriented by the blow, Thorismud was rescued by his troops and withdrew from the front lines. Aetius, too, had his own night-time adventure. Jordanes records that "Aetius was separated from his host in the confusion of the night, and went wandering through the midst of the enemy, trembling lest some untoward event should have occurred to the Goths, and ever asking the way, till at length he arrived at the camp of his allies, and passed the remainder of the night under the shelter of their shields." The picture of the Roman general wandering among the enemy troops in the middle of the night is most peculiar. Some credibility for this account is gained, however, if we recall that Aetius had been a boyhood hostage in both the Gothic court of Alaric and the Hunnish court of Rua; he no doubt spoke both languages fluently.

Something odd happened that night. The reference in Jordanes to Aetius wandering through the enemy ranks must preserve some authentic tradition since it serves no obvious purpose in the story; and yet what Jordanes tells us doesn't seem to be complete. That's usually Gibbon's cue to step in and develop the romantic possibilities of the text. Instead, he takes the strange details and weaves them into a credible account of a chaotic battlefield.

> In the same manner, but on the left of the line, Aetius himself, separated from his allies, ignorant of their victory, and anxious for their fate, encountered and escaped the hostile troops that were scattered over the plains of Châlons; and at length reached the camp of the Goths, which he could only fortify with a slight rampart of shields, till the dawn of day.

Some have wondered if Aetius and Attila came face-to-face one last time. The Spanish chronicler Hydatius (c. 400–69) started the speculation when he reported that Aetius paid a nocturnal visit to both the Hunnish and Visigothic camps, from whom he extorted ten thousand pieces of gold as the price of an honorable retreat. Obviously, Hydatius has given us a fanciful account. But it's a little shortsighted to reject him out of hand as modern historians do. In the nineteenth-century world of historiography, a story is either right or wrong. If only it were that simple. Today we're more open to the idea that a story can be true or false, depending on what you're trying to extract from it. If you're looking for an objective battlefield account, then you'll reject Hydatius. But if you're looking for a record of what people believed, then there's a lot here that's true. Hydatius is grappling with the inconclusive nature of the battle; he's filling an explanatory gap. Who won and who lost? How did Attila manage to escape? Why did the Visigoths suddenly retreat? The story simplifies these complexities to a personal encounter. Even though false, at least by one set of standards, the story dovetails truthfully with the mystery that Jordanes relates—the disappearance of Aetius.

The greater historical mystery, of course, is why Aetius let Attila leave Gaul with the remnants of his army. Once again, this is what Hydatius is trying to explain by reference to a bribe. But with tens of thousands of dead soldiers lying on the battlefield, it's unlikely that a bribe would have mattered much either to Attila or Thorismud, the son of the fallen Theodoric. The best explanations here are political. When dawn broke the next day, the Goths searched for their king and found him dead among the corpses. Still reeling from the head blow he'd sustained, Thorismud knew that he would have to return home to Toulouse and assert his claim to his father's throne. Jordanes (who was himself a Goth) preserves the Gothic version of these events, which are largely exculpatory for Thorismud. The new Gothic king "was eager to take vengeance for his father's death on the remaining Huns." He consulted with Aetius. The general "feared that if the Huns were totally destroyed by the Goths, the Roman Empire would be overwhelmed, and so he urgently advised Thorismud to return to his own dominions to take up the rule which his father had left." The bald truth is that Thorismud must have deserted the battlefield, leaving Aetius with no option but to let the Huns retreat.[180]

There was no miscalculation by Aetius. What happened, rather, was that the political realities of the alliance had overtaken his grand strategy. The death of Theodoric had been a devastating blow. The allied army was immediately disbanded as Thorismud marched home to look after his own political future. Attila had been checked, if not checkmated, and he was no longer an immediate threat. At first, Attila believed that the Gothic withdrawal was a ruse; but when it became apparent that the fighting was over, he gathered up his ragged army and returned home to Pannonia. He would return the next year, but this time to Italy. And this time Aetius would be on his own, without the vast army of German *foederati* to support Rome's defense.

Not all the Huns went home that year. Some remained in Gaul, where they turned their swords into ploughshares and pursued quiet lives as French farmers. Some areas in Champagne register a higher than normal incidence of the so-called Mongolian "blue spot"—a birthmark found on the buttocks of some newborn babies—an indication perhaps of remote Hunnish ancestry. Place-names in Switzerland may also point, though not conclusively, to an early settlement of Huns in the Alps. Others still were left behind as ghosts, at least as legend would have it. A ghost story to this effect has come down to us from an unexpected source, a Neoplatonist philosopher named Damascius who believed that the world was alive with spirits.[181] Damascius was the last director of Plato's Academy in Athens, which Emperor Justinian closed down for good in 529. In one of his books, a collection of 570 "stories from beyond," the pagan philosopher relates what he had heard in the East about the Battle of Châlons. The violent clanging of swords could be heard throughout the countryside as the ghosts of the dead kept on fighting for three days and three nights, unaware that the battle was over. Historians blandly note that the fabulous tale demonstrates the great reputation of this battle throughout the world. I give Damascius more credit than that. He basically got it right: the world is alive with spirits. Languages and legends are proof of that.

THE GOLDEN VOICE

News of the great battle was welcomed in the East like summer rain. The action in the West gave Marcian and Pulcheria time to deal with heretics. Leo was delighted that the imperial team was committed to purifying the Church; he applauded the new emperor for his "strong eagerness for the

Church's peace." What concerned Leo, though, were the political dynamics lying beyond his control. He feared that the Council of Chalcedon might enhance the prestige of the Eastern Church and thereby weaken his authority. One of Leo's great contributions to the medieval Catholic Church was his tireless advocacy of Rome's primary status throughout Christendom, and by extension the authority of the bishop of Rome. He was among the first bishops of Rome to claim Petrine authority for his office—the Catholic doctrine that Christ bestowed his authority on Peter and every bishop of Rome who has succeeded him. At first Leo objected to the idea of a council, arguing that it wasn't really necessary; all Marcian and Pulcheria needed to do, he wrote, was to endorse his own decrees on the subject of Christ's nature. That would give them the basis they needed to root out heretics from the Eastern Church, powerful figures such as Dioscorus in Alexandria. Finally, Leo gave in to Marcian's insistence, provided the council did not entertain any new theological arguments. The council's purpose was merely to codify the orthodox position that Leo had already articulated.

In the summer of 451, while the Western army was battling Attila in Gaul, delegates began arriving in Nicaea. This city to the southwest of Constantinople was where the First Ecumenical Council had been held in 325 and it's where the new council was expected to be convened as well. Those plans changed, however, and the council was first postponed and then moved to Chalcedon, just north of Constantinople, to accommodate the needs of the emperor. A small detachment of Hunnish troops had raided the eastern Balkans in September 451—a shot across the new emperor's bow, as it were—and Marcian seized the opportunity to define himself as a leader who was very different from Theodosius II. Taking personal command of his troops, the sixty-year-old rode out to battle like the great soldier-emperors of old. Aspar's son Ardabur fought alongside Marcian in the Balkan campaign and earned for his effort a promotion as *magister militum per Orientem*, military commander for the East.[182] (It is in this capacity that we see Ardabur a year later when Maximin and Priscus traveled through Damascus.)

The delegates were restless and the council was finally convened on October 8, 451.[183] We would be wrong to see this event in simple isolation from everything else occurring throughout the Roman world. Leo had made it clear in his letter to Marcian that he saw religion and politics as part of the same equation, and that's how we have to read the histories of the time as well. We have already seen this intermingling of religious and political values in the history of Socrates Scholasticus. The deaths of Octar and Rua were understood as divinely orchestrated events. The stories of their deaths are told only because they play some explanatory role within ecclesiastical history. Octar died strangely under the same circumstances as Attila himself, at a propitious moment. The sudden death from "natural" causes (though it was really supernatural, if God willed it) thwarted a military campaign and led to the conversion of the Burgundians. Rua's death, too, was a divine intervention. His death by lightning was accompanied by other signs and wonders that were interpreted in light of Ezekiel's prophecies in the Old Testament.

Religion had become the essential filter through which the world was understood. The histories written in Constantinople—all the histories, not just the ubiquitous "ecclesiastical" ones—were anchored to this worldview. There existed no independent set of facts about the world; there was only the world as seen through the grid of an imperialistic Christianity. How well we understand Priscus—the characters he describes and the events he narrates—depends largely on how we handle this grid. We can't just look *through* it to the "truth," the way a Russian peasant prays *through* an icon to God. It doesn't work that way. The icon is what you see—and what you "see" always gets in the way. The story of Attila's death, how he drank too much and died of a hemorrhage, is so blindingly simple that we think we're seeing the truth, when we're just looking at a picture, a grid, a story propped up in front of us like an icon for our edification.[184]

But Priscus was a pagan. Or was he? We don't know and it doesn't really matter. His boss was the most Christian of emperors. Pagan or Christian, Priscus knew more about Attila's death, and told more, than what the record has preserved. The inconsistencies in Jordanes have pointed unmistakably to that conclusion. There must have been a murder account that was also preserved and that was suppressed. But we still have the story of natural causes sitting before us. It's time to get rid of it altogether, and we can do that by demonstrating how that story came into being. But to do this, we'll have to go back a generation into the homiletic literature of Constantinople, back to one of the great figures of the Eastern Church. St. John Chrysostom, dubbed the Golden-Voiced Preacher, was the patriarch of Constantinople from 398 to 404 and is remembered as one of the "four great doctors" of the Church. Popular among the people for his eloquence, John earned a lot of enemies at the court of Emperor Arcadius for his strongly worded denunciations of luxury, wealth, and gluttony.

EXHIBIT THIRTEEN

The basic elements of the account that Priscus wrote about Attila's "natural death" can be found in the homilies of John Chrysostom.

Gluttony and drunkenness—the very things that killed Attila, according to Jordanes—recur over and over again in John's preaching.[185] He returned almost obsessively to the theme, inveighing against the materialistic excesses of his city and its rulers. "For just as the uproar is great in a city under attack by its enemies," John preached, "so also is the soul under invasion by wine and luxury." Whether he's picturing a strong city or (more often) a strong man, the key lesson is always that strength is overcome by dissipation. "If you place a burden on a very strong and large man which is greater than he can bear, then you will see him with his burden lying prostrate on the ground." Elsewhere John develops more fully this picture of the spiritually dead man who is consumed by the lusts of the flesh: "A man who lives in pleasure is dead while he lives, since he's only living for his belly. He's like a man stretched out on a bed with his eyelids closed tight, perceiving nothing that's happening around him." The central details of Attila's death are outlined here in the vivid metaphors of John Chrysostom: a strong man consumed by drunkenness, lying flat on his back.

John is more specific about the physiological effects of gluttony. "The more luxuriously we live," he preached, "the more harmful are the odors with which we're filled." He goes on to develop the graphic metaphor:

> The body is like a swollen bottle, *overflowing in every direction*. The violent belching is enough to pain the head of a bystander. From the heat of fermentation within, vapors are sent forth, as from a furnace. If bystanders are pained, how do you think the brain feels when it's constantly assaulted by these fumes?—*to say nothing of the channels of the heated and obstructed blood*. . . . We're careful to keep the drains in our streets from getting obstructed. We clean out our sewers with poles and drags, so they won't get stopped up and overflow; but we don't bother to keep the canals of our bodies clear, but instead obstruct and choke them up. . . . What disorders do you think are produced in body and soul when all this stuff is pent up inside the body and can't find an outlet?

In other words, gluttony and drunkenness make the body, with its "channels of the heated and obstructed blood," explode. So, taking John's metaphors and applying them to Attila, now we have a strong man consumed by drunkenness, lying flat on his back, with overflowing channels of blood in his head. Sounds like what Jordanes records and attributes to Priscus.

Already the parallels are striking; but there's an even more explicit parallel found in Homily LXX, which John preached on the text of Matthew 22:15. The passage reads: "Then went the Pharisees and took counsel how they might entangle him in his talk." You wouldn't think this verse could take you all the way to gluttony, but if it's your favorite topic, you'll find a way. John begins by depicting the warfare between the spirit and the flesh in terms of a military campaign, much as the fourth-century Spanish poet Prudentius depicted the *Psychomachia*, or battle in the psyche, between the virtues and vices. The spiritual camp needs no spears or shields "to conquer all the lusts that are plotting against us." Wherever you see "a multitude of dead lying there, slain by the sword of the Spirit," you know that there is no drunkenness or gluttony where the victorious stand. In fact, drunkenness and gluttony (personified in the manner of Prudentius) "lie dead, put to the rout by the drinking of water"! Drunkenness and gluttony are a "many-headed monster" from which all the vices ultimately spring. And then John returns to the picture of a strong man once more:

> The very giants, the heroes, those that do countless brave deeds, you will find without chains bound by sleep and drunkenness, *without slaughter or wounds* lying like the wounded—or rather in a more grievous condition. For the wounded have at least struggled; but these don't even do that, but immediately give up.

The images all come down to this: a humiliating picture of strength subdued by debauchery. Or, as Chaucer would later put it in his "Pardoner's Tale":[186]

> Looke, Attilla, the grete conquerour,
> Deyde in his sleepe, with shame and dishonour,
> Bledynge ay at his nose in dronkenesse.
> A capitayn sholde lyve in sobrenesse.

By Chaucer's time Attila had become an exemplum (a moral story) of drunkenness in medieval homiletic literature. The "shame and dishonor" is much more than the shame of the sin itself; the real shame lies in the fact that the "great conqueror" has been denied a heroic death. There is no greater glory for the hero in a warrior society than to die in battle in the full vigor of manhood. Dying on your back in bed—your marriage bed no less!—is as far from the heroic ideal as you can get. Here's where our modern sensibilities can trip us up again, since we think that dying comfortably in our sleep at an advanced age is the best we can hope for. Not so for Attila—and not for the heroes of medieval literature such as Beowulf (who died old, but in battle) or Roland—for whom the only way to go is with swords blazing and dripping with gore.

We should look again at what Jordanes has written and compare it closely with the composite picture provided in the homilies of John Chrysostom.[187] Jordanes writes that Attila

> had given himself up to excessive joy at his wedding, and as he lay on his back, heavy with wine and sleep, a rush of superfluous blood, which would ordinarily have flowed from his nose, streamed in deadly course down his throat and killed him, since it was *obstructed* in the usual passages. Thus did drunkenness put a disgraceful end to a king renowned in war. On the following day, when a great part of the morning was spent, the royal attendants suspected some ill and, after a great uproar, broke in the doors. There they found the death of Attila accomplished by an effusion of blood, *without any wound*, and the girl with downcast face weeping beneath her veil.

In both texts we find a strong man, a "giant" of the world (as John puts it), who dies on his back, subdued by wine and an effusion of blood. The clincher, though, is this: In both texts we read that the body is "without wound." The amazing correspondence of images and phrases drives us to one conclusion. The official story of Attila's death is not a set of objectively presented facts. It is, rather, a homiletic exemplum meant to puncture the myth of his invincibility. Attila is a "type" of the fleshly man who is brought down to destruction by his own lusts. The phrase "thus did drunkenness put a disgraceful end to a king renowned in war" should have put us wise to that strategy from the start. Attila's uncle Octar met the same fate for the same reasons when he led his army against the Burgundians. We noted with suspicion back in Chapter Five the odd coincidence that both uncle and nephew died in much the same way. But when we find their deaths sketched out in a homily delivered a generation earlier, we must move from suspicion and doubt to outright rejection of the "historical" account. In so doing, we've managed to expose one of the main techniques of propaganda—the use of a formulaic story, an interpretive set piece as I call it, to render the world intelligible within the boundaries of an already accepted ideology. We've delivered a death blow to the official version, by showing that it's no different

MICHAEL A. BABCOCK

from the broken bow in the sky, or the eagle hovering over Marcian's head. It's propaganda pure and simple.

But just to remind ourselves: Priscus had told us more about Attila's death—that is, in the original form that Priscus wrote, before his text got snipped up into little pieces. Recall again how Priscus described the treacherous death of Bleda and promised us that "by the balance of justice" Attila would reap "the hideous consequences of his own actions." Priscus must have placed two accounts side by side, which is not an uncommon thing in ancient histories;[188] or possibly, these two accounts appeared in separate editions of his history. One was a violent plot; the other was a homiletic exemplum about drunkenness. The exemplum may have been published during Marcian's reign, along with the other official stories that enhanced the emperor's reputation. The world was to take note that God's hand was guiding his reign. As a youth Marcian had been saved from certain execution in Philippopolis and was designated an Augustus by an overshadowing eagle in Libya (or was it Persia?). Not even Attila could confront the Christian warrior. The Hun's bow was broken in the sky at the very moment Attila died on his back in a drunken stupor. That's the gist of the imperial message.

Though remembered as a doctor of the Church, John Chrysostom was a controversial figure in his own day. Emperor Arcadius banished him in 404 because he wouldn't stop condemning—from the pulpit no less—the exorbitant lifestyle of Empress Eudoxia. John died in 407 in the remote region of Pontus along the Black Sea. Some thirty years later his body was brought back to Constantinople. The story is told that the patriarch's coffin could not be lifted from its burial place until the emperor, Theodosius II, had issued an apology on behalf of his late mother, Eudoxia. Once that was done, the coffin was lifted and returned to the capital. The current patriarch opened the box and found that John's body was perfectly preserved. Theodosius broke down in tears and apologized again as he gazed upon John's corpse. After a day or so during which grief and guilt were publicly displayed, the body was removed to the Church of St. Irene for final burial. Before the casket was closed, the patriarch and the other clergy standing around witnessed a won-

216

der. The Golden Mouth opened one last time and spoke a benediction: "Peace be to all."

John was back in favor and he still had plenty to say. Damascius would understand this; Chrysostom was just another ghost who couldn't stop talking. Even now, crack open Edward Gibbon's *Decline and Fall of the Roman Empire*, or any other authoritative source, and read about the death of Attila the Hun. As you read, you'll be hearing the voice of John Chrysostom speaking beneath the historical account. But what of the violent story that Priscus had promised us—the story that got silenced because John wouldn't shut up? That's the last part of the puzzle, and we'll turn to it next.

SEVEN

IN THE LAND OF DEATH

W HAT started off as a routine excavation suddenly became far more interesting when an infant's skeleton turned up in the storerooms of an
ancient building.[189] In the early 1990s American archaeologist David Soren
had been asked to come to Lugnano, a little town nestled in the hills seventy
miles north of Rome where a fifth-century villa had been uncovered by local
archaeologists. The little body had been pressed into an amphora, a clay
storage jar, and buried. Seven more skeletons were found before the day was
out. In all, forty-seven remains were identified, ranging from stillborn in-
fants to a three-year-old child. Especially puzzling were the raven's claw,
burnt plant offerings, and the decapitated skeletons of puppies that had
been ripped apart and placed into the graves—evidence, Soren believed, of
a terror so great that the Christian population had reverted to pagan prac-
tices.

What caused the sudden deaths of so many children in Lugnano? New
research techniques in the field of biomolecular archaeology have yielded
the surprising answer: malaria. Among the nearly fifty skeletal remains
found at the site, only the leg bones of the oldest child were sufficiently de-

veloped for microscopic analysis. Fragments of leg bone were ground into powder and subjected to a new laboratory technique, polymerase chain reaction (PCR), which has been described as "the most important new scientific technology to come along in the last hundred years."[190] PCR enables researchers to generate unlimited copies from minute traces of DNA. After months of analysis, the most virulent form of human malaria, *plasmodium falciparum*, was positively identified in the child's remains. It was the first proof of what had long been suspected, that malaria had swept through Italy during the final decades of the Roman Empire.

The children's cemetery in Lugnano has been dated to A.D. 450, which is right around the time Attila was threatening the West, first with an invasion of Gaul in 451 and then, like a bad sequel, the invasion of Italy in 452. Attila had left Gaul defeated; but why he left Italy the next year, especially why he left it so suddenly at the urging of a holy man, has always been a mystery. Vague allusions to plague and famine do exist in the historical record;[191] what David Soren dug up in Lugnano, however, was the first solid evidence that raw fear, more than anything else, turned Attila away from certain victory in Italy. With plague ravaging his troops, he may have considered it a wise strategic withdrawal; in reality, his enemies were maneuvering him into position so they could kill him. He signed his own death warrant by doing so.

Attila spent the winter of 451–52 licking his wounds back home in Pannonia and regrouping his forces. He was restless to get back on the battlefield and avenge the losses he had suffered in Gaul. Waiting made it a long winter, for Attila and for anyone forced to share his company. But spring finally came with its birds, its flowers, and its fresh opportunities for pillage and plunder. And so he turned his attention to Italy, the crown jewel of the Empire. Gibbon is completely wrong when he writes that "neither the spirit nor the forces nor the reputation of Attila were impaired by the failure of the Gallic expedition."[192] On the contrary, Attila felt compelled to invade Italy—not for the love of a woman (as Gibbon, the hopeless romantic, would have it) but precisely because his spirit, forces, and reputation had suffered greatly in Gaul. Sure, he must have renewed his demand for Honoria; but he had a defeat to avenge and soldiers who had to be paid. If we're looking for a motive, we can't do any better than what the Spaniard Hydatius tells us in his *Chronicle*. Writing in the middle of the fifth century, Hydatius expresses what must have been obvious to all: "Attila was furious about the unexpected defeat suffered in Gaul and he turned to Italy in his rage."

Attila's route through northern Italy in 452 was determined less by a coherent military strategy than by his need for personal vindication. He would pursue a methodical revenge, city by city. Gaul had been a very different campaign, governed (as best we can tell) by a clear objective: to wrest territory from the Visigoths and to smash their capital of Toulouse. Cities that could easily be plundered were taken; others like Paris were left alone. When stiff resistance was encountered at Orléans, Attila refused to commit his forces to take the city. Not so in Italy where the first stop was the nearly impregnable "virgin fortress" of Aquileia, near the modern resort city of Trieste on the border between Italy and Slovenia. This important and well-defended city held out for three months—sufficient time, ordinarily, to outlast the impatient Huns. In fact, Attila was readying his troops for withdrawal when an omen changed everything. As he took a final walk around the wall, he saw storks evacuating the city with their young. Birds can see the future, of course—that's where we get our word *auspicious* from—and so Attila took heart that the city would soon be his. The battering rams were readied for a final push and the walls were breached. The Roman garrison was slaughtered and the city was utterly destroyed. Writing a hundred years later, Jordanes claimed that you couldn't find as much as a trace of Aquileia anymore. It was an exaggeration; Aquileia was rebuilt, but it never became an important city again.

Modern historians, beginning with Gibbon, have described how Emperor Valentinian III fled from Ravenna along with Aetius as the Huns began their march through northern Italy. The charge is false, as we'll soon see, but it's rendered believable by the puzzling absence of an effective Roman defense. After their victory at Aquileia the Huns swept like a firestorm from city to city, destroying at will. The small city of Concordia, thirty miles away, was next on the list. Roman sarcophagi have been excavated along the roads leading into Concordia that show evidence of violent plundering: heavy marble lids were torn from their boxes by blunt tools wielded perhaps by Huns searching for buried treasure.[193] Another thirty miles brought them to Altinum, a coastal city with charming white villas perched along a lagoon. Yet another thirty miles or so and they reached Patavium, the modern city of Padua, famous as the birthplace of the Roman historian Livy. Each city, rich in the legacy and lore of Rome, was demolished. The violence served the Huns well: Farther down the road the population capitulated with less of a struggle. Vicenza, Verone, Brescia, Bergamo, and Milan opened their gates and were sacked, though they were spared the fury that had leveled Aquileia.

Where was Aetius in all this? Why hadn't he posted garrisons in the Julian Alps leading into Italy? The general who had defended Gaul so ably the year before is all but absent from the ancient and modern historical accounts of the Italian campaign of 452. Edward Gibbon scarcely mentions him as he narrates the events in Italy; others mention him in passing, and then only by way of referring to his "abandonment" of Italy (a common theme in the histories that rests more on the silence of our sources than anything else). The conduct of Aetius in 452 has always been the one embarrassing line on his résumé. On the thinnest thread of evidence (silence) we are to accept his "failure" to anticipate Attila's next move, his "negligence" in not defending the alpine passes, and his decision to "abandon" Italy and flee with Emperor Valentinian. Even the eminent Theodor Mommsen, the greatest nineteenth-century classicist, prolific editor of ancient texts, and second winner of the Nobel Prize for Literature in 1902—*even Mommsen* seems to have gotten Aetius all wrong.[194]

But there was one scholar (there always has to be one, or the story couldn't advance) who challenged the orthodox line. He was a philologist and historian, and his shrewd reconstruction of these events makes it clear that Aetius did not make an amateur's mistake.[195] It's important for us to dig into this matter, to challenge and correct the record, not so that we can right a wrong and rehabilitate the reputation of a Roman general. Rather, a clearer understanding of the Italian campaign will let us close the conspiracy's loop. Italy is the key to understanding Attila's death. A rich choreography of interests brought Aetius and Marcian together in a plot that is still discernible, though barely, in these shadowy events that took place in the summer of 452.

THE PROFESSOR'S CLUTTERED OFFICE

Early in January 1969 Professor Otto Maenchen-Helfen of the University of California at Berkeley walked into the offices of the university press with a thick manuscript tucked under his arm.[196] As his colleagues would later remark while toasting his memory at the faculty club, the professor had completed his life's work; he had completed a sweeping synthesis of "the world of the Huns." He placed his manuscript on the desk, walked out, and died a few days later. But the manuscript wasn't quite complete, as a peek inside his office soon revealed. Documents, articles, handwritten notes, early drafts, and photographic negatives were stacked from floor to ceiling. Still, the book was far enough along to be published after some creative editorial reconstruction.

The professor's office was a reflection of his life; and his life, in no small measure, was a dynamic reflection of how he viewed history. The smallest detail—a weapon culled from an archaeological dig, an overlooked passage in an ancient text—might form the basis of a bold rethinking of "received knowledge." Otto was born in Vienna, in a house that stood two blocks from the ancient wall that once protected the city from Turkish cannons. "All my life," he wrote, "I have been fascinated by the problems of the frontier."[197] The confrontation of East and West that kindled his youthful imagination would become the main focus of his life's research. As a young scholar he traveled far and wide throughout the East—Mongolia, Kashmir, Nepal, Kabul—learning the culture of the steppes that centuries before had spawned Attila's hordes.

He was cut from the same academic mold that produced Julius Moravcsik, another versatile scholar with a prodigious grasp of languages and a keen interest in the East. Moravcsik was the more systematic of the two, believing that we can know the past if we're just thorough enough, and connect the dots accurately. What Maenchen-Helfen lacked in organization (note again his cluttered office) he made up for in creativity. Connecting the dots is one thing; Maenchen-Helfen, however, could see dots that no one had ever noticed before, like constellations that can be seen only by squinting. His take on the Italian campaign of 452 is typical. Was Aetius out to lunch when the invasion occurred? The weight of historical opinion has always said yes. Maenchen-Helfen evaluated the arguments, reconsidered the old texts, and said no.

It's time to put him on the witness stand.

Maenchen-Helfen's testimony rests on three arguments that, taken together, overturn the common historical judgment about how the Western government responded to the invasion.[198]

- Emperor Valentinian III did not flee from Ravenna, and Aetius never intended to abandon Italy to its fate.
- It is wrong to fault Aetius for failing to defend the alpine passes against an invasion.
- Aetius was actively involved in providing a vigorous and clever defense of Italy.

Although it nicely fits our conception of Valentinian as a craven and dissolute ruler to imagine him fleeing from the invading army, it doesn't square with the facts. Historians who should have known better have continued to peddle this line, although a fairly ample paper trail places Valentinian in Rome for most of the time between 450 and 452. All of Valentinian's laws in 451 and 452 were issued from Rome, and Marcian's imperial portrait was sent to the Western emperor in Rome, not Ravenna. Aetius, too, was in the old capital in the summer during the invasion. How do we know this? Very little documentary evidence survives from this time, but we do have one piece of evidence that has often been overlooked: one of Valentinian's laws, or a *novella* as they were called. The *Novella Valentiniana* of June 29 spells out the duties of the swine, cattle, sheep, and goat collectors in the city. What makes this revision of the municipal code noteworthy, however, is that it contains the only contemporary reference we have to the great war then raging in Italy. In the preamble, the emperor praises Aetius, who "among his warlike troubles and the blare of trumpets" was able to tend to the food needs of the city's population. An uncomplicated reading of this law leads to two conclusions: first, the swine, cattle, sheep, and goat industry in Rome was a bureaucratic nightmare; and, second, Aetius was busily engaged in the defense of Italy.

Why then has he come under such harsh criticism? Aetius could have stopped the invasion dead in its tracks, we are told, if only he had posted garrisons in the Alps. Historians have not made up this charge out of the clear blue; they point to a contemporary source, the *Chronicle* of Prosper of Aquitaine, as evidence that the general had been grossly negligent. Here's what Prosper says:

> After Attila had made up for the losses suffered in Gaul, he intended to at-
> tack Italy through Pannonia. Our general had not taken any provisions as
> he had done in the first war, so that not even the defenses of the Alps, where
> the enemy could have been stopped, were put to use. He thought the only
> thing he could hope for was to leave Italy together with the emperor. But
> this seemed so shameful and dangerous that the sense of honor conquered
> the fear.

As we've cautioned before, one shouldn't challenge an ancient authority lightly; but Prosper seems especially open to criticism for commenting on things he knew nothing about. Most modern historians have believed Prosper without bothering to check if he had any axes to grind. The rare exception was Edward Gibbon, who understood that Prosper's account was a "rash censure" of Aetius that must be "counterbalanced" by other contemporary sources—one of the many cases, it's worth pointing out, where Gibbon's judgment was right on the money.[199]

Even if expecting an invasion (as Aetius surely was), he would not necessarily have mounted an alpine defense. The Italian border was not as easy to defend as Prosper claimed. Writing in the eighth century, Paul the Deacon describes the geography well: "Yet from the eastern side by which Italy is joined to Pannonia it has an approach which lies open more broadly and is quite level." Maenchen-Helfen points out that the several times Italy was invaded, including by Alaric in the early fifth century, the Julian Alps were never defended. The charge of negligence is simply insupportable.[200] Aetius was a chess master in the geopolitical sphere: he was always thinking several steps ahead. He had learned the art of war as a young hostage in the service of Alaric the Visigoth; later on he served under Rua, shared meals with Bleda and Attila, and learned the techniques and tactics of the Huns. He rose to power in Italy through the calculated elimination of his opponents, one by one. Unprepared for Attila's invasion? Not a chance. Aetius simply had limited resources at his disposal after the exhausting defense of Gaul the year before. The mainstay of his Gallic strategy, the Visigoths, had retired to their capital in Toulouse, and the Western Roman army was virtually nonexistent without its *foederati*.

EXHIBIT FOURTEEN

Marcian and Aetius had cultivated a close political
alliance that culminated in the defense of Italy.

Despite his limited resources, Aetius was very much in the thick of the action, leading a counterstrike, commanding troops that had been sent by Emperor Marcian to aid in the Empire's defense. Only one sentence in the

Chronicle of Hydatius bears witness to this heroic struggle; no other account survives.

> Auxiliaries were sent by the emperor Marcian, and under the commandership of Aetius the Huns were slain. Likewise they were subdued in their own territory, partly by plagues from heaven, partly by Marcian's army.

This passage has given rise to some amusing bouts of confusion. British historian E. A. Thompson, for instance, follows earlier historians, compounding their errors and ending up in the process with *two* different generals named Aetius. Thompson's interpretation of Hydatius? "In these circumstances, an East Roman force crossed the Danube under the command of an officer who, *curiously enough*, bore the name of Aetius."[201] Curious indeed, considering how Aetius is one of the least frequently encountered names in late antiquity. We're dealing with a very different class of name than, say, all the Constantines in the Byzantine Empire or all the Michaels in my kindergarten class. The idea that two generals named Aetius were commanding troops against the Huns in 452 is utterly preposterous. It's best to let Occam's razor cut through to the simplest explanation.[202] Applying the standard that "plurality is not to be assumed without necessity," we must conclude that Marcian sent troops to the West that were placed under the command of Aetius—the one and only.

A defensive counterstrike such as this could not be improvised on the fly if it were to have any chance of success. The only available port of entry would be Ravenna, a fortress even more impregnable than Aquileia; extensive planning would have been required to mount the operation, to assemble the fleet, and to stockpile food for the soldiers and horses. In other words, everything must have been planned well in advance of Attila's invasion. The letters of Pope Leo reveal that the Western Romans had believed that Italy, not Gaul, was going to be invaded in the summer of 451.[203] There was, then, plenty of time to make adequate preparations for what finally did happen the next year when Attila crossed the Alps. None of this would have been possible—troops, equipment, rations—if the invasion had truly "struck the patrician with the violence of a thunderstroke," as Thompson glibly claims.[204] Maenchen-Helfen bluntly replies: "Nothing could be further from the truth."

This is much more than a scholars' dispute; it's a pivoting point for our understanding of Attila's death a few months later. The striking conclusion that Maenchen-Helfen reaches from these scattered pieces of evidence is that "Aetius and the government in Constantinople must have worked out a plan of coordinated action against the Huns, should Attila invade Italy." But we can go one step further. We can make out the blueprint of a larger coordinated effort to deal with Attila decisively. Aetius may have made his first contact with the Eastern court in June 450 when the mysterious messenger arrived from Rome. Who sent the message informing Theodosius of Honoria's intrigue with Attila? We don't know, but Aetius was the one person who would be hurt most by an alliance between Attila and Valentinian. It's quite possible, though just conjecture, that Aetius was cultivating a political connection with Constantinople before Marcian ever came to power. The Western court at Ravenna had not been on very good terms with the Eastern court at Constantinople for years, and Aetius was probably attempting an end run around Valentinian. Even after Marcian came to power, Valentinian refused to recognize the new emperor for almost two years, so it's not at all surprising that Aetius would capitalize on the icy relationship between the two capitals to forge a personal alliance that cut Valentinian out of the loop.

More hints lead to more possibilities. We are reasonably sure that Maximin and Priscus were in Rome in 450, and the first communication between Marcian and Aetius must have occurred at this time. In September 451 Marcian personally took the field against the Huns in the Balkans. Though it was not militarily necessary to do this, Marcian was signaling a new aggressive posture against Attila—evidence, perhaps, of a coordinated strategy to squeeze the Huns from both sides. We know as well from Hydatius (once he's been rescued from his misinterpreters) that Marcian delivered troops to Aetius for the defense of Italy. Still more evidence of an East-West alliance can be teased from the culminating event of the Italian campaign. It would not be an encounter of armies as in Gaul but an encounter of personalities between the Holy Father and the Scourge of God. Attila wouldn't get reli-gion, but he would get a good case of the jitters.

THE GENERAL, THE POPE, AND THE BARBARIAN

Leo, bishop of Rome, had taken the invasion of Gaul in stride; but he must have been less sanguine about what was happening throughout northern Italy in 452. The invasion had proved devastating to the Church. The once important ecclesiastical center of Aquileia lay in ruins. Attila had strutted through the very palace in Milan where the edict had been signed legalizing Christianity. What was one to make of the disturbing fact that the heavenly sign by which Constantine conquered, the sign of the cross, had failed to prevent the barbarian onslaught? With convenient simplicity, the propagandists of the fifth century (Leo among them) could move back and forth between victory and defeat, finding in either circumstance the invisible hand of God. The language of the Old Testament prophets was easily adapted to any situation. In the good times, God rained down his judgment on the barbarian host, Gog and Magog, who were invading from the North. In the bad times, God chastised his people for their wickedness and heresy.

Even more distressing to Leo must have been what was happening in Lugnano and the other communities around Rome that were ravaged by malaria. Christians were abandoning their prayers to Christ and were reverting to the pagan sacrifices of their ancestors. In every province of the Empire, the Church was still battling tenacious heresies such as Arianism and Monophysitism. No wonder Leo described the office he held as "a burden to shudder at." More was resting on his shoulders than the administrative and ceremonial functions of the Church; the very fate of Christianity itself was at stake. And to top it all off, the Scourge of God was now headed toward Rome.

Jordanes tells us (with Priscus backing him up) that "Attila's mind had been bent on going to Rome." It wasn't the tug of old acquaintances drawing him back, despite what persistent legends claim about young Attila living as a diplomatic hostage among the Romans. Attila had never been there before. Medieval chroniclers, nationalistic scholars, and Hollywood screenwriters have all found the romance of this story line irresistible.[205] But it's not true. (This is one legend I'm not buying into; it has no ancient authority and can be shown to arise from the need of Hungarian historians, medieval and modern, to ennoble their "first king" with a good Roman education.) Attila's mind was bent on going to Rome for the same reason Willie Sutton robbed banks. The accumulated spoils of centuries of Roman conquest made the city a very attractive target indeed. The Temple of Jupiter Capitolinus even had a gold roof on it! Gaiseric was so impressed in 455 that he tore half the roof off and took it with him back to Africa. But Attila never saw the city's glories, either as a youth or as an old warrior at the end of his life. Taking Rome would have been a cakewalk. Unlike Constantinople, Rome had no natural defenses; nor did Rome need, for most of its history, massive walls like the kind Theodosius II had built along the Bosporus.[206] Rome's army had always been her defense; but the fabled legions of Rome existed now in name only. Without the Visigothic *foederati*, the Western Empire could muster an army only with help from the East. Even Marcian's auxiliaries could not have prevented the Huns from marching straight into the heart of the Roman Forum. Still, when Attila considered his options, he decided at the last minute to pack it in and go home.

The about-face is puzzling, though we have several explanations to choose from. The first comes from Jordanes, who refers us back to the authority of Priscus:[207]

> Attila's followers, as the historian Priscus relates, took him away from Rome, not out of regard for the city to which they were hostile, but because they remembered the case of Alaric, the former king of the Visigoths. They distrusted the good fortune of their own king, inasmuch as Alaric did not live long after the sack of Rome, but straightway departed this life.

Jordanes goes on to say that "Attila's spirit was wavering in doubt between going and not going." This man who was ordinarily so decisive had now become Hamlet. What Jordanes gives us is pure commentary—an ancient form of pop psychology—and it goes back directly to what Priscus wrote. Priscus had taken the ancient Greek historians Thucydides and Herodotus as his models; Thucydides especially would weave interior motivations into his narration of public events. How indecisive Attila was could be debated; certainly Priscus never once sensed that Attila was indecisive when he observed him in person. His manner of dispensing justice when he held court outside his tent was rather cut and dried; his response to diplomatic messages was drop-dead blunt. The two images of Attila are inconsistent—decisive and indecisive—just as we have a hard time reconciling how the sober Attila could drink himself to death.

We do know that Attila was deeply superstitious, and what Priscus calls indecisiveness may best be described as a healthy respect for omens. The story of Alaric's sudden demise was widely known among Attila's followers, and the ghost of Alaric would have exercised a powerful sway over his thinking. Shortly after sacking Rome in 410, Alaric loaded up his ships at the southern tip of Italy and prepared to cross over to Africa by way of Sicily. But a storm came up and destroyed his fleet. Jordanes describes how Alaric "was cast down by his reverse and, while deliberating what he should do, was suddenly overtaken by an untimely death and departed from human cares."[208] His men buried him in the bed of the Busento River, diverting the water and filling the grave with treasure. Then they released the waters once again and the servants who prepared his grave were killed to conceal the location.

Somebody close to Attila told him this story. But who and why? Perhaps his Roman advisors, Orestes and Constantius, were the ones who warned him about an ancient curse on anyone who dared to violate the sacred city. They may have embellished the story with credible eyewitness accounts that had circulated among the Romans—the kind that Galla Placidia herself must have brought back from exile.[209] If it was Orestes and Constantius who talked to Attila and "took him away from Rome," then are we really to believe that they were motivated by concern for Attila's welfare as Priscus claims? The explanation Priscus gives us ("they distrusted the good fortune of their own king") is not entirely convincing.[210] There's a better way to interpret this, one that explains more effectively the oddities of the text and of the event itself.

EXHIBIT FIFTEEN

With limited military resources to defend Rome, Aetius conspired with Attila's Roman advisors to persuade the Huns to withdraw from Italy.

Aetius knew these men. He knew their families. He had sent Constantius to Attila some years before. We can be sure that Aetius had maintained a degree of leverage over each of these men—influence that he could tap at just the right time. Rome in the summer of 452 was definitely the right time and the right place. The master game of outbribing and outmaneuvering your opponent was in full swing. Attila had tried to do the same thing when he invaded Gaul, making deals with the king of the Alans, sending separate letters to Theodoric and Valentinian. Gaiseric had also played the game, trying to move the players around on the chessboard to his own advantage. Aetius, too, was a master of the game: his scheming had led to the destruction of his chief rival, Boniface. Aetius had few military options available to him, and so he orchestrated instead the withdrawal of the superstitious Attila from Italy. Somehow Aetius got to Orestes in the summer of 452 and turned him back to the Roman side. Even J. B. Bury, the eminent Irish scholar and a rationalist who believed almost nothing, acknowledged that "there may be something" to what Priscus has recorded about the Alaric curse, since "Attila's secretaries were doubtless open to bribes."[211]

By the time of the Italian campaign in 452, Aetius had joined the ranks of those seeking Attila's death. It was quite a reversal for the general. Early in his career Aetius had deployed the Huns as his allies; later on, when they were Rome's enemy, the Huns were still useful to Aetius as an insurance policy. As long as Attila was a threat to Rome, Valentinian would need the general at his side. But now two things had changed. Aetius had a powerful new friend in Constantinople; and his son Gaudentius was betrothed to the emperor's daughter Placidia. The political fortunes of his family seemed assured. With Gaul and Italy now devastated, it made sense (for the first time) to eliminate Attila.

Attila's Roman advisor, Orestes, could not have been happy with his current lot. Though he was probably not a patriot, the destruction of Italy and the threatened destruction of its glorious capital must have been disturbing to him. Orestes had many friends and even family in Rome. Recall that his father-in-law, Count Romulus, had headed up the Italian embassy that Maximin and Priscus ran into during their diplomatic mission in 449. Recall as well that Orestes's father, Tatalus, and the secretary Constantius were also traveling with the Romans. Priscus tells us that these two, Tatalus and Constantius, were friends of the ambassadors, which suggests that both Orestes and Constantius had deep personal connections to Italy. The names and relationships are hard to keep straight, but the only thing that's necessary to see here is the high probability that Aetius would have had considerable leverage over these Roman advisors to Attila.

More evidence suggests that Orestes nurtured a secret allegiance to Rome. An obscure sixth-century writer, the so-called Anonymous Valesianus, reports that Orestes, the father of the last Western emperor Romulus Augustulus, "joined with Attila and became his secretary (*notarius*) at the time he, Attila, came to Italy."[212] This could not have been in 452, as Orestes had been with Attila for a number of years already by this time; obviously, then, Attila had been to Italy at least once before. Anonymous Valesianus is implying that Orestes, though born in Pannonia, was actually living in Italy when he became Attila's *notarius*. Over time, Orestes had risen through the ranks to become one of the five named *logades* ("chosen men") of Attila, along with Edecon, Onegesh, Scottas, and Berica. But not everyone thought that Orestes held equal rank. Back in Sardica in 449, Bigilas explained to Maximin that Orestes had not received the same treatment in Constantino-

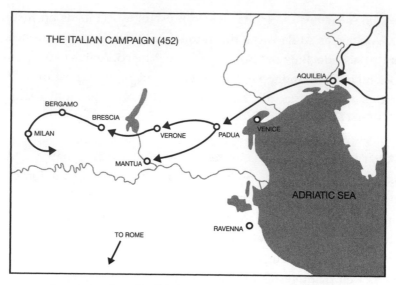

A reconstruction of Attila's invasion of Italy in A.D. 452. The map
suggests two possibilities: Attila either went directly from Padua to his
meeting with Bishop Leo near Mantua, or he met Leo after progressing
first through Verone, Brescia, Bergamo, and Milan.

Map by Matthew Pamer

ple because he, Orestes, was a secretary and a Roman. Class snobbery and
racial prejudice must have factored into the hostilities between Orestes and
Edecon. We don't know the degree to which Orestes himself still *felt* Roman
in 453, but it's obvious that his Roman blood had to start stirring at some
point for him to maneuver his son onto the throne two decades later.[213]

Betrayal had become a much easier option after Gaul and Italy, since it
was obvious that Attila was at the end of his career. Orestes was looking beyond Attila to his own future when he agreed to steer the Huns away from
Rome. Constantius, too, may have been easily persuaded to change loyal-
ties, especially when the appeal came directly from his old patron Aetius.
Unlike Orestes, we know nothing certain of what happened to Constantius
after Attila's death. There is an Italian tombstone from the early fifth
century—or rather, there *was*, as it's now been lost—which commemorates a
general and senator named Constantius. Some highly respected historians

have sought to connect this inscription to the secretary who served Attila.[214] According to the inscription, Constantius "was as much burning in love and devotion to the Romans as he was bringing terror to the Pannonian tribes." It's tempting, but foolhardy, to connect the two names; Constantius was an extremely common name in the fifth century, as we've already seen. Not to mention, how could the Constantius who served Attila be described as a "terror" to the Huns? Let's suspend our disbelief (and better judgment) for just a moment. If Constantius joined Orestes in betraying the Huns, then he, too, would have gone on to a political and military career in the West. Under these circumstances, it's quite easy to imagine how he could be described as a Roman patriot and a terror to the enemy.

Aetius was confident that his disinformation campaign would work on Attila, especially since malaria was then raging throughout the district. Plagues and comets don't normally register as anything but coincidences to the modern mind. To the ancient mind, however, plagues were engineered by vengeful deities and comets appeared over battlefields as if penciled in by God on some cosmic calendar. Attila looked around and saw that some of his own troops were dying from plague. He hesitated, and that gave the emperor time to confer with the Senate and organize the defense of the city. After much deliberation, the best plan they could come up with was to send the Holy Father and two patricians out to meet Attila. This is one of those rare cases where History does a better job than Hollywood in producing a scene that's too well choreographed to be true. Surely only legend could stage an encounter this improbable. And yet it really did happen near Mantua, along the banks of the Mincio River north of Rome. As it turned out, Leo reinforced the message—either by accident or design—that was already planted in Attila's ear. Here's what Priscus has to say, as related to us by Jordanes:[215]

> Therefore while Attila's spirit was wavering in doubt between going and not going, and he still lingered to ponder the matter, an embassy came to

him from Rome to seek peace. Pope Leo himself came to meet him in the
Ambuleian district of the Veneti at the well-traveled ford of the river Min-
cius. Then Attila quickly put aside his usual fury, turned back on the way he
had advanced from beyond the Danube and departed with the promise of
peace.

What's especially striking here is the sparseness of detail. Neither Priscus
nor Jordanes had any reason to lionize the pope, so we get just the facts: Attila threatened Rome, Leo led an embassy, Attila went home. No motives
and no miracles.

We have an even older account, though—older than Priscus. Within
three years of the encounter, a resident of Rome and protégé of Leo described the scene that he might have witnessed himself. That would be Prosper of Aquitaine (c. 400–65), whom we earlier found so unreliable in his
testimony about the Julian Alps. Prosper's *Chronicle* is an invaluable source
of information for events occurring in the Western Empire in the fifth century, though he must be read cautiously with an eye to his personal agendas.
His writing career began with an impromptu letter to St. Augustine in 427 in
which he asked the great theologian to clarify his views on free will and
grace, central issues in the Pelagian heresy then stirring in the West. Prosper
ended up in Rome around 430 and would eventually become Pope Leo's *notarius*. Though he doesn't seem to have been a clergyman himself, his life
and writings were devoted to fighting heresy. He held strong political
views, and a constant theme in his *Chronicle* is the disastrous jockeying for
power among Rome's leading generals. These well-defined religious and political views must be kept in mind when we read Prosper's nearly contemporary account of the event.[216]

Now Attila, having once more collected his forces which had been scattered
in Gaul, took his way through Pannonia into Italy. To the emperor and the
senate and Roman people, none of all the proposed plans to oppose the enemy seemed so practicable as to send legates to the most savage king and
beg for peace. Our most blessed Pope Leo—trusting in the help of God,

who never fails the righteous in their trials—undertook the task, accompanied by Avienus, a man of consular rank, and the prefect Trygetius. And the outcome was what his faith had foreseen; for when the king had received the embassy, he was so impressed by the presence of the high priest that he ordered his army to give up warfare and, after he had promised peace, he departed beyond the Danube.

We can assume that Prosper intended to magnify his patron's reputation. The Roman "victory" in Italy was Leo's to claim; Aetius had nothing to do with it at all. Attila turned away from Rome because he was "impressed by the presence of the high priest," whom Attila must have viewed as a shaman. If Aetius had posted troops in the Julian Alps (as Prosper claimed), then none of this would have been necessary. Aetius was just another one of the power-hungry generals whom Prosper decries in the long history of the Roman state. Once we've redlined these agendas, we can extract the valuable authentic details, such as the role of the Roman senators Avienus and Trygetius.

The embryo of a legend is already here in Prosper's account. Two hundred years later, Paul the Deacon would tell us what he heard from oral legends: an old man stood beside Leo, brandishing a sword.[217] Perhaps this was a classical figure, Mars the warrior; or perhaps it was St. Peter, whom Leo had claimed to be his special companion "in all emergencies."[218] The legend continued to grow and merge with the earlier historical accounts. In the anonymously written *Life of Leo the Great*—a typical piece of medieval hagiography written to showcase Leo's claim to sainthood—we find an amplified version of Prosper's account. "The old man of harmless simplicity, venerable in his gray hair and his majestic garb, ready of his own will to give himself entirely for the defense of his flock, went forth to meet the tyrant who was destroying all things." It is apparent that the anonymous hagiographer knows both Prosper and Jordanes; but he also knows the legends that grew up and flourished around this event, legends that Leo himself was keen to foster. The hagiographer puts an impossible message in Leo's mouth—an appeal for self-control and mercy! "Now we pray that you, who have conquered others, should now conquer yourself. The people have felt your scourging; now as suppliants they would feel your mercy." The response was just as unexpected.

> As Leo said these things, Attila stood looking upon his venerable garb and aspect, silent, as if thinking deeply. And lo, suddenly there were seen the apostles Peter and Paul, clad like bishops, standing by Leo, the one on the right hand, the other on the left. They held swords stretched out over his head, and threatened Attila with death if he did not obey the pope's command. Wherefore Attila was appeased—he who had raged as one mad. He by Leo's intercession straightway promised a lasting peace and withdrew beyond the Danube.

Leo was a great Church leader and, by all accounts, a great man. He was also a tireless self-promoter. His justification for pumping his own career—endlessly asserting his authority over the bishops in the East—had much to do with his firm conviction that he stood in a line of succession reaching clear back to St. Peter. Leo was one of the first bishops of Rome to claim Petrine authority: "You are Peter, and upon this rock I will build my church and the gates of hell will not prevail against it" (Matthew 16:18). With Peter at his side, and Paul thrown in for good measure, the gates of hell were pushed back from Rome—the clearest indication yet, for all who doubted, that Leo stood in Peter's stead, doing God's work on earth. The prestige of the medieval papacy owes much to this encounter.

The story of Leo's embassy, then, is *historical*, but it offered Leo and the Church a windfall of propaganda. Leo would be less successful three years later when he tried the same thing against Gaiseric. His subsequent failure, though, seems not to have tarnished his reputation. His legend grew. Rarely do we get so clear a picture of how history is transformed into legend. Leo himself contributed to the growth of the legend, asking in a sermon he delivered a few years later: "Was it the circus games or the protection of the saints that delivered Rome from death?"[219] The two patricians at Leo's side—Avienus and Trygetius—lived on in memory as the two founding pillars of the Church, Peter and Paul. They survived the same way "the boy at the table" did in Germanic legend, evidence again of how much truth lurks beneath the miracles of saints and the raw imagination of poets.

There's one more wrinkle to the story of Leo and Attila. In a letter written around 513 by the Western bishops to Pope Symmachus, we learn that Leo had negotiated with Attila for the release of those taken hostage in the Italian campaign.[220] It's a passing reference in an obscure letter that survived by accident. We're not told what the outcome was, but it's reasonable to assume that Leo paid a large ransom. So then why did Attila withdraw from Rome? Probably for every reason mentioned, excluding the appearance of Peter and Paul. Attila's troops were suffering from famine and plague; the evidence from Lugnano certainly supports the view that malaria helped drive Attila out of Italy. Marcian's troops (under the leadership of Aetius) were now offering a stiffer defense of Italy. Attila was probably impressed by Leo and bribed by him as well. All in all, he had many reasons to leave this *regio funesta*, this "land of death." The story about Alaric—planted by his advisors at the instigation of Aetius—was the final straw. Fearing the same fate, he went home to Pannonia, only to die there in a few short weeks.

WHAT STORYTELLERS DO

According to Jordanes, Attila left for home spouting "threats that he would bring worse things upon Italy, unless they sent him Honoria, the sister of the Emperor Valentinian and daughter of Augusta Placidia, with her due share of the royal wealth." Whatever happened to Honoria? Was she ever married off to Flavius Bassus Herculanus?[221] We know that Herculanus was elected consul of Rome in 452, the same year Attila invaded Italy. Was the old senator rewarded with the consulship for taking on such a difficult project and giving Valentinian the cover he needed? Perhaps. If Honoria were the wife of another man, then the emperor would have stronger grounds for refusing Attila's matrimonial demands.[222]

The ghost of Honoria haunted the Italian memory for centuries. This according to a distinguished American medievalist whose name, unfortunately, was Krappe. In a 1931 article, Professor Krappe analyzed the legendary accounts of the miraculous birth of Attila that circulated in late medieval Italy. He concluded that they may reflect some remote memory traces of Honoria being locked away in a tower under house arrest.[223] We hear nothing about her after 452. John of Antioch (seventh century) offers a few dark hints when he mentions how her life was spared in 450. *"On that occasion,"* John writes, "she escaped chastisement." The implication is clear: later on, she was not so lucky.[224] (It wouldn't be the first time a Roman emperor had dealt so severely with his sister.) There's one more ominous hint. Honoria is conspicuously absent from the list of Roman nobles carried off by Gaiseric to Carthage in 455. If she had been in Rome, she would have been taken. If she had been taken, she would certainly have been mentioned in the list of noble hostages.

In the winter of 452–53, the working assumption was that the world had not seen the last of Attila the Hun. "So Attila returned to his own country," Jordanes writes, "seeming to regret the peace and to be vexed at the cessation of war." Who would feel his wrath when spring came around—Rome, Toulouse, or Constantinople? Though he was still breathing threats against Rome when he left Italy, Attila never considered returning to this land of pestilence and holy men. He had even less incentive now that Honoria was out of the way. The Visigothic capital of Toulouse was never an option either—too far away—though Jordanes surprises us with a story about a second Battle of Châlons. After returning from Italy, Attila supposedly marched straight back to Gaul and faced the Visigoths once again. It's a ridiculous account fraught with problems: the battle was fought in the same place and in the same manner, we're told, as the great showdown with Aetius! This second Battle of Châlons, in which Attila was once again defeated, is rightly rejected by historians as an improbability. Always the patriotic Goth, Jordanes is magnifying the history of his people at the expense of the truth. The Visigothic king Thorismud is thus given an opportunity to make good for his earlier desertion of Aetius in Gaul.

Constantinople had the most to fear as a new year approached. Though

Attila was determined to teach Marcian a lesson, one gets the impression that the emperor was not nearly as "disquieted about his fierce foe" as Jordanes claims. Already Marcian had twice refused to pay tribute. He had personally led a counterstrike against the Huns in 451 and he had forged an alliance with Aetius during the Italian campaign. These were not the actions of a timid emperor like Theodosius II. That much Attila knew. But for all his fabled cleverness, the extremely preoccupied Hun never figured Marcian out. Attila never absorbed the fact—he didn't have time to—that he had been outmaneuvered by the wily emperor in Constantinople. Attila clearly underestimated Marcian; if he had known how great a danger Marcian was, he surely would not have ventured west. Historians have followed Attila's error, badly underestimating Marcian and seeing rashness instead of resolve in his defiance of the Huns. According to this view, Marcian had benefited from good timing; he was "lucky" that Attila had died a "providential" death. The modern endorsement of chance as a historical force doesn't serve us well here. The fortuitous timing of Attila's death, unlike the appearance of Halley's Comet, was not determined by statistical chance but by human manipulation.

As soon as he arrived back home in Pannonia, Attila took a new wife, a young woman named Ildico. We know next to nothing about her from the historical record, though we've already seen that what she lacks in history she makes up for in legend as Kriemhild and Gudrun. Jordanes tells us that she was beautiful. The fact that she's mentioned by name may suggest that she came from a prominent royal family. Most likely she was German, in which case her name would probably have been Hildico, or the very Wagnerian-sounding Hilde. Attila never married for love, and so we should assume that she was part of some larger political plan. Attila had been greatly weakened by his adventures in Gaul and Italy. He had led his German allies into defeat and had very little to show for it. Widespread dissatisfaction must have existed among his followers and even among the *logades*.[225] This marriage was an attempt to stop the bleeding, so to speak.

Jordanes describes the ceremony with a single statement: "Attila gave himself up to excessive joy at his wedding." But there's a problem with this: it doesn't square at all with what Priscus had witnessed at the diplomatic feast. Perhaps we shouldn't expect that Attila was *always* sober and humorless, the way he was when Priscus watched him sipping from his wooden mug. Priscus saw Attila at a diplomatic feast, not a private wedding celebration. It is nonetheless difficult to reconcile the separate pictures of self-control and reckless abandon, especially as our doubts are fueled by more than just a single impression. Every piece of evidence from Attila's career suggests that he cultivated an austere public persona. In the "horseback negotiations" at Margus in 435, and in every subsequent diplomatic encounter, Attila conveyed supreme self-confidence and self-control. Priscus observed his haughty gait as he strode forth in public view to hold court and issue judgments. Attila was very different from his older brother, Bleda, both in policy and style; we see this most clearly in how they treated Zerko the dwarf. Bleda was (if it's not too wrenching a description) a happy-go-lucky Hun. Attila was all business.[226]

EXHIBIT SIXTEEN

Attila had been significantly weakened by his back-to-back adventures in the Western Empire and was now politically vulnerable within his own ranks.

"Overcome by the blond radiance of her beauty," Marcel Brion gushed in 1929, "he disrobed her with impetuous violence and carried her to the bridal chamber." Once our heart rate has returned to normal, we can see all that's wrong with this silly picture. For starts, Attila didn't have to carry her far as his bed was already set up in the middle of the dining hall, elevated and surrounded by curtains. This simple but important spatial detail allows us to see how Attila could have been poisoned in plain view of all the revelers. Poisoning Attila during the public feast, just steps away from his bridal bed, would have been as easy as bribing or coercing the cupbearer. Priscus described in great detail the elaborate formalities of the diplomatic feast he witnessed. Each guest was recognized individually with a toast, and "it was not right for him to sit down until the king had either tasted the wine or drunk it up and given the cup back to the cupbearer." The wedding feast probably followed a similar ritual. Even a sober man such as Attila could be killed this way, sip by sip, if the cup were spiked with poison.

Of course, Jordanes doesn't say anything about poison. Let's look once again at his famous account, reading it not as a historical analysis that's meant to inform but as a story that's meant to persuade:

> Shortly before he died, as the historian Priscus relates, he took in marriage a very beautiful girl named Ildico, after countless other wives, as was the custom of his race. He had given himself up to excessive joy at his wedding, and as he lay on his back, heavy with wine and sleep, a rush of superfluous blood, which would ordinarily have flowed from his nose, streamed in deadly course down his throat and killed him, since it was hindered in the usual passages.

The next scene occurs on the following day. At this point we're drawn in as spectators through the magic of storytelling. We find ourselves outside the room facing the closed door. We stand there along with Attila's advisors, wondering why the chieftain is sleeping so late. When they break in the door at last, their discovery becomes ours.

> On the following day, when a great part of the morning was spent, the royal attendants suspected some ill and, after a great uproar, broke in the doors. There they found the death of Attila accomplished by an effusion of blood, without any wound, and the girl with downcast face weeping beneath her veil.

How we read this passage depends entirely on what we want to see. Historians who are steeped (like Gibbon) in the rationalism of the modern age, have always been impressed by the apparent neutrality of the account. (In particular, the absence of miracles—hovering eagles and prophetic dreams—always impresses the modern historian.) The details are convincing, the tone is dispassionate, and the "objective" source (Priscus) is unimpeachable. With these presuppositions guiding us, the account is validated as an accurate, one-to-one rendering of historical truth. By contrast, the postmodern approach begins by questioning whether "truth" is the first order of business in the text at all. Truth can be excavated only after the propaganda has been dealt with, only after the text has been handled first *as a story*.

It's a tidy story—no loose strings. It was this narrative efficiency, more than anything, that first provoked my suspicions many years ago, back in Anatoly's seminar on the Gothic language. Only later did I find the devastating literary parallels that confirmed, to my mind anyway, that this was an ecclesiastical cover story. But my first doubts were prompted by the story itself. There are too many holes in the record, too many nagging questions that it raises. The death scene has been staged too well. The details aren't neutral descriptions; they sound as if they've been conveniently planted in the testimony for the very purpose of steering us away from any suspicion of murder. The bride weeping beneath her veil, the doors that must be broken in, the body that shows no wound—all these details are purposely arranged to *persuade* us that Attila died of natural causes. The testimony is so dogmatic that it becomes suspicious. Other things don't seem right, either. I wondered, for example, why Ildico didn't scream.[227] Why didn't she alert somebody that Attila was in distress? Why did she sit there all night long next to the bed and the body with the stench of vomit and blood hanging in the air? Was she so paralyzed with fear that she didn't know what else to do? Or was she told to wait until morning?

Let's take one detail—the locked door. It seems obvious to us that the doors would be locked and that the royal attendants would have to break in. Attila was in his bridal chamber, after all. But it's extremely unlikely that the door was locked, or even had locks. Edecon told Chrysaphius back in 449 how security around Attila worked. He had bodyguard detachments posted outside his doors at all times. No one could disturb him. Checking on him in the morning would have been as easy as knocking two or three times and then opening the door. The locked door is a validating detail, meant to confirm Attila's death by natural causes. It's the original locked-door mystery, familiar to us from Agatha Christie's novels. *How could it be murder*, we ask, *when the door was locked from the inside?*

What Priscus originally wrote, and what Jordanes preserved, is not so much a historical account as a hermeneutical parable, complete with doors and veils. Priscus stages the event as a theatrical set piece. Why? Because that's what storytellers do. The doors are forced open and we see a tableau meant to be interpreted and validated. Priscus builds his audience into the text, a "dramatic audience" as the device is sometimes called. These characters are meant to stand in *our* place, letting *us* experience the event vicariously. Our involvement is heightened as we see what they see, hear what they hear, think what they think. Looking over their shoulders, we, too, find Ildico cowering beneath her veil. *We* participate in lifting the veil. *We* see the fear on her face and *we* rubber-stamp the conclusion: Ildico is ruled out as a suspect. The body is then examined and the initial postmortem is meant to become the final judgment of history: we join in confirming that Attila's body was found *sine ullo vulnere*, "without a wound." Of course, we're not supposed to raise our hands and say, "Didn't John Chrysostom say something like that half a century before?" (Scholars are *always* doing that— always ruining the story, that is.)

Theological necessity, not medical accuracy, is generating this death scene. We would be wrong to look for a specific medical condition here, such as esophageal varices, a rupturing of the vessels brought on by chronic alcoholism. There's no reason to believe that Attila was a chronic drinker; if he was, then he certainly hid it well. Far from being a convincing piece of evidence, the emphatic denial of any wound may also be something of a diversion. Poison, of course, doesn't leave a wound the way a dagger does, and poisoning is not specifically refuted by the passage at all.

Any of the poisons commonly used in the Roman world might have been slipped into Attila's wedding cup: monkshood, hellebore, hemlock—all of which lead to nausea, vomiting, paralysis, and respiratory failure. Of course, Ildico was innocent, but that's not why she was spared. Her survival is one more detail, if a red herring, that authenticates Attila's death by natural causes.

EXHIBIT SEVENTEEN

The official description of Attila's death scene and the funeral that followed show evidence of a cover-up.

The story protests too much. It's so forthright and specific that it must be answering a rumor that was already brewing in the Gothic camp, the proto-legend that would eventually give us Kriemhild and Gudrun. Though many scholars have acknowledged that the rumor of Attila's murder must have begun circulating immediately, most have explained this away as the natural byproduct of a collective mythmaking mind. There was a quirky nineteenth-century historian, though, who allowed his suspicions to take him one step further, right up to the line of alleging murder. Amédée Thierry was a French journalist, historian, and politician. A romantic and a liberal, Amédée was the younger brother of an even more famous historian, Augustin. Among his many publications, Amédée Thierry's three-volume *History of Attila and His Successors* (1856) stands out as the first major historical study of Attila. Thierry took seriously the vast legendary materials found among the Germans, Italians, French, and Hungarians. He believed that they were worth studying in their own right, but he also felt that these legends sometimes give us back-door access to the truth. This blending of legend and "fact" probably explains why Thierry is seldom cited in serious studies of the Huns.

A postmodern approach, however, is more accepting of Thierry's method. Thierry, of course, was no postmodern, but he was the next best thing. Both brothers, Amédée and Augustin, were romantics and liberals, which meant basically the same thing in the early nineteenth century. Both were ardent supporters of the legacy and humanistic ideals of the French Revolution. Not surprisingly, the groundbreaking histories that each brother wrote were sweeping interpretations that pivoted around a single idea. Whether it was Anglo-Saxon England facing the Normans (Augustin) or the Celts withstanding Julius Caesar in Gaul (Amédée), the drama was always the same: humanity's unending struggle for liberty. Amédée's fascination with Attila was probably rooted in his love for old Gaul. But the impressive figure of Attila was also cut from a romantic mold, a figure every bit as big as Prometheus, Dr. Faust, or Napoleon. Thierry was bound to see the grand story of revolution—the oppressed throwing off the yolk of the oppressor—framing the story of Attila's death.

As every other historian before and after has done, Thierry cites the relevant passages that speak of Attila's murder: Marcellinus Comes, Malalas, and the *Chronicon Paschale*. But where others see nothing but groundless rumors behind these accounts, Thierry wonders if they might possibly be true. "What happened that fatal night?" he asks.[228] "The rumors that circulated outside the palace were diverse and contradictory; but the fact that the leaders took such care to prove that Attila's death was *natural* makes the sinister version all the more believable. The Latin texts," he continues, "allow one to imagine a homegrown plot of the type which Theodosius had instigated four years earlier—but a plot more insidious and better planned." It's clear that Thierry suspects Edecon and possibly Orestes, though he never translates his suspicions into an operative theory. The story that Attila died of a hemorrhage was "intended no doubt to prevent accusations and inquiries that were dangerously destabilizing, or perhaps to forestall an immediate collapse of the empire." Thierry's instincts are worth following here, as he's looking beyond the rhetoric to the propaganda behind it. "This account," he writes, "is what Attila's sons and the *logades* of the court would repeat everywhere, out of political considerations as well as pride; and this would become the officially sanctioned account of Attila's death." Thierry must have believed (deep down in his romantic heart) that Attila was murdered. And so do I.

THE SUMMATION

It's time to sum up the case. Seventeen pieces of evidence point to an assassination plot that was sponsored by Emperor Marcian in the East, facilitated by Aetius in the West, and executed by Edecon and Orestes within Attila's court. We found that it was necessary first to discredit the official account of Attila's death before a murder allegation could be lodged. What I've called the official, or orthodox, version of Attila's death—the version everyone believes—can be shown to rest upon a single uncorroborated account that has suffered from textual corruption (Exhibit 1). Priscus was in Egypt when Attila died; and though he speaks with the authority of an eyewitness in many instances, he had to rely on secondary sources for what he knew of Attila's death. What Priscus knew and passed on was gathered secondhand upon his return to Constantinople. We don't even have the full record of what Priscus wrote, as his history was adapted by Cassiodorus in 525 and Jordanes in 550. For his account of Attila's death, then, we have only what Jordanes has chosen to pass on to us.

Even if this account faithfully preserves what Priscus wrote, it still has all kinds of credibility problems. It's a literary treatment of Attila's death and it's been deliberately crafted to persuade the reader. The narrative details (such as the locked door, the weeping maiden, the inquisitive attendants who examine the body) are all meant to rule out anything but death by natural causes (Exhibit 17). Other literary influences can be seen in the account as well. The official story has been shaped within an ecclesiastical culture of propaganda. The circumstances of Attila's death are remarkably similar to what Socrates Scholasticus wrote about the death of Attila's uncle Octar (Exhibit 8). The story of Octar dying after a gluttonous feast is preserved within an ecclesiastical source, and it represents a moralizing commentary about the enemies of the Church and Empire. This cultural, social, political, and religious background in Constantinople—what German higher critics call the *Sitz im Leben* (or "life setting") of a text—provides us the framework for understanding Marcian's motives and his methods for covering up the assassination.

The most significant evidence of ecclesiastical tampering comes from the homilies of St. John Chrysostom. The very details that historians have found most credible in this account of Attila's "natural death" can be found in the sermons that John famously delivered in Constantinople a generation before (Exhibit 13). John often railed against the vices of gluttony and drunkenness, describing their effects in terms of a strong man (who illustrates the godless, carnal man) dead on his bed, his blood hemorrhaging from his head, no sign of wounds upon his body. The metaphor echoes the official account of Attila's death—or, more properly stated, Attila's death echoes what Chrysostom wrote. The official version, then, can be dismissed on several grounds as a cover story modeled on ecclesiastical rhetoric.

But that still doesn't amount to murder. It turns out, however, that the allegation of murder existed from the beginning and was not concocted later in the poetic imagination of the Germanic tribes (Exhibit 7). We've seen that the fantastic stories told by the Germans about Attila's death are of great antiquity. But we also have some very early references to murder in various historical accounts that may ultimately be dependent on the testimony of Priscus. The most notable of these is the *Chronicle* of Marcellinus Comes, which is dated to the early sixth century. Here Marcellinus claims that a woman stabbed Attila "at the instigation of Aetius." This last part may be spurious—the product of textual corruption—but the suspicions that Attila was murdered and that Aetius was involved cannot be dismissed so easily. The often unreliable Malalas gives additional witness to the antiquity of the murder rumor. Possible hints of an unnatural death can also be found in the brief notices of other early historians, such as Isidore and Hydatius, though no other early author is so specific and credible in his claims as Marcellinus.

But shouldn't we dismiss the murder story as a base rumor? Priscus, after all, was an objective and reliable eyewitness historian and he doesn't mention anything about murder. Well, actually he *does*, though indirectly;

but before we get to that we should remember that Priscus was not an objective narrator at all but a government employee who was skeptical, inquisitive, self-serving, and rhetorical (Exhibit 2). As we follow his eyewitness narrative—a narrative so beguiling in its candor and specificity—we begin to realize that Priscus is not always trustworthy. We must constantly reconstruct the circumstances behind everything he tells us, deconstructing the motives, isolating the filters of memory, and parsing out the narrative gimmicks. He was also a historian in the ancient Greek tradition, which means that he was constantly looking for explanations, trying to link up causes with effects. He brought a finely tuned skepticism to this task, a skepticism that had been sharpened in part by the deceptions that he himself had witnessed. When we match his skepticism with our own, we realize that Priscus must have known more and must have written more about Attila's death than what has survived in the fragments of his history.

It can be shown through a philological analysis of Jordanes's text that Priscus must have originally written a second account of Attila's death in which the Hun died violently (Exhibit 4). This second account was suppressed as the text was adapted and abbreviated by Jordanes. Still, there are hints in what remains of what was originally recorded. Jordanes records that Bleda died treacherously (killed by his brother, Attila), and that "by the balance of justice" Attila later would receive "the hideous consequences" of his action. But Jordanes never follows through on this claim, which suggests that the alternative account was edited out from the original text that Priscus had written.

In this second account, Attila's death must have been linked to Bleda's treacherous death in 445 (Exhibit 3). The evidence shows that Bleda, the older brother, was the first in command and that the two brothers had severe disagreements about foreign policy. We catch a few scattered rumblings of dissent among the Huns, most notably in the stories of noble fugitives such as Mama and Atakam. The "chosen men," or *logades*, who surrounded Attila were drawn from different backgrounds—Hunnish, Roman, and Gothic; the political grievances they had with one another, and even with Attila, were kept in check through the exercise of autocratic power. A deadly hatred, though, had been kindled by the murder of Bleda. Someone in the inner circle was waiting for the right time to avenge Bleda's death.

That someone was Edecon. We see him first in 449 when he is bribed by the Eastern eunuch Chrysaphius to join in a plot to assassinate Attila. This failed assassination plot provides the blueprint for understanding what would happen four years later when Attila died (Exhibit 9). Priscus reconstructs in minute detail how the plot was hatched during a diplomatic mission to Constantinople and why it ultimately failed. The evidence clearly shows that Edecon's initial commitment to the plot was genuine, which leads us to conclude that if he could betray Attila once, then he could betray him again. Why did Edecon agree in 449 to assassinate Attila? And, more importantly, why would he conspire again in 453 to carry out the deed? The odd little saga of Zerko, the Moorish dwarf, provides some unexpected evidence that Attila's death, in part, was a revenge killing (Exhibit 6). Zerko was captured from Aspar's forces in the Balkans in the early 440s, after which he belonged to Bleda. Attila didn't want Zerko around after Bleda's death and so he packed him off to Aetius. Aetius didn't want him either and so he returned him to Aspar in Constantinople. While in Constantinople on a diplomatic mission, Edecon told Zerko that he would intervene with Attila on the dwarf's behalf if he wanted to return to Pannonia. Edecon's interest in Zerko is best explained not as a humane expression of compassion but as loyalty to their mutual benefactor, Bleda. That loyalty would lead Edecon to avenge Bleda's death.

The accession of Marcian in 450 marked a turning point in the Empire's relations with Attila. The new emperor had several interlocking motives—financial, military, and religious—for plotting Attila's death (Exhibit 10). Marcian was a resolute, battle-hardened soldier; he was a strategic thinker who was able to calculate the tangible benefits of a policy, project its costs and benefits, and then fashion the means to implement it. Within a year of taking office, Marcian had shut off the cash flow out of the treasury and personally commanded troops against the Huns. Of course, he was risking war—and he knew it—but it was a risk worth taking. One of Marcian's main domestic goals (a stable fiscal policy) could be more easily achieved if gold weren't constantly being drained from the treasury and sent north. Attila's death would remove even the risk of war. Marcian's new advisors, Maximin and Priscus, briefed him extensively about Attila, the inner workings of his court, and the contacts that Aetius maintained within Attila's retinue. No doubt Marcian began plotting Attila's death from the early months of his reign.

Marcian's religious motivations were equally strong. The letters flowing back and forth between Marcian and Pope Leo reveal a pattern of thinking in the late Roman Empire in which the defense of the Church was explicitly equated with the defense of the Empire (Exhibit 11). Marcian took this challenge seriously and would become known as the Second Constantine. He earned his reputation by convening and presiding over the Council of Chalcedon as well as defending the Christian Empire from external threats. Furthermore, Marcian seems to have been an active promoter of his own reputation, no doubt sponsoring the various biographical legends that conferred upon him a divine mandate to lead and conquer. Marcian saw it as his destiny, his calling, to defeat the enemies of the Empire. The stories told about Marcian were shaped by these values—and so were the stories told about Attila's death.

Marcian would need an ally in the West if any plan were to succeed against Attila. He would find that ally in Aetius (Exhibit 12). The Hunnish invasion of Gaul in 451 and Italy in 452 completely changed the political dynamics of the late Roman world and made it clear that Attila was no longer a threat just to the Eastern Empire. Aetius had always pursued a policy of balancing one power against another; until the invasion of Gaul he had no intention of seeking Attila's death. But with his own political future seemingly assured, Aetius saw Attila as a threat to the Empire he hoped his son would someday rule. Protected (as he wrongly thought) by his son's betrothal to Valentinian's daughter, and by a private back-channel alliance with Marcian, Aetius was now free to move against Attila.

Evidence of an alliance between Marcian and Aetius can be seen in the events that unfolded in Italy (Exhibit 14). The relationship dates back to the beginning of Marcian's reign in 450. Priscus records that he and Maximin were in Rome in 450, probably soon after Marcian's accession, and they probably met with Aetius at this time. Maximin and Priscus were now both working directly for Marcian, having been promoted within the bureaucracy after the death of Theodosius. As Marcian's close advisor, Maximin was well positioned to inform the emperor of the complex relationship that Aetius had maintained with Attila's inner circle. Specifically, they could have told Marcian how Aetius provided Roman secretaries to the barbarian king and how Aetius was well connected to one of Attila's top advisors, Orestes. Marcian would have recognized the unique leverage that Aetius had with members of Attila's inner circle; he secured the cooperation of Aetius right from the start as part of his policy to keep Attila in check.

With limited military resources to defend Rome, Aetius conspired with Attila's Roman advisors to persuade the Huns to withdraw from Italy (Exhibit 15). Attila was apparently convinced to withdraw from Rome not just by Leo, and not just by a malaria epidemic, but by his Roman advisors, Orestes and Constantius. They reminded Attila of what had happened to Alaric the Visigoth when he sacked Rome in 410: he died several months later of natural causes. Were these Roman advisors thinking of Attila's or Rome's interests when they urged him to retreat? At this point, there already existed a secret security agreement between Marcian and Aetius—one that guaranteed help for Marcian against the Huns and help for Aetius in his political maneuvering in Italy. Aetius was the classic Roman conspirator. It's likely that Aetius had struck a deal with his contacts inside Attila's court even before the Huns had left Italy for home.

Edecon and Orestes, the once and future enemies, were now working together, though for different reasons. Edecon would seek Attila's death as payback for the crime against Bleda. Orestes, the Roman, would be helping to save Rome and assure his own political future. Attila had been significantly weakened by his back-to-back adventures in the Western Empire and was now politically vulnerable (Exhibit 16). There had been heavy losses in Gaul; plague had claimed many more in Italy. By the end of 452, the Gothic tribes that Attila had led to disaster must have been chafing under his leadership. Within weeks of returning home to Pannonia, Attila took another bride, a Gothic princess. The fact that her name, Ildico, is preserved in the historical record suggests the importance of her family. Attila was trying to shore up his political base through a strategic marriage. The wedding would provide the ideal cover for poisoning Attila; and, even though suspicions would naturally point to the young woman, she would be protected.

The chieftain who took a young bride that night in early 453 was very different from the drunken, partying sot we see in the official account. The one time we get a glimpse of Attila at a feast—the diplomatic feast that Priscus attended—we see a man who is a model of sobriety and self-control (Exhibit 5). He was not a chronic alcoholic who might have died from esophageal varices. But he could have been poisoned, sip by sip, during the kind of ceremonial toasts that Priscus witnessed at the banquet he attended in 449. Edecon and Orestes controlled the bodyguards; it would have been an easy thing to bribe the cupbearers and usher out the guests so that Attila could die on the wedding bed unattended by all but his new bride.

In the end, a theory should be tested by whether it answers more questions than it raises. When we place this new theory over these old events and use it as an interpretive grid, we can explain some of the unexplained oddities of texts and events. We can explain why Jordanes contradicts himself by promising one thing and delivering another. We can explain why the official account reads a lot like an ecclesiastical homily and why it protests so loudly about the circumstances of Attila's death. We can explain the curious events in Italy—why Attila suddenly left at the urging of his advisors. (In particular, the story about "the curse of Alaric" begins to look like a preemptive attempt to control the "spin" after Attila's death.) We can explain why Attila died within a narrow window of opportunity: after withdrawing from Italy and before invading the East. We can explain Marcian's dream about the broken bow. We can also explain the curious reappearance some twenty years later of Edecon and Orestes—or, more accurately, the appearance of their sons in the final drama of the Western Empire that played out in 476.

EIGHT

A CONSPIRACY OF SILENCE

A dictionary of Attila's language would contain a single word, *strava*.[229] That's the word Jordanes gives us in his detailed account of the funeral held for Attila. We read that the body was taken out onto the plains where it lay in state beneath a silken tent. Men plucked out their hair and cut their faces with swords. While servants prepared the burial mound, skilled horsemen rode around the tent "in the manner of a circus," which probably refers to ceremonial horse races of some kind. And then a *strava* was celebrated over the body, though we don't know specifically what the word is meant to describe. Is it a feast? Does it refer to the pyre itself? Philologists have flocked around this single specimen for generations, like nineteenth-century naturalists observing some exotic insect brought back from the jungle. Despite all the attention it's received, nothing certain can be claimed for the word. We don't even know if it's Hunnic. Jakob Grimm thought it was a Gothic word that could be reconstructed from the verb *straujan*, the same root that, in English, gives us the verb "to strew." What strewing has to do with burial has never been satisfactorily explained. Others have sought to construe the word as Turkish or Slavic. Our imaginary dictionary, then, would list many possibilities under its one and only entry, but nothing *definitive*.

Whatever a *strava* was, it was "celebrated over Attila's tomb with great reveling." Over the body, too, was sung a funeral hymn that has come down to us through a line of transmission as tortured as Busbecq's lexicon.[230] It's always been assumed that the poem was originally sung in Hunnic, and then recited to Priscus by a Gothic informant, translated by Priscus into Greek, and preserved by Jordanes in Latin. Here's how it reads in English:[231]

> *The chief of the Huns, King Attila,*
> *born of his father Mundiuch,*
> *lord of the bravest tribes,*
> *sole possessor of the Scythian and German realms—*
> *something never before seen—*
> *captured cities and terrified both empires of the Roman world,*
> *and, appeased by their prayers,*
> *took an annual tribute to save the rest from plunder.*
> *And when he had accomplished all this by the favor of fortune,*
> *he fell not by wound of the foe,*
> *nor by the treachery of his friends,*
> *but in the midst of his people at peace,*
> *happy in his joy and with no sense of pain.*
> *Who can even call this a death,*
> *when no one believes it calls for vengeance?*

Amédée Thierry, the French historian whom we encountered in the last chapter, felt that these lines were teeming with ulterior motives. Great pains had been taken to explain the death, and that was evidence, he believed, of a plot involving several of Attila's officers. The funeral hymn was a key element in the cover-up and was "destined to become the official version of the event." We can hear denials couched within the boasting lines—"a noticeable affectation," as Thierry calls it, "the declaration of a natural death that requires no vengeance." There must have been a political motive behind these words, a need "to dispel some vague accusations among the Hunnish vassals."[232] As far as hunches go, this is a pretty good one in light of the political instability that followed the death of Attila.

It's quite remarkable that a Goth should walk into Constantinople and recite a poem like this word for word. The poem, like the death account, is simply too detailed to be believed. The claim that "no wound" was found on his body is a suspicious echo of the death account; this alone should make us wonder if the funeral hymn were actually composed in Constantinople, not improvised on the plains of Hungary. For all his inquisitiveness, Priscus was not a philologist like Grimm or a Renaissance collector like Busbecq whom we can picture scouring the marketplace for scraps of Hunnic or Gothic poetry. Our Greek historian was a propagandist. The funeral hymn is the death account rendered into verse for distribution among the barbarians. If there's one thing the Germans knew, it was revenge. Their poetry testifies to that. But not to worry: "Who can even call this a death," the poem asks, "when no one believes it calls for vengeance?"

We had earlier discovered that Priscus must have written a second account, one that specifically ties Attila's death to Bleda's murder. It's a little hard to imagine how the violent story of murder could sit side by side with the ecclesiastical exemplum and the funeral hymn. The one account completely undercuts the other. That's a problem we'll tackle when we come back to the conspiracy of silence that has kept the plot hidden, like Attila's grave, over the centuries.

By nightfall the burial mound had been prepared. Attila's body was removed from the tent, placed in the mound, and his casket was covered with gold, silver, and iron. Weapons and the treasures looted during his conquests were placed beside the body. Finally, the servants who had prepared the mound were slain and buried with their chieftain so that the final resting place would forever be concealed. "And so it has remained until this day," is what most histories say next. But that's not entirely true. Every twenty years or so, Attila's grave gets discovered, usually in Hungary, but sometimes in the former Yugoslavia, Slovakia, Germany, or even the Ukraine.

One of the most recent "discoveries" came in 1975, in a sugar-beet field in northern Yugoslavia, where engineers working on a dam project unearthed some human bones, shards of burial urns, and other ancient artifacts.[233] It was believed to be an early Hun settlement from the late Roman period. Laszlo Szekeres, the archaeologist who took charge of the excavation, made a claim sensational enough to be picked up by *The New York Times*: even the grave of Attila the Hun might be found, he said. The archaeological finds extended over two miles, indicating a significant settlement from the early centuries of the Christian era; but it was the site's proximity to the Tisza River (a breeding ground for burial legends) that made everybody think that Attila might be buried nearby.

It seems that 1975 was an especially productive year for finding Attila. Only a few months earlier, Yugoslavian archaeologists had reported that remote sensors had detected a suspicious object inside a small hill outside the Yugoslavian village of Martonos—an object "which could possibly be the fabled coffin of Attila."[234] Using a proton magnetometer, scientists detected what they thought was a large iron object, some ten feet by ten feet, buried twenty-five feet inside the mound. Nothing came of it. The scene has been repeated many times since 1874, when newspapers in Vienna reported in a matter-of-fact way that the triple sarcophagus of Attila had been found by fishermen in the Tisza River. The dispatch from the Austro-Hungarian capital was very precise: "On striking with poles, a ringing sound was produced resembling that of brass. The length and width of the object discovered suggests the idea of a coffin."[235] Such stories, referred to as fishermen's stories by one scholar, seem to have been quite common in the late nineteenth century around the Tisza River in southern Hungary and northern Yugoslavia.[236] To this day these stories are passed down as part of the lore of the region.

Some of these "discoveries" are rooted in actual archaeological finds; many, however, spring from local legend and the credulity of the public. In March 1955, in the German town of Niederrimsingen, a bulldozer excavating in the cliffs along the Rhine exposed a rectangular block of limestone roughly the shape of a coffin.[237] What the workmen jokingly called "Attila's tomb" was a trick of nature, like the "face" on Mars or the skull we know as Golgotha. The local newspaper reported the discovery of Attila's tomb in its April Fool's edition, and the public immediately embraced the account as fact. Even after the truth had been revealed, and the immediate flux of tourists, schoolchildren, and amateur archaeologists had subsided, the city continued to embrace the myth wholeheartedly. An enormous sculpted bust of Attila the Hun stands today in the center of the town—a comically ambiguous commemoration. Is it a monument to an important figure in Western history and lore? Or is it a monument to tomfoolery and gullibility?

OPEN FOR BUSINESS

As I'm writing these words, 1,552 years have elapsed since Attila the Hun was buried somewhere on the great Hungarian Plain. Halley's Comet has come and gone twenty times since it blazed above the fields of Châlons, and Attila's hold on the Western imagination hasn't waned much at all. In memory, at least, Attila has been a survivor. He outlived his role in ecclesiastical literature as the Scourge of God. He outlived the legends of the Middle Ages and the tragic plays of the Renaissance. He's even survived, in recent times, a handful of movie portrayals so bad they'd kill anyone's career. You have this kind of staying power only when you've become an icon.

And that leads us to a paradox. Given his enormous reputation, you would think Attila affected the course of history much more than he did. You would think that the crumbling Western Empire would have received a boost from his death. But it didn't happen that way. The Western Empire had been dying, in slow motion, for a long time. Edward Gibbon even went so far as to claim that "if all the Barbarian conquerors had been annihilated in the same hour, their total destruction would not have restored the empire of the West."[238] When Attila died, the fools in Rome and Ravenna might actually have believed that the Empire could yet be salvaged. Attila's death—or rather his *murder*—was a desperate effort to change the inevitable direction of history; but the Western Empire was so preoccupied by its own considerable problems, such as the ongoing power struggle between Valentinian and Aetius, that the happy event was hardly noticed. This is suggested by the odd fact that the chronicles in the West barely mentioned it, relegating it to a terse sentence, *"Attila occiditur,"* "Attila died."

Of course, the level of interest was much higher in the East, where a new round of slashing and burning was expected by spring. The timely death of Attila was a factor, if only a small one, in the survival of the Eastern Empire. Marcian got exactly what he was aiming for, and the Eastern Empire lasted for another thousand years. Ironically, though, Attila's death provoked the opposite effect in the West, hastening the collapse of Roman rule. That's largely because Aetius was far less successful than Marcian in making his transition to the post-Attila world. Within a year he would be murdered himself, stabbed by a suspicious and ungrateful emperor who now viewed him as expendable. Aetius had held the West together for over two decades; if he had lived, and if he'd been able to guide his son Gaudentius to the throne, perhaps Rome might have survived to see another century.

The Empire's borders had been shrinking for decades. The provinces had been divvied up one by one. Pannonia had gone to the Huns, Britain to the Saxons, Gaul and Spain to the Visigoths, and North Africa to the Vandals. Gradual encroachments had turned into full-scale invasions by the fifth century. Rome tried to curry favor with barbarian chieftains by doling out imperial titles and pretending that tribute money was a salary paid for services rendered to the state. The legions of Rome were no longer an effective defense, and so the Empire fielded armies that were less and less Roman as though there would never come a time when those armies would refuse to fight for the ancient imperative. The Roman capital itself was not naturally well defended. But then, for most of Rome's history it didn't have to be, since no enemy could possibly set foot in Italy, let alone approach the walls of the city. But during the fifth century, Rome might as well have

THE DAY ROME DIED

When Aetius walked into the palace that day in 454, all the great battles of his life were behind him. He had struggled with the imperial house, dueled the greatest Roman generals, and defeated the Empire's fiercest enemies. Sometimes he had been on the wrong side and sometimes on the right, but he had always survived. Now Aetius, the man of war, walked into the emperor's chamber to discuss—what was it?—either tax policy and the financial health of the Empire or the planned marriage of his son to Valentinian's daughter. But Valentinian wasn't listening; his fingers were twitching by the sword at his side. Our main source for the story is the seventh-century Byzantine writer, John of Antioch. No doubt John relied on earlier accounts that are now lost (Priscus perhaps?); obviously, what we'd like is much more information about this richly motivated event—the assassination of Flavius Aetius, the last of the Romans.

Some never forgot or forgave Aetius for appearing first in Italy as the leader of sixty thousand Huns. Even after saving the West at Châlons and arranging Attila's withdrawal from Rome, Aetius was still the dangerous outsider. His power had always come from beyond the senatorial and imperial classes, from the barbarian armies Rome loathed but needed. More than anyone else, Aetius knew he'd have to reinvent himself one last time if he were to survive; he would have to become, of all things, a court insider. That's what the marriage deal with Valentinian was all about. His son, Gaudentius, was to marry Valentinian's daughter and the Theodosian House would survive for another generation. It sounded good to Aetius and Galla Placidia, but it threatened a lot of vested interests. Valentinian feared for his own throne. His chief advisor, a eunuch named Heraclius, feared the fate of Chrysaphius. And then there was a sixty-year-old senator named Petronius Maximus, who should have been content to be well respected and filthy rich, but who threw it all away on a scheme to become emperor himself. The senator Maximus and the eunuch Heraclius teamed up and together they convinced Valentinian that Aetius was plotting to kill him and seize the throne.

posted a big sign in German along the northern highways reading Open for Business.

There were a few men—precious few—in the fifth century who saw clearly what was coming. St. Augustine was one of those. He died a generation before Rome's official "fall," but not before he had been able to take the measure of what was happening. The sack of Rome in 410 convinced him that an epoch was passing. Inspired to write *The City of God*, Augustine placed current events within the cosmic framework of Christian theology and drew out the trend lines: the City of Man must give way to the City of God. The Romans had always seen themselves as a people of destiny with a divine mandate to conquer and rule. Augustine turned the Roman hubris on its head and claimed that Rome was destined no longer to reign but to fall into ruin. Even the Eternal City must bow to the counsels of God.

St. Jerome's response to the sack of Rome in 410 was just as profound and grave: "My voice sticks in my throat; and, as I dictate, sobs choke my utterance. The City which had taken the whole world was itself taken."[239] But for the Roman aristocracy in the palaces and villas of Italy, the "Fall of Rome" hadn't even crossed their minds as a relevant category of thought. There's a wonderful little story that captures the trivial preoccupations of the ruling class during this time. (Gibbon relegates it to a footnote since it's pulled from the fertile imagination of Procopius, the often unreliable historian of the sixth century.) Emperor Honorius was in his palace in Ravenna when Alaric sacked Rome. The emperor's chamberlain came running to tell him the terrible news.

"You say Rome has perished?" Honorius cried. "Not quite an hour ago she was eating from my hand!"

"No," the chamberlain said. "Not your pet chicken. The *city* Rome, the *city* has perished."

"Thank God! I thought I'd lost my little bird!"

The story is apocryphal, but like all good myths it comes loaded with truth. Lulled into a stupor by centuries of security, Rome's upper classes were unable to fathom the predicament they were in. Indifference to calamity was something of a stoic Roman attribute to be sure, a learned behavior that was now an anachronism. Back in olden times, one *could* be indifferent to the occasional setback when the great idée fixe of Roman civilization—the destiny of Aeneas—was confirmed by Roman victory. Rome had not really fought for her survival since the days of Hannibal, over six hundred years before. The Roman nobility had forgotten how to feel desperate and how to act properly, like Romans, in desperate times. Instead, they were blinded by their own history and the myth of their invincibility.[240] Alaric's sack of Rome, or the Gothic defeat of the Roman army in 378, might have been the proverbial wake-up call. But still the giant slumbered, dreaming the same imperial dreams of manifest destiny that Virgil had first sung about during the reign of Caesar Augustus. The dreaming is all too apparent in that last pathetic scene that played itself out in 476, when the young and preposterously named Romulus Augustulus was deposed by a barbarian chieftain. Romulus? Little Augustus? Distant—and mocking—memories of Rome's glorious past.

Edward Gibbon is usually credited with popularizing the idea that Rome "fell" in 476. He didn't pull that date out of a hat; Gibbon's was the judgment of ancient historians as well. Writing not quite a generation after the event, Marcellinus Comes explains the significance of the date with mathematical precision:

> *Thus the Western Empire of the Roman race,* which Octavianus Augustus, the first of the Augusti, began to govern in the seven hundred and ninth year from the founding of the city, *perished with this Augustulus* in the five hundred and twenty-second year from the beginning of the rule of his predecessors and those before them, *and from this time onward kings of the Goths held Rome and Italy.*

Still, historians continue to ask if Rome really fell or if it merely evolved into something different. The most ambitious challenge to Gibbon came in the 1930s from a Belgian historian, Henri Pirenne, who claimed that the ancient world didn't really come to an end until the rise of Islam in the seventh

and eighth centuries.[241] But regardless of how we negotiate the ambiguities, hindsight clearly shows that the world in which Attila lived and died was undergoing a major transition. Priscus might have been among the few who understood this as he journeyed down the Nile in 452 past pyramids and desert monasteries. The ancient world and its classical ideals were disintegrating, and the medieval world, governed by the dogmas of the Church, was being built in its place.

In the late nineteenth century, Thomas Hodgkin opted for the grandest explanation of all for why Rome fell—this after 1 million words and eight volumes. Hodgkin's view, boldly if quaintly stated (from a modern perspective), is that Rome fell because God willed it.[242] It's a refreshing take on the old problem, especially in our day of increasingly narrow microhistories that attempt to slice out a piece of the past thin enough to be analyzed scientifically—say, the role of malaria or lead poisoning in Rome's decline. What historians are far less prone to offer nowadays is a broadly articulated thesis beginning with the phrase "Rome fell because." These new histories scale down the challenges to something "manageable," thereby implying rather optimistically that the historical method can indeed recover the past; but this abandonment of grand theories also signals, paradoxically, a kind of historical agnosticism about ultimate answers. Hodgkin had no such misgivings. He appealed to a higher authority, like Augustine before him. And though Hodgkin's explanation may seem at first glance to be a throwback to Augustine, it's also quite compatible with postmodern skepticism. Who, after all, can know the mind of God?

The problem is intractable, so much so that one is tempted to throw the date 476 out altogether. I'm with Gibbon on this one, though, and I think that Marcellinus Comes got it essentially right. Something significant *did* happen in 476—a legal transaction of sorts whereby the government passed from Roman to German hands. One could argue, however, that Rome had already died a few years before, on a crisp day in late September 454, and that Attila's death had more than a little to do with it.

It wasn't too difficult to convince Valentinian. His whole life had been lived under someone else's shadow, and he saw this as an opportunity to declare his independence.

While Aetius was presenting his case, whatever case that was, Valentinian suddenly jumped up from his seat and shouted that he would no longer be abused by the general's treacheries. Aetius was to blame for all his personal problems and, for that matter, all the problems of the Empire. A torrent of accusations followed, including the claim that "Aetius desired the power of the Western as well as of the Eastern Empire." Aetius was dumbfounded by the irrational outburst. The emperor had come unhinged, and all Aetius could think to do was speak reasonably and try to calm him down. He could not have expected Valentinian to pull his sword—a sword that had never once been wielded in battle. Heraclius, too, pulled a cleaver from his cloak and "both of them together directed their blows against the head of Aetius and killed him." Forensic psychiatrists might see evidence in this one detail—striking Aetius in the head—that the murder was not just a political calculation but a deep homicidal rage that expressed itself against the *person* and all he represented.

What did Valentinian mean when he accused Aetius of desiring the power of *both* the Western and Eastern Empires? John of Antioch was a Byzantine writer, and he may be placing these words in Valentinian's mouth so as to make the event more significant to his Eastern audience. On the other hand, Valentinian's accusation (whether historical or not) may reflect a trace memory of the political alliance between Aetius and Marcian, which resulted in the salvation of Italy in 452 and the assassination of Attila in 453.[243] Recall that Valentinian had praised Aetius in his *Novella* of June 29, 452, for his untiring civic devotion in the midst of crisis. Valentinian didn't *have* to write that, but he did, and it seems to indicate that the relationship between the two men had become practical, if not affectionate. Things quickly soured once Italy was saved and Attila was dead. The alliance between Aetius and Marcian, once revealed, could only strike the emperor as a disturbing development, especially when he recalled the decades of suspicion and animosity between the two courts.

Now the savior of the West lay dead in a pool of blood on the palace floor. Valentinian was apparently pleased with himself. He turned to a chamberlain, and said, "Wasn't that well done?" The chamberlain supposedly replied: "I'm not sure if you know it, but you've just cut off your right hand with your left." This remarkable exchange never happened, but it's true all the same. As with the emperor's chickens, the story is an interpretation of an event. The significance of what happened is acted out in the pithy exchange between a clueless emperor and a bold chamberlain who speaks with the voice of History. The chamberlain's judgment was echoed by Marcellinus Comes, who recorded in his *Chronicle* that "the western realm fell with Aetius and since then it has not had the strength to be revived."

A few months later, right around the Ides of March, 455, Valentinian went riding out to the Campus Martius, the Field of Mars, on the north side of Rome. A couple of things should have made Valentinian think twice about his leisurely afternoon. It *was* the Ides of March, after all, and you didn't have to be a scholar to think immediately of Julius Caesar. Valentinian was going to an unfriendly neighborhood, too, a field where the military hung out, a place where he'd be as vulnerable as Caesar on the Senate floor. The emperor dismounted with his bodyguards and began some archery practice. Two followers of Aetius were also in the field that day, barbarian soldiers named Optila and Thraustila. John of Antioch states that they had accompanied Valentinian and his bodyguards to the field, something that makes no sense at all. Are we to believe that the emperor was now surrounding himself with the general's aides less than six months after he had slaughtered Aetius? Not hardly. But Gibbon believes John, and he tries to wrench meaning from the improbable account: "Valentinian, who supposed that every human breast was devoid, like his own, of friendship and gratitude, had imprudently admitted among his guards several domestics and followers of Aetius."[244] Whether Valentinian was really that stupid or not is something we'll come back to in a moment.

As Valentinian drew back his bow, Optila lunged out and struck him on the side of the head. The emperor turned to see his attacker and he was struck a second time in the face. Thraustila drew his sword and felled Heraclius the eunuch. The emperor's bodyguards stood and watched the whole thing without breaking a sweat. As soon as Valentinian slumped to the ground in death, a swarm of bees appeared and sucked up his blood—a "divine sign," John of Antioch writes, though heaven knows what it meant. Optila and Thraustila scooped up the imperial diadem and ran straight to Petronius Maximus, who (John claims) had convinced them to assassinate the emperor. Valentinian had been the senator's target all along; Aetius had to be removed first so as to clear the path to Valentinian. Since "our information is dark and imperfect," to quote Gibbon, what we choose to believe about all this becomes a matter of personal judgment. We can all agree that the swarm of bees is definitely out; Gibbon, too, got that one right. But he's wrong about Optila and Thraustila and he completely misreads what John is up to. The barbarians needed no convincing by a Roman senator; their own code of tribal honor demanded that they avenge the death of Aetius. John is writing a story—a soap opera, actually, with a perverse and complex plot. The ambitious figure of Petronius Maximus, pathetically overreaching his destiny, ties everything together and explains the deaths of Aetius and Valentinian, the sack of Rome and its subsequent collapse.

Let's back up and see how John pulls this off. The months following Attila's death were calm times in the Roman capital. John tells us that Petronius Maximus used to drop by the palace to play checkers with the emperor. The old senator was flattered by the invitation, but Valentinian was only interested in his wife. When Maximus lost a game and didn't have the money to pay his bet, the emperor took his ring instead. Valentinian immediately sent the ring to the senator's wife, without his knowledge, and summoned her to dinner. When she came to the palace, she thought she was going to dine with her husband; but Valentinian intercepted her at the door—again without the knowledge of Maximus—and seduced her. After Valentinian had ravished the senator's wife, she came weeping out of the private chambers, met her husband, and cursed him as her betrayer. Maximus was humiliated and vowed from that day on to seek the emperor's destruction. Aetius stood in his way, however, and would have to be killed first.

Once Aetius was killed, Maximus began to plot the emperor's death. He found his opening when Valentinian received some of the general's followers (Optila and Thraustila) into his inner circle; and so the senator started to work on them. Presumably these Germanic warriors, for whom honor was everything, had to be persuaded to get off their lazy butts and avenge their leader. Since none of this is believable, let's approach it from a different perspective. It makes no sense that Valentinian would entrust his safety to the partisans of Aetius, so we must assume that what happened in the Campus Martius was a chance encounter. Optila and Thraustila may have heard that the emperor was coming to the fields that day, but they certainly hadn't accompanied him. For six months they had been waiting for an opportunity to avenge Aetius. But why does John claim that "Valentinian rode in the Campus Martius with a few bodyguards *and the followers of Optila and Thraustila*"? Because this is the only way he can stage the murder as a conspiracy that's traced back to Petronius Maximus. For some reason, John wants to hang everything around the senator's neck, including the Fall of the Roman Empire. If John can put the barbarians in Valentinian's court, then Maximus can conspire with them the same way he did with Heraclius the eunuch.

John is not finished telling his story. Petronius Maximus was proclaimed emperor and he immediately commanded Valentinian's widow, Eudoxia, to quit her mourning and become his new bride. (We're not told what happened to the senator's wife, since she's not useful to the story any longer.) Perhaps Maximus was trying to connect himself by marriage to the Theodosian House; perhaps he was trying to pay back the late emperor for the seduction of his wife. Distraught, Eudoxia did what her sister-in-law, Honoria, had done: she appealed to a barbarian chieftain for help, sending a messenger across the Mediterranean to Gaiseric the Vandal.[245] Petronius Maximus didn't live long enough to see how the disastrous chain of events played out. He always wanted to end his life as emperor. He got his wish.

He became emperor, and seventy days later, with the Vandal fleet bearing down on Rome, a mob ended his life. His body was ripped apart, publicly desecrated with no imperial burial, and thrown into the Tiber River.

Like the official account of Attila's death, John's story became authoritative not because it's true but because it survived. You can take the same basic set of facts and tell a completely different story. Valentinian needed no prodding to kill Aetius, and the soldiers certainly had motive enough to avenge their leader's death. Maximus was nothing but an opportunist. Everything was set in motion when Attila died, and not (as John would have it) when the senator lost a game of checkers. Years later, we catch a fleeting glimpse of Thraustila.[246] He survived and flourished as a general in the East. Instead of being punished as the murderer of Valentinian, he was given sanctuary as the avenger of Aetius. Marcian never formally responded to the death of Valentinian, his cousin by marriage. Perhaps Thraustila's success in the East can be interpreted as Marcian's response: "Good riddance to the man who destroyed Aetius, and with him, the Western Empire"—a rough paraphrase of Marcellinus Comes.

THE FINAL CURTAIN CALL

The bloated body of Petronius Maximus may have reached the Mediterranean seaport of Ostia just about the time Gaiseric the Vandal was setting foot on the docks. Ostia was Rome's outlet to the world. Located fifteen miles down the Tiber, this busy port was where the goods poured into Italy from all around the Empire: grain, glassware, leather, olive oil, perfumes, silk, spices, timber, and wine. But on June 2, 455, it was Vandal soldiers, not sacks of grain, that were being unloaded from the North African ships. Everyone in Rome knew that the barbarians were coming; but since it took only three or four days to sail from Carthage, there wasn't enough time to mount a credible defense. Emperor Maximus didn't even try. He issued an edict that gave the citizens of Rome "permission" to run for their lives. Which is what they did after ripping the emperor limb from limb and throwing his body in the river. As the Vandals advanced from the south, the roads leading north from the city were clogged for miles with wagons loaded down with treasure.

It was time for Leo's old magic. The pope came out to meet the invading army, just as he had done when Attila threatened three years before. But this time he had nothing going for him. Aetius was dead. There was no Eastern army waiting in the wings. The Vandals were healthy and well victualed. Peter and Paul didn't show up. Gaiseric, too, was very different from Attila. He was a Christian, though of the Arian variety, that persistent strain of heresy so entrenched among the Germanic tribes. Gaiseric wouldn't have seen Leo as a terrifying shaman, the way Attila must have, but as a Catholic with whom he had specific doctrinal and political differences. It's remarkable that Leo managed to extract any concessions at all from Gaiseric. The city would not be spared from plunder, but Gaiseric agreed not to destroy the buildings and not to torture or kill anyone to find out where they buried their treasure.

For fourteen days the Vandals picked the city clean. Despite their name and reputation, the Vandals were "methodical and leisurely" in how they approached the task.[247] The palaces and churches were emptied of their riches. Statues were lifted off pedestals, loaded onto barges, and taken down the Tiber to Ostia. The spectacular roof of the Temple of Jupiter Capitolinus— at least half of it—was pried off. This temple on the Capitoline Hill of Rome was one of the most remarkable buildings of the ancient world. Successive temples had stood on the hill since well before the time of Christ, but the final structure was completed by Emperor Domitian around A.D. 82. The doors were covered with gold and the roof was made of copper tiles also overlaid with gold. We don't know why Gaiseric took only half the tiles; perhaps the effort was too great for the amount of gold extracted. In the following century, the temple was still a marvelous sight, even after the Gothic conquest. But over the centuries it fell into complete ruin and became the foundation for a great Renaissance palace built by the Caffarelli family in 1584. By a curious irony, this palace built over the ruins of Jupiter's temple passed into Prussian hands in the nineteenth century and became the symbolic residence of the German emperor in Rome.

No inventory exists of what the Vandals crated up and packed into their galleys during those two weeks. But our curiosity is stoked a little by something Procopius tells us. Seventy-nine years after Gaiseric came and went, the Eastern Roman army commanded by General Belisarius finally defeated the Vandals in Africa. Belisarius walked into the palace of the great-grandson of Gaiseric with Procopius at his side. Procopius, who is described by Gibbon as a "fabulous writer for the events that precede his own memory,"[248] might at least be given some credit for the things he witnessed, such as this remarkable scene in Carthage. They opened the doors to storerooms brimming with silver talents, golden vessels, and jewelry studded with precious stones. They found ceremonial saddles and carriages made out of pure gold. The most intriguing find of all was the golden lampstand from Herod's Temple in Jerusalem and all the other sacred vessels that Titus had looted in A.D. 70 and carried through the streets of Rome in a triumphal parade. One can still see today how these artifacts were represented on the Arch of Titus, but the originals, it would seem, have been lost for good. Procopius tells us that they were taken back to Jerusalem, where they were placed in Christian churches for safekeeping. It was their fate, presumably, to be stolen one last time by a greedy crusader or a Turkish sultan.

One of the richest ships to leave Ostia during that fortnight of plunder was packed with Rome's finest statues. The ship was lost—the only one in the fleet to go down—and its priceless cargo now lies somewhere on the bottom of the Mediterranean Sea between Rome and Carthage, awaiting discovery. Human cargo was carried off as well—hundreds, perhaps thousands of Romans who were destined to lives of servitude in North Africa, where the genes of the Roman upper classes have been passed down in the populations of Libya, Tunisia, and Algeria. Among the nobility taken captive were Valentinian's widow, Eudoxia, her daughters Eudocia and Placidia, and Gaudentius, the son of Aetius. Priscus tells us that Marcian sent embassies to Gaiseric demanding, to no avail, that the royal family be released.

Eudoxia and her daughter Placidia languished for eight more years before they were sent to Constantinople; the other daughter, Eudocia, was given to Gaiseric's son in marriage. We don't know what happened to Gaudentius. If only Valentinian had allowed this son of Aetius to marry his daughter Placidia, then none of this might have happened.[249] When he lifted his sword in the palace that day, he brought down a terrible fate upon his family and his Empire.

We must be a little surprised when in this vast Empire everyone seems ultimately to know everyone else, something you might expect from a badly written play. Perhaps it's only the highly selective nature of our sources that makes it seem as though a handful of people keep running into each other. Orestes and Edecon are a particularly interesting example of this phenomenon. We see them first in 449, embroiled in the Chrysaphius Affair. We see them again—or, more accurately, their sons—at Rome's demise in 476. What accounts for the success of Orestes and Edecon in the quarter century following Attila's death? Is it just "a strange irony" that the sons of Edecon and Orestes should meet decisively as the curtain falls on the Western Empire?[250]

About 50 million people lived in the Empire at its height, but only a thin slice at the top were involved in affairs of state. Throughout the Empire's long history, the Roman aristocracy maintained this privileged position through wealth and marriage. But in the late Roman Empire another route to political power had opened up: military patronage. Henchmen, in particular, were well looked after. After Heraclian beheaded Stilicho in 408, he was rewarded with the governorship of Africa. Thraustila was one of the assassins of Valentinian and he shows up later as a general in the Eastern army. Orestes, too, went on to a spectacular military career in the Western Empire. Like his patron, Aetius, Orestes knew the ways of the barbarians; he could speak their language, and this intimate knowledge would become his secret weapon as he rose rapidly through the ranks of a military that was increasingly German. Eventually, Orestes achieved the title master of soldiers and was powerful enough to depose Emperor Julius Nepos in 475. As a Roman, Orestes could have placed himself upon the throne, but he chose instead to promote his son, Romulus Augustulus, to the office.

It's hard to believe that this could be the same Orestes we first ran into in Sardica in 449.[251] Back then he was bitterly complaining like a child about the gifts he didn't get in Constantinople. He was petty, to be sure, but he was also ambitious—ambitious enough to set aside his rivalry with Edecon and go after the sweet commission that Aetius probably dangled in front of his face. Priscus might not have lived long enough to see the Fall of Rome, to see the fruit of all this irony; and that's a real pity, since Priscus, more than anyone, would have enjoyed the narrative closure that was so tragically Greek. Orestes reached the pinnacle of his power in 474 and 475. Interestingly, Priscus never once mentions that the lowly advisor skulking around the campfire in Thrace was the same master of soldiers who would someday depose a Roman emperor. From his silence, then, we might conclude that Priscus had already published his history and (perhaps) joined his old partner Maximin in death.[252]

Edecon is something more of a cipher.[253] He remained with the Huns after Attila died, having decided against the life of luxury that once looked so good to him back in the eunuch's chambers. But then, it was always revenge, not wealth, that he was really after. As the head of Attila's bodyguard units, Edecon was able to strengthen his position after the chieftain's death; and so he stayed on, even as the coalition of Germanic tribes broke apart. At the Battle of Nedao in 454 the Ostrogoths and other Germanic tribes defeated their Hunnish overlords and reasserted their independence. The Scirians under Edecon's control were among the only members of the old alliance to stick with the Huns through this and subsequent battles with the Ostrogoths. The last we hear of Edecon is when the Scirians were crushed near the Bolia River in 468. Edecon apparently perished in this battle, though his two sons survived.

One son, named Hunoulphus or Onulf, went east to Constantinople where he was welcomed as a mercenary; the other son, Odovacer, went west to Italy and rose through the ranks of the powerful kingmaker, the

German commander of the Roman army, Ricimer. By the time Orestes deposed Emperor Nepos in 475, Odovacer was already a force to be reckoned with in the Western army. Orestes made a fatal decision—and gave Odovacer his opening—when he replaced Nepos with his own son Romulus. "Little Augustus" is what the troops derisively called the boy-emperor, who was just a teenager. A rebellion began to brew in the ranks and Orestes quickly lost control of the army. Orestes was presented with a blunt demand: "Give us one-third of Italy as our just inheritance," the German troops demanded. After all, the Ostrogoths had Pannonia, the Visigoths had Gaul, and the Vandals had Africa. When Orestes refused to capitulate to the demand—an impossible demand, as Orestes knew, since it would mean the end of the Empire—Odovacer played the discontent to his advantage. If the troops would only follow *him*, then he would give them the land they desired.

On August 23, 476, Odovacer, the son of Edecon, was promoted by his troops to the position of commander. Five days later, Orestes was captured in central Italy and beheaded. Orestes's brother, Paulus, managed to hold Ravenna for a few days before the city was taken and he, too, was beheaded. The young emperor, however, was spared. Odovacer took pity on the youth—admiring his beauty, we're told—and sent him to live with his mother in a splendid villa near Naples.[254] Thus the Roman Empire expired with a whimper. The personal conflict between Orestes and Edecon, first witnessed by Priscus in Sardica, had culminated in the confrontation of their sons in 476. The feud between these two families was the Fall of Rome in miniature: the Roman giving up his throne to the German.

Attila's sons, too, pursued military careers, but these were far less noteworthy. Ernach, the "boy at the table," never lived up to his father's expectations. Though the oracles had prophesied his restoration of the Hun Empire, he died in obscurity and may even have become a mercenary in the Eastern army.[255] Another one of Attila's sons, Dengizech, had his father's temperament, but without the talent. He demanded land and money from Emperor Leo and treated Roman ambassadors with contempt. Leo judged rightly that

Dengizech was no great threat. Like his predecessor Marcian, Leo refused the Hun's demands. Dengizech invaded Thrace in 469 and was easily defeated. The head of Attila's son was brought back to Constantinople on a stick and was carried with great fanfare down the Mese, that broad avenue where Edecon had once walked when Attila's name meant terror.

VICTORIES OF THE PEN

Why is it that Marcian didn't own up to the plot and take credit for saving the Eastern Empire? We don't know that he didn't. We don't know, for example, that the dream of the broken bow isn't just that—an implicit claiming of credit. As always, we're completely at the mercy of what survives. What we have of documentary evidence is largely due to the accidents of history. Much of what survived into postclassical times was no doubt destroyed in 1453 when the Ottoman Turks overran Constantinople and burned its archives. But Marcian probably didn't claim credit for the assassination, nor did the histories record it. The ecclesiastical message would have been blunted, after all, if Attila's death turned out to be of human design.

Priscus *did* record a second account of Attila's death. This account probably didn't circulate during Marcian's reign, but it would have been found in the book Priscus published in the early 470s, shortly before his death. It is not at all surprising that multiple accounts of the same event should be found in one book; ancient histories often give alternative versions side by side. In the surviving fragments we have of Priscus, there are two different descriptions—one from Fragment 8 and one from Fragment 9—of Attila's wooden palace. These may have been written at different times, or placed in the narrative at different places, or quite possibly they may represent different drafts or editions of the book. The same must be true of what Priscus wrote about Attila's death. This is the only satisfactory way to explain the textual inconsistencies we uncovered back in Chapter Three—the unfulfilled "promise" that Attila's death would somehow be linked to Bleda's murder. This is also the best way to explain why some ancient historians, Marcellinus Comes and Malalas among them, deviate from the orthodox line and present more than one version of Attila's death, even though these accounts admittedly became colored by all kinds of fantastic poetic detail never found in Priscus.

The second account Priscus wrote surely implicated Edecon (as the avenger of Bleda) and may well have pointed to Aetius, too. Marcian was not listed among the conspirators, even though the propitious dream of the broken bow implies his participation. How do we account for the text as we now have it? Why was it necessary for Jordanes to expunge the violent details Priscus had written almost a century before? Once again, it all comes back to propaganda. Jordanes was a barbarian, a Goth, and he was employed in Constantinople by Justinian the Great. Around the time Jordanes was writing his *Gothic History*, Justinian was trying to recapture Italy, which had been in Germanic hands ever since Odovacer deposed Romulus in 476. Justinian's army was having a hard time of it. The Gothic king in Italy was a formidable opponent, a fierce warrior with a name that sounded oddly familiar: Totila. The parallel between *Totila*, king of the Goths, and *Attila*, king of the Huns, was obvious to all.[256] Attila's death had to be portrayed to the rebellious Goths as a divine retribution orchestrated by God's hand alone, not a political assassination. And his death had to be disgraceful: drunk and flat on his back. In this manner, Totila and the Goths were being sufficiently warned not to challenge Justinian's divine rule over Italy.

This is the old propaganda about Alaric all over again; and it's the same story that had been written about Attila's uncles, Rua and Octar. It's the message, too, of the ecclesiastical cover story told about Attila. If you challenge God's divinely appointed rulers, he will judge you and strike you dead. Ultimately, this is the message of all imperial histories. The barely human enemy must be confronted by all means necessary—by the power of the sword and the power of the pen. Rome's propaganda victories (what we call official history) have lasted far longer than her victories on the field.

And yet the battle rages on, since we'll never stop writing histories, no matter how familiar the material. We *can't* stop writing them, since we're convinced that voices long silent might still be heard, like ghosts on some distant battlefield.

EPILOGUE

ON January 26, 457, Marcian was walking in a procession toward the Hebdomon, seven miles outside the gates of Constantinople, when he became too ill to continue. He returned to the palace, where he died the next day. We know a lot about this procession; it was held every year to remember the great earthquake that struck Constantinople on January 26, 447, destroying the walls of the city just as Attila's Huns were advancing against the capital. Emperor Theodosius II had appeared in public with his feet bare—a sign of contrition and humility as he, along with the Senate and clergy, begged God to save their city. After sixty days of hard work, the walls were repaired and Attila turned his army away from the capital. The procession to the Hebdomon became an annual commemoration, one of the distant links that the Byzantine Empire maintained with its remote Roman past. We know from a tenth-century liturgical calendar that Byzantine emperors were still leading this procession five hundred years later.

Marcian was an old man, but he always insisted on walking the entire seven miles and handing out gifts along the route. But this time, in 457, he

The Column of Marcian is the only remaining monument in Istanbul (Constantinople) dating from Marcian's reign (450–57). Located in the Fatih District of the city, the column was originally topped by a statue of the emperor.
Frimart S.R.L. (Milano, Italy)

couldn't finish the walk. He lingered through the night and died the next day, January 27. Priscus recorded the details of his death; but once again, his original account is lost and we're at the mercy of those who plagiarized him in later years. That would include, unfortunately, the Monophysites in Egypt who hated Marcian's theology and did everything they could to defame him in death. One of the most venomous of these writers pictured Marcian "the Schismatic" hanging from a hook in hell.[257] (The Orthodox Church remembered him more fondly; he was canonized along with Pulcheria, and their feast on the liturgical calendar is February 17.) Other sources, drawn again from Priscus, speak of the acute inflammation that he suffered in his legs. It seems clear enough: Marcian couldn't finish the procession because he was suffering from an advanced case of gout. He was among that rare class of Roman emperors who died an ordinary death.[258]

In the Fatih District of Istanbul you can see the only remaining artifact, a single column, that's directly connected to the seven years of Marcian's reign. The Column of Marcian is the best preserved of the four honorific columns surviving in the city from Roman times. Tucked away in a private garden for centuries, the column was unknown to Western visitors until it was "redis-covered" in 1675. In 1908 the district was completely redesigned after a dev-astating fire, and the column has stood ever since in the center of a bustling neighborhood square. The statue that once stood atop the column has long since disappeared—the victim of an earthquake, or a windstorm, or the Crusades. But the inscription on the base can still be read: "Erected by the Prefect Tatianus in Honor of the Emperor." Turks have long credited the col-umn with the power of telling true virgins from false ones, which is entirely possible, considering who Marcian was married to.[259]

Once there were statues on every corner in Constantinople. We get some idea of all we've lost from an inventory of the city's monuments written down in the eighth century.[260] We're told, for example, that a statue of Mar-cian stood in the "Tribunal of the Palace," in the august company of Con-stantine's portrait and other imperial images. We learn as well that a statue of Marcian and Pulcheria once stood in the Theodosian porticoes where the public could honor their memory. None of these statues survives, which is a real shame considering that the images of so many lesser lights fill the world's museums. There is one possible portrait of Marcian, however—the colossal imperial statue in Barletta, Italy, which has been variously identified as a portrait of Valentinian I, Honorius, or Marcian. I'd like to think it's Marcian. Holding a cross in his outstretched right hand, the fifteen-foot statue represents a Christian emperor confidently leading the Empire for-ward. The statue ended up on the shores of Barletta when a ship that was re-turning from the 1204 sacking of Constantinople foundered on the Adriatic coast. The colossal figure lay on the shore for many years until it was finally fitted with new legs and mounted in its current location.

Marcian's body was interred in a porphyry sarcophagus in the Church of the Holy Apostles, one of the great churches of ancient Constantinople and the resting place of countless other Roman and Byzantine emperors. The Empire he defended from heretics and barbarians stood for a thousand years, through eighty-five more rulers. At some indeterminate point it had

Late imperial bronze statue, believed by some to represent Marcian, emperor in the East (450–57). The colossal statue (more than fifteen feet tall) has also been identified as Valentinian I and Honorius. It was brought from Constantinople around 1205 in a ship that foundered off the coast of Barletta, Italy. The statue lay abandoned on the beach for years until it was fitted with new legs and erected in the city square where it can be seen today.

Erich Lessing / Art Resource, NY

become the *Byzantine* Empire, but its roots were still Roman. Occupants of the sprawling palaces along the Bosporus still called themselves Caesar, just as Augustus had first done in 27 B.C.

That changed in 1453. Exactly one thousand years had passed since the night Attila died, one thousand years since Marcian dreamed of a broken bow in the sky. The Gate of St. Romanus was breached by the "infidels" on the night of May 29, and the Ottoman army swarmed through the ancient Theodosian Walls. The city that Marcian had loved and defended now succumbed to the Turks, a people who, like the Hungarians, proudly name their sons Attila. Mehmet the Conqueror converted churches into mosques, including the Church of the Holy Apostles, which was already falling into ruin. Remnants of the old church were recycled as building material, and a few original columns can still be seen today. The bones of the Second Constantine, Marcian, are probably strewn somewhere in the rubble beneath this impressive mosque where worshippers gather five times a day to pray to Mecca.

Two hundred yards south of the Fatih Mosque, the bare Column of Marcian stands with no statue on top and a simple inscription at the base. It's a silent witness, in a busy city square, to what time has almost managed to obliterate: the memory of a remarkable man whose single greatest accomplishment—the destruction of Attila the Hun—has never been acknowledged by history.

ENDNOTES

CHAPTER ONE

1 *"Regio funesta."* the phrase comes from the fifth-century poet Claudian.

2 "One scholar has even written." Arthur E. R. Boak in the "Foreword" to C. D. Gordon, *The Age of Attila* (1966), p. x.

3 The quote is found in the preface to Nietzsche's *Daybreak: Thoughts on the Prejudices of Morality*, translated by R. J. Hollingdale (1982). The emphasis has been added.

4 "Grandfather's furniture." Nietzsche's advice in a letter he wrote in 1869 to a young student. This is exactly what has happened to philology. In the early editions of the *Encyclopedia Britannica* (pre-1926), philology was defined as "the generally accepted comprehensive name for the study of the word or languages; it designates that branch of knowledge which deals with human speech, and with all that speech discloses as to the nature and history of man." That last phrase, especially, points us toward the rich cultural dimension of philological inquiry. In the 1926 edition, however, the definition was noticeably altered: "Philology: a term now rarely used but once applied to the study of language and literature. It survives in the titles of a few learned journals that date to the 19th century." (These observations are indebted to Jack Peradotto of SUNY at Buffalo, as found in an online discussion.)

5 *Indo-European* is a scholar's word for the ancient language spoken by the distant ancestors of a widespread group of people stretching from the British Isles to the Indian subcontinent. The Indo-European hypothesis was first suggested by Sir William Jones in the late eighteenth century as a way to account for the remarkable similarities between Sanskrit, the ancient religious language of India, and ancient Greek and Latin.

6 *"Ætla weold Hunum."* from the Old English poem *Widsith*, which lists the typical repertoire of an Anglo-Saxon poet.

7 "Attila was credited with founding Venice." a persistent legend that is treated seriously by Edward Gibbon among others. The claim was popular fare in Renaissance Italy (as in Machiavelli's *History of Florence*).

8 *Zeitschrift* (pl. *Zeitschriften*) is the German word for "academic journal." These journals are disintegrating faster than libraries can microfilm them; meanwhile, the medieval manuscripts whose knowledge these journals seek to preserve are getting along just fine with their nearly indestructible sheets of vellum parchment.

9 J. Moravcsik, "Attilas Tod in Geschichte und Sage," *Körösi Csoma Archivum* 2 (1926–32): 83–116. Also published in the same year and reaching many of the same conclusions about Attila's death was: Helmut de Boor, *Das Attilabild in Geschichte, Legende und heroischer Dichtung* (Bern 1932).

10 The biographical details are based on Moravcsik's own reminiscences as related to a friend and colleague. János Harmatta, "Byzantium and the Ancient Hungarians: The Life-Work of Gyula Moravcsik." In: *Mélanges à la mémoire de Gyula Moravcsik à l'occasion du centième anniversaire de sa naissance* (Szeged 1994).

11 One of the most important historical sources for the late Roman period and the early Germanic tribes. The standard Latin edition is by Theodor Mommsen (Berlin 1882); the standard English translation is by C.C. Mierow, *The Gothic History of Jordanes* (1915), which is in the public domain and is widely available online in full text. Throughout the book, my direct quotations from Jordanes come from Mierow's translation. The death account is found in ¶254.

12 Gibbon's history, a masterpiece of style, was published in six volumes between 1776 and 1788; Le Nain de Tillemont's history, which is *not* a masterpiece of style, was published in six volumes between 1670 and 1738.

13 Klaeber discusses Jordanes in his essay, "Attila's and Beowulf's Funeral," *Publication of the Modern Language Association* XLII (1927): 255–67. Biographical details are taken from the "Inventory of the Frederick Klaeber Papers" (University of Minnesota Archives), written by Carol O'Brien and revised by Karen Spilman.

14 "The history Priscus published": Scholars commonly refer to the "publishing" of ancient works, even for the centuries before Gutenberg invented printing. We don't know the title of this work by Priscus, so it will be consistently referred to in this generic manner. The dates given for Priscus, Cassiodorus, and Jordanes are round approximations. Priscus published his history sometime in the early 470s; Cassiodorus

*Read the "¶" symbol as "paragraph."

probably wrote his twelve-volume *Getica* between 519 and 533; the usual date given for the *Getica* of Jordanes is 551. Cassiodorus was an extremely important and versatile writer who served Theodoric the Great, the Ostrogothic king who ruled Italy in the immediate aftermath of the Roman era. Scholars have expended great effort on the problem of how these sources relate to one another; but very little of the argument presented in this book depends on whether or not something should be attributed to Jordanes in 551 or Cassiodorus in 526.

15 "His vivid paraphrase of Jordanes." found in Vol. 3, Ch. 35. Gibbon's *Decline and Fall* has been published in so many editions and is so widely available on the Internet that I cite all passages by volume and chapter only.

16 "Gibbon had personal reasons." Gibbon's *Memoir of His Life and Writings*, commonly referred to as his *Autobiography*, was first published in 1796.

17 "Will and Ariel Durant." Actually, Will Durant wrote the first six volumes by himself, after which he apparently needed help—history *is* a big subject. His wife Ariel joined him on Volume 6, which is entitled (ironically?) *The Age of Reason Begins*. The passage on Attila's death is quoted from Vol. 4, Ch. 2.

18 *The Heavenly City of the Eighteenth-Century Philosophers* (1932), p. 44. Becker acknowledges paraphrasing Voltaire ("History is after all a pack of tricks we play on the dead"), though Becker actually *means* it, whereas Voltaire was probably framing a witticism.

19 *Gothic History* ¶ 255.

20 "One of many flattering stories." The claim will be explored in Chapter 5.

21 *Attilas Tod*, p. 91.

CHAPTER TWO

22 The surviving fragments of the narrative history of Priscus are collected and translated in C. D. Gordon, *The Age of Attila: Fifth-Century Byzantium and the Barbarians* (Ann Arbor 1966). This extraordinary narrative is the main source of information for Chapters 2, 3, and 5.

23 The central texts about the very obscure Blemmyes are found in Stanley Burstein, ed., *Ancient African Civilizations: Kush and Axum* (Princeton 1998).

24 Information on the hieroglyphic and demotic texts at Philae can be found in Richard Parkinson, *Cracking Codes: The Rosetta Stone and Decipherment* (Berkeley 1999): 178–79.

25 On the datable evidence at the Temple of Isis at Philae, note Maenchen-Helfen, *The World of the Huns* (Berkeley 1973), p. 143, in which Maenchen-Helfen concludes that "the peace cannot have been concluded later than in October or November" of 452. This is significant in that this dating all but conclusively places Priscus in Egypt when Attila died.

26 "Ambrosius Aurelianus." My statement is a bit more dogmatic than the facts will allow. There are some chronological problems, though they're not insuperable; it does appear likely that the exploits of Ambrosius Aurelianus were at least *transferred* to whatever historical personage Arthur was.

27 "Hopelessly inept." Not a judgment shared by all historians. My view is based on the domination of his court by corrupt advisors, his management of the fiscal policy of the state, his waffling on ecclesiastical matters, and his consistent appeasement of the Huns.

28 Panium was located about 100 miles west of Constantinople along the Sea of Marmara.

29 Vol. 3, Ch. 34, note 42.

30 "Dull registers of doubtful facts." Aptly described as "laconic and artless chronicles" by Stewart Oost, *Galla Placidia Augusta: A Biographical Essay* (Chicago 1968): 20.

31 Some historians argue for 448, but I follow the dating promoted by E. A. Thompson, "The Camp of Attila," *Journal of Hellenic Studies* 65 (1945): 112–15; also in his *Attila and the Huns* (Oxford 1948).

32 The largest surviving fragment, the famous journey to Attila's court, was preserved in a work commissioned by the Byzantine emperor Constantine VII (913–959)—a compilation of extracts drawn from early histories that dealt with diplomatic missions.

33 Gibbon records the facts about Maximin's promotion: Vol. 3, Ch. 34, note 41.

34 Gibbon is cited from Vol. 3, Ch. 34, note 42. Hodgkin is cited from Vol. 2, Ch. 2 of *The Barbarian Invasions of the Roman Empire*. J. B. Bury (*History of the Later Roman Empire* [Dover edition, 1958]) adds the slight evidence that Priscus uses a word for "Greek" that may denote pagan affiliation: Vol. 2, p. 287n. More discussion can be found in R. C. Blockley, *The Fragmentary Classicising Historians of the Later Roman Empire* (Liverpool 1981); and J. Martindale, ed., *The Prosopography of the Later Roman Empire*, Vol. 2 (Cambridge 1980).

35 St. Jerome mentions Theotimus, the Goth, as a successful, or at least persistent, missionary to the Huns.

36 One of the best surveys of the early history of the Huns is found in Maenchen-Helfen, *The World of the Huns*. Maenchen-Helfen largely endorses the thesis, first proposed in the eighteenth century, that equates the Huns with the "Hsiung-nu" referred to in early Chinese chronicles.

37 Edward Gibbon's judgment was that Ammianus was "an accurate and faithful guide, who composed the history of his own times without indulging the prejudices and passions which usually affect the mind of a contemporary" (Vol. 2, Ch. 26). It is exactly his prejudices that are most on display in what he says about the Huns. A standard edition can be found in the Loeb Classical Library published by Harvard UP.

ENDNOTES

38 This description of the Huns is found in Jordanes ¶ 127.

39 The saying was analyzed by Archer Taylor, "Attila and Modern Riddles," *Journal of American Folklore* 56 (1943): 136–37. Gibbon also uses this expression in Vol. 3, Ch. 35.

40 "A respectable dinner." Priscus notes that the locals gave them sheep and cattle. These typical dishes, though not mentioned in Priscus, are suggested by a Roman cookbook of the first century, *De Re Coquinaria* by Marcus Gavius Apicius.

41 The anecdote is related in Jordanes ¶ 143.

42 Priscus had a low estimation of court eunuchs (see his depiction of Chrysaphius as discussed in Chapter 5). Priscus also writes: "Eunuchs are terrible in sewing up their hurts when the promise of gold lies before them. The race is insatiable and always open for gain, and there is nothing wicked accomplished within the palace without their evil influence." Gordon, *The Age of Attila*, p. 51. The attribution of this fragment to Priscus is uncertain, though plausible.

43 "Historians have seldom pointed out." We'll note an exception in Chapter 7: the nineteenth-century French historian Amédée Thierry.

CHAPTER THREE

44 The words Hitler wrote describing his experience in the museum could have been taken right out of Attila's mouth: "I knew that this was an important moment in my life. . . . I stood there quietly gazing upon it for several minutes, quite oblivious to the scene around me. It seemed to carry some hidden inner meaning which evaded me, a meaning which I felt I inwardly knew, yet could not bring to consciousness. . . . I felt as though I myself had held it in my hands before in some earlier century of history— that I myself had once claimed it as my talisman of power and held the destiny of the world in my hands. What sort of madness was this that was invading my mind and creating such turmoil in my breast?"

45 The fragments of Priscus are cited throughout from Gordon's translation in *The Age of Attila*.

46 The source is Socrates Scholasticus, available in the multi-volume *Nicene and Post-Nicene Fathers* (the full text is available online).

47 "His brother Octar had ruled jointly with him." This is a supposition, advocated by many historians. We know next to nothing about the political structures of the Huns. In addition to Mundiuch, there was a fourth brother, Oebarsius, who was still living in 449 when Priscus journeyed to Attila's court. He must have been considerably younger than his siblings, as he did not assume power after Rua died.

48 "Trading posts like this." These markets were ultimately closed down by Emperor Leo in 468, which "dealt a deadly blow at the continuance of Hun society in the form which it had reached under Attila." E. A. Thompson, *The Huns* (1996): 198–99.

49 This edict is discussed by Maenchen-Helfen, p. 110n.

50 One of Gibbon's many memorable phrases, which is frequently quoted: Vol. 3, Ch. 34.

51 See Gordon, *The Age of Attila*, p. 67.

52 The reference to "royal Scythians" who refused to serve in the war is found in Gordon, p. 67.

53 Amédée Thierry makes the logical point that Edecon revealed the conspiracy at this point when he went ahead of the rest of the party. *Histoire d'Attila et de ses successeurs* (Paris 1856), Vol. 1, p. 78.

54 Gibbon's judgment, based on the fact (as recorded by Priscus) that wood and stone were not plentiful in these parts.

55 This division of rulership is scholarly conjecture. See J. B. Bury: "We may *conjecture* that he [Bleda] ruled in the east . . . and Attila in the west" (Vol. 1, p. 275).

56 Bury's conclusion is widely held: "The indications are that Bleda was older than Attila" (Vol. 1, p. 272n).

57 The Latin title is *De Excidio Britanniae*. The history of Gildas (c. 516–570), which was published in the 540s, provides some of our only information on early Britain (including the life of Ambrosius Aurelianus). He was canonized by the Catholic Church.

58 "The Venerable Bede." The traditional appellation for Bede (c. 672–735), who published his *History* around 731.

59 "There *was* a change in policy." Oost speculates on this: "Since by 448 Attila was known, or thought, to be contemplating a reversal of his policy toward the Western Empire, the possibility suggests itself that the policy favoring the Western Empire may have been Bleda's primarily, and Attila, not long after his assumption of sole power, began to change this" (281–82).

60 This same sequence—*Bleda et Attila*, in the Latin—is found in a much earlier source, the *Chronicle* of Marcellinus Comes (early sixth century), as listed under the year 442.

61 "How much is later commentary?" Not to complicate this unnecessarily, but Cassiodorus (now lost) stands between Jordanes and Priscus, so there's really another set of questions that have to be asked in sorting all this out. When I speak of Jordanes cutting material about Bleda, etc., it might have been Cassiodorus before him who did this.

62 "Though Bleda was never completely forgotten." Evidence of this comes from the spelling of Bleda's name in the Old English translation of Bede's *Ecclesiastical History*. In this vernacular text Bleda's name is not given as it's found in the historical sources; instead we read *Blaedla*—a form of the name that shows that it had undergone continuous development as spoken in the mouths of Germanic poets over the centuries. The vowel sound in the name changed in concert with other natural linguistic changes in Anglo-Saxon. This means one simple thing to the philologist: The name Bleda was

not being reintroduced back into the text after centuries of obscurity. He had been re-membered all along as a fit subject of Germanic heroic poetry in his own right—something conceivable only if he had occupied an important role. A similar phenomenon can be demonstrated in the Old Icelandic and Middle High German stories about Attila, where Bleda survived (again, in the mouths of poets) as Budli and Blödelin respectively.

63 How can we be sure that this interpretation of Bleda's death goes back to Priscus and was not made up by Jordanes? How can we be sure it was not made up by Cassiodorus? We can see Priscus in the highly rhetorical nature of the passage. In particular, the use of *sententiae* (sententious, or moralizing, statements) is a hallmark of the Greek historian's style. See Babcock, *The Stories of Attila the Hun's Death: Narrative, Myth, and Meaning* (2001), pp. 41–43, where the argument is laid out in greater detail.

64 "*fraudibus*." For example, Jordanes writes that Amalaric "was ensnared by the *plots* of the Franks in early youth and lost at once his kingdom and his life." And, more significantly, after Attila's death his subjects sang an elegy at his funeral, assuring the world that the chieftain had fallen "not by wound of the foe, nor by the *treachery* of his friends, but in the midst of his nation at peace." And then the song ends with the ultimate spin job: "Who can even consider it death, when none believes it calls for vengeance?" It sure doesn't sound like the "balance of justice" that we were promised.

65 We can show more definitively in another passage that Jordanes falls victim to the very same editing glitch. In paragraph 58 of the *Gothic History*, Jordanes writes that "the Getae we have proved *in a previous passage* to be Goths, on the testimony of Orosius Paulus." At no point in the previous text, however, do we find what Jordanes is alluding to; that "previous passage" was edited out and he forgot to take out the later reference to the passage that no longer existed. This is what happened as well with his account of Attila's death.

66 About the only historian who believes that this interview took place as recorded is the British historian E. A. Thompson, whose Marxist leanings predisposed him to view favorably the social and political critique implicit in the passage.

67 The description of Constantius is found in fragment 23 of Olympiodorus. The quotation is taken from Gordon's translation (*The Age of Attila*), p. 38. This Constantius will reappear in Chapter 5 as the husband of Galla Placidia and father of Emperor Valentinian III.

68 Priscus identifies this messenger as Tatalus, the father of Orestes.

69 Discussed in great detail by Thompson, "The Camp of Attila," *Journal of Hellenic Studies* 65 (1945): 112–15.

70 The details about the Libyan campaign, including the fabulous story about Marcian,

are recorded by Procopius, *De bello Vandalico* III, iii, 35 (available in the Loeb Classical Library edition).

71 Thompson (*The Huns*) suggests that the story of the hovering eagle was "designed to explain his [Marcian's] policy of non-interference in Africa" (302n).

72 The passage from Prosper is discussed by Thompson, *The Huns*, p. 97 and 293n.

CHAPTER FOUR

73 The historical content of myth and legend has been superbly argued by G. Shoolbraid in *The Oral Epic of Siberia and Central Asia* (1997). Shoolbraid submits the following conclusions that bear directly on the method of Chapter 4: ". . . [T]raditional stories should not be inconsiderately rejected as a basis for a hypothesis" (2). "For all [their] drawbacks, ballads, folktales, and epics are, from a historical point of view at least, a valuable record of the social, moral, and spiritual consciousness of a nation" (4). "The modern scholar can be grateful for such historical germs and by careful linguistic, folkloristic, and archaeological analysis he can elicit these germs from the surrounding accretion of later material" (6). "So history may lie at the back of mythological epic, no matter how far-fetched the story may seem" (7).

74 Most of the tribal names that end in *i* in the Latin texts (the Heruli, the Sciri) are here consistently Anglicized (e.g., Herulians, Scirians), the one exception being the Alemanni.

75 "Great Migrations." The term *Völkerwanderung* was used primarily by Germanic philologists in the nineteenth century. It has fallen out of use, along with other terminology from that era that came loaded with a nationalistic ideology. In the context of nineteenth-century ideas, this term was seen to express the living vitality, the irrepressible dynamism of the Teutonic people. This idea in turn led to a political and military policy of the Nazis, *Lebensraum*, the notion that the German people needed "elbow room" on the continent. Most scholars today have simply abandoned the old term altogether in light of these unavoidable connotations, opting instead for more neutral terms, such as "the period of Migrations."

76 *Visigoths* literally means "good Goths" or "noble Goths" and *Ostrogoths* literally means "eastern Goths."

77 Numerous examples could be cited from late antiquity of the cultural intermingling of names. Note the extensive discussion of Attila's name (specifically on the problem of a Germanic name for a Hun) in Maenchen-Helfen, pp. 382–387.

78 Jordanes ¶ 58.

79 All the Germanic languages experienced umlaut, but modern German records these changes in vowel sounds as follows: ä, ö, ü. The type of umlaut I am illustrating is also called *i-mutation*.

80 Though Attila's name was largely fixed and stable in written texts, we see in Renaissance manuscripts a few orthographic conventions altering the form: Athila, for example, in the Hungarian Chronicles.

81 This account of Crimean Gothic is indebted to Jared Diamond, "Deaths of Languages," in *Natural History* (April 2001). Diamond notes that additional information comes from the work of linguist MacDonald Stearns, Jr., of UCLA.

82 We're wise to be skeptical since this information comes largely from Procopius. "Heruli" derives from a Germanic root *harjilaz* meaning "belonging to the marauders." The root survives in the archaic Modern English word "to harry."

83 The evidence for claiming that Edecon was a Scirian (that is, a German and not a Hun) is not conclusive, and a number of scholars reject the identification, believing that when Priscus wrote "Scythian," he meant to describe Edecon ethnologically.

84 "As I have said, *gepanta* means something slow and stolid, [and so] the word Gepids arose as a gratuitous name of reproach. I do not believe this is very far wrong, for they are slow of thought and too sluggish for quick movement of their bodies." Jordanes ¶ 95. Gepids formed the right flank of Attila's troops in the Battle of Châlons.

85 "Something that is like a genius for law." The phrase is attributed to F. W. Maitland, *The History of English Law* (1895).

86 Moravcsik is the primary advocate of this view.

87 The *Lex Burgundionum* (Laws of the Burgundians), which was compiled before 516, lists "Gundaharius" along with three of his predecessors; Latin chronicles record the Burgundian conflict in which Gundahar died.

88 "The poets dovetailed." Note what Shoolbraid writes about this tendency of epic poetry: "From the point of view of a 'primitive,' time is foreshortened, and the events of centuries ago are as one with those of recent times, for the events happened 'long ago,' in that indeterminate period before living memory. Thus events taking many years to work themselves out (as a long series of wars) may be telescoped into one major battle" (5).

89 Because of the energy of nineteenth-century Germanic philologists, we know more about the evolution of this poem than of any other great heroic epic (A. T. Hatto, trans., *Nibelungenlied*, Penguin edition, p. 370). Scholarly work on the *Nibelungenlied* formed the methodological foundation for philological reconstructions of medieval legends, just as Wulfila's Gothic New Testament is the foundation for the linguistic reconstruction of the Germanic languages.

90 Shoolbraid, once again, has stated this well: "Epics as such tend to embroider until any historical underlay is well hidden, and most examples of the traditional type are so overgrown with imaginative greenery that it is frequently impossible to believe that there has ever been a factual basis" (3–4).

91 "Strange non sequitur." A. T. Hatto in his translation of the *Nibelungenlied* (Penguin), p. 302.

92 I have not found this reconstruction suggested in any of the scholarship, though chances are some tireless philologist, say, in the 1860s tucked a similar thought into a footnote in one of those crumbling *Zeitschriften*. The Germans thought of everything at least once.

93 The "problem" of Etzel's survival is discussed further in Babcock, *The Stories of Attila the Hun's Death*, pp. 83–104.

94 These taut poems with their clipped lines became the basis of another Scandinavian account, the prose version found in the *Völsungasaga*, or "Saga of the Volsungs." Here Atli is described as "a fierce man and grim," responsible for the murder of his brothers—a telling detail that is echoed in the earlier Eddic poems and that may recall the historical traditions about Bleda's death.

95 The translated text is from Ursula Dronke, *The Poetic Edda* (Oxford 1969). The poetry is even more compressed, and the syntax is even more tortured, in the original Old Icelandic.

96 The history of Socrates Scholasticus can be found in translation in the multi-volume *Nicene and Post-Nicene Fathers* (which is in the public domain and available online).

97 John of Antioch is quoted from Gordon's translation, *The Age of Attila*, p. 28.

98 Vol. 7, Chs. 42 and 43 of the *Ecclesiastical History*, where Socrates refers to Rua as Rougas. Thompson discusses the ecclesiastical legend of Rua's death (*The Huns*, pp. 80–81). In the "Introduction" to the standard translation of Socrates (*Nicene and Post-Nicene Fathers*, Second Series, Vol. 2), A. C. Zenos notes: "It cannot be said that . . . Socrates either thoroughly realized or attempted any systematic treatment of his subject from the point of view of the true relations of church and state; he simply had the consciousness that the two spheres were not as much dissociated as one might assume" (xiii). This conclusion doesn't square with the evidence here proposed.

99 "*Wie es eigentlich war*." The phrase of Leopold von Ranke (1795–1886), the leading German historian of the nineteenth century. Ranke believed that history could be reconstructed on purely rationalistic (which is to say, objective) grounds, once it had been extracted from the detritus of legend and tradition.

100 "A tale about his brother, Octar." Found in Vol. 7, Ch. 30. Socrates calls him Uptar, but there's no doubt that the historical Octar is indicated. (See Maenchen-Helfen's discussion, pp. 81–83; also Thompson, *The Huns*, pp. 72–75; on the name, see Maenchen-Helfen, pp. 381.)

101 Maenchen-Helfen, p. 83.

102 *Die letzten Jahre Attilas*, p. 54.

103 Maenchen-Helfen, p. 130.

104 This reconstruction is summarized in Gareth Morgan, "Hagen and Aetius," *Classica et Mediaevalia* 30 (1974): 440–50.

105 Gareth Morgan lays out the argument, first proposed in 1885, that Hagen is Aetius. The evidence is quite strong—involving thematic, narrative, and linguistic parallels— though in the end the theory remains highly speculative.

CHAPTER FIVE

106 On these *logades*, see Maenchen-Helfen, pp. 192–95.

107 Thomas Hodgkin remarks that this speech by Eslas has all the earmarks of having been written by Attila. *The Barbarian Invasions of the Roman Empire* (1880), Vol. 2, Ch. 2.

108 An inference drawn from the fact that Priscus never condemns the plot that might have cost him his very life.

109 Priscus refers several times in his narrative to later conversations with the interpreter.

110 "Attila's phrase." At least as translated and filtered through Priscus; that is, it's not presented as a literal transcription of something Attila said.

111 An amusing anecdote is told of the pagan Cyrus, newly installed as a priest, being forced by his congregation in Phrygia to preach his first sermon. He reluctantly stood up in the robes of his office and spoke the following: "Brethren, let the birth of God, our Saviour, Jesus Christ be honored by silence, because the Word of God was conceived in the holy Virgin through hearing only. To him be glory for ever and ever. Amen." And then he sat down. The congregation was astonished at his erudition and he was welcomed to his new post with wild applause. The anecdote is related by John Malalas, as translated by Bury (Vol. 1, p. 228).

112 The *Vita S. Danielis* is the ancient source that points a finger at Chrysaphius.

113 John of Antioch, cited in Gordon's translation, p. 70.

114 These ethnic and national identities are hard for us to pin down with certainty. Edecon's nationality is somewhat a matter of dispute; however, I am taking the position that he was a Scirian, one of the Germanic tribes. That Priscus calls him a Scythian means very little except that he was not Roman or Greek. Orestes is universally conceded to be of Roman birth. There were many such Romans in the fifth century whose national origin was not expressed in allegiance to the Empire. (At times in his career, this was true of Aetius.) Sebastian, the son of Boniface, was also a mercenary to various Germanic warlords, among whom were Theodoric the Visigoth and Gaiseric the Vandal. A leading authority on Hun burial sites, Joachim Werner [*Beiträge zur Archäologie des Attila-Reiches* (Munich 1956)], argued that the *logades* that Priscus describes were members of an international (i.e., not exclusively Hunnish) ruling group.

115 "This was not Edecon's first trip." Priscus notes (frag. 7 in Gordon, p. 70) that in 448 "Edecon came *again* as ambassador."

116 Much of the description of ancient Constantinople and its monuments is indebted to Hillary Sumner-Boyd's *Strolling through Istanbul* (1972).

117 *"Agent provocateur."* John Julius Norwich's description, in *Byzantium: The Early Centuries*, Vol. 1, Ch. 7.

118 I base this claim that Priscus *would* have told us if Edecon were only feigning treachery on the manner and style of his narration in other passages, in which he is quick to question whether Bigilas did something "truly or falsely." Priscus would not have withheld this information if he had it. His failure to do so suggests that it should be taken as a self-evident fact that Edecon was recruited and later reneged on his pledge of cooperation.

119 Thompson illuminates the social structure for us: "A portion of the horsemen seems to have been under the direct orders of Edeco[n], and, when the murder of Attila was suggested to him, his first thought was to assure the co-operation of the men under his immediate command. It is clear that, although each of the *logades* was assigned a military force of its own, that force was well aware to whom it owed its first loyalty" (181). The bribery money, then, was a necessity.

120 *"Audagjan."* Winfred P. Lehman, *A Gothic Etymological Dictionary* (Leiden 1986). Entry for audagjan: to be blessed. My interpretation of Edecon's name is eccentric, and there are phonological difficulties in relating the words.

121 Amédée Thierry (1856) is in the minority by believing that Edecon was recruited and got cold feet in Sardica (Vol. 1, p. 78–79).

122 Gibbon is quoted from Vol. 3, Ch. 34; Hodgkin's more dogmatic assertion—the "probable supposition" being that Edecon had "feigned compliance"—is found in Vol. 2, Ch. 2.

123 Oost points out, however, that sexual relations with the princess of an imperial house had been considered "high treason" for hundreds of years—an offense punishable by death (p. 283); as a practical matter, however, the law was seldom enforced at the end of the Roman Empire.

124 There's much confusion about the chronology and exact location of Honoria through all this. Marcellinus Comes always gets the dates wrong, so his dating of the Honoria affair is not to be believed. J. B. Bury dealt a fatal blow to Gibbon's and Mommsen's belief (based on Marcellinus) that the affair with Eugenius occurred in 434 and that Honoria was thereafter sent to Constantinople. See Bury, "Justa Grata Honoria," *Journal of Roman Studies* 9 (1919): 1–13. Oost complains that because of this error Marcellinus "is implicitly or explicitly ignored by some modern scholars." He goes on to argue that although the date is wrong, "this does not mean that as an Easterner, drawing on Eastern sources, he is in error as to the fact of Honoria's presence in Constantinople." Oost concludes that it would be "peculiarly fitting under the circum-

stances that she should be exiled to the custody of Pulcheria" (283n). Oost is among those who believe that Honoria was sent immediately to Constantinople and from there she sent Hyacinthus to Attila; both Honoria and Hyacinthus were then sent back to Rome, where Hyacinthus was executed and Honoria imprisoned. (There's no documentary evidence for this, however, as Oost readily admits.) The other extreme position is staked out by Maenchen-Helfen, whom I greatly respect, but who is probably wrong when he writes: "I disregard the often told melodramatic story of the vicious Princess Honoria, her clandestine engagement to Attila, and what follows from it. It has all the earmarks of Byzantine court gossip" (130). I take a middle approach in my assumptions. The story about Honoria is fundamentally true; she may have been in Constantinople years before, but almost certainly wasn't rushed off to Pulcheria's care in 450. Honoria's treachery occurred within the sphere of the Western Empire, even though most of our sources view this event from an Eastern perspective.

125 Bury believes that the message came from Attila, though there seems to be no documentary evidence to support this claim (Vol. 1, p. 290). I think this is unlikely, though; what John of Antioch tells us is that the message arrived "concerning events in Rome."

126 The description of Pulcheria's court is based on details from Sozomen's *Ecclesiastical History* (fifth century), as summarized by Hodgkin (Vol. 2, Ch. 2).

127 The ancient sources mention only the fall without specifying the injury. The details are derived from a Greek source of the fourteenth century, Nicephorus Callistus. But as Bury suggests in his notes to Edward Gibbon, "the consequence was so likely to happen, and so unlikely to be invented" that we should probably accept its authenticity.

128 The heresy was generally known as the Eutychian heresy; later on, it was referred to as Monophysitism. (I follow the *Catholic Encyclopedia* in using the terms almost interchangeably.) The intricate interweaving of politics and theology is powerfully demonstrated by this: Chrysaphius the eunuch was the *godson* of Eutyches the heretic.

129 We have no contemporary record of the coronation except for the detail about Pulcheria placing the crown on Marcian's head. We do have, however, an extensive record of the coronation at the Hebdomon of Marcian's successor, Emperor Leo. I have adapted this description. See Oost, p. 55, and Bury (Vol. 1, Ch. 10). It is surmised that Anatolius presided at Marcian's coronation, though no historical document attests to this.

130 Bury, Vol. 1, p. 236n.

131 Maximin probably wasn't designated to fill the same office as Chrysaphius, though the symmetry of these changes is intriguing. The Chrysaphius Affair had affirmed the integrity of Maximin and Priscus. Gibbon cites the proclamation in which Maximin's promotion was declared (Vol. 3, Ch. 34).

132 The opening sentence of Vol. 3, Ch. 35 (Gibbon's *Decline and Fall*).

133 "Remarkable stability and clear sense of direction." This has been the general view since Gibbon, but not everyone agrees. Thompson offers a minority view about Marcian's new boldness toward Attila: "It is difficult to avoid the impression that Marcian's display of audacity was to the last degree untimely. Within a few months of his accession he had brought the East Romans to the edge of the abyss, and all but lost what Theodosius had won by eleven years of patient, exacting, and costly effort" (148). (A. H. M. Jones echoes Thompson when he speaks of Marcian's "rash gesture of defiance" that managed to "turn out luckily" when Attila died.) All of this criticism brashly disregards what actually happened in history: Attila never again threatened the Eastern Empire, and Marcian left 100,000 pounds of gold in the treasury when he died. And, of course, if Marcian did conspire to kill Attila, as I allege, then this also puts the emperor's boldness in a different light. Thompson's views are unduly governed by his Marxist political philosophy, as when he sneers at Marcian's claim that the emperor's duty "is to provide for the utility of the human race." Thompson counters that Marcian's legislation "was aimed almost exclusively at furthering the interests of the landed gentry," and he goes on to cite his tax policies as evidence. Finally, Thompson says that it's unfortunate that more historians have failed to challenge Bréhier's conclusion that Marcian "shows himself as one of the best emperors to have reigned at Constantinople" (cited in Thompson, p. 211). A. H. M. Jones, too, doesn't give Marcian credit for any original thinking at all: "Marcian's defiance of Attila was probably designed to win the favour of the senatorial order," he writes cynically. And a paragraph later: "Marcian's ecclesiastical policy was probably inspired by Pulcheria." (*The Later Roman Empire*, 284–602 [1964], Vol. 1, p. 219.) So there you have it. Marcian did nothing out of conviction. He was an amiable dunce blessed with good luck.

134 Flavius (literally, "Golden-haired") was a name that had been generalized into a meaningless title held by just about everybody in the fifth century who was somebody—a status-name of the upper classes in late antiquity.

135 Book 2, Ch. 1, as translated by E. Walford (1846). The text is available online.

136 This anecdote from the *Chronographia* is translated by John Wortley and is available online in his collection of Byzantine *"Beneficial Tales."*

137 This is according to John Lydus (sixth century).

138 Procopius is often described as an indiscriminate peddler of legend. It's very likely, however, that he had good sources for much of what he wrote down; other stories he must have lifted from popular legends that circulated in oral form. Trying to tell which is which is nearly impossible. Procopius was not far removed at all from the

events that he narrated (a mere hundred years) and he was a very well connected court insider. Undoubtedly, one of his sources was the earlier court historian, Priscus. Most of these stories recorded by Evagrius, Theophanes, and Procopius probably do derive from the history that Priscus wrote (Evagrius says as much); the stories were intended to flatter his patron. The stories are no different from the dream of the broken bow that Jordanes attributed to Priscus. Each story speaks of divine favor; and each story points to a campaign of propaganda officially sanctioned by Marcian and facilitated by his handpicked historian.

139 Thompson, in particular, offers a moralizing censure of Priscus (pp. 210–11).

140 Her connection to Constantine was distant but legitimate: Placidia's half-uncle, Emperor Gratian, was married to Constantine's granddaughter.

141 It may have been 389.

142 It can surprise us to remember that late Roman emperors often never even visited Rome.

143 "The story was later told." The source is Orosius, though the authenticity of the story is subject to doubt. See Oost, pp. 124–25.

144 In Chapter 3 we compared this description of Constantius to the description of Attila. The translation of Olympiodorus is from Gordon, p. 38.

145 Olympiodorus mentions the magician by name: Libanius. Discussed more fully in Oost, p. 144.

146 My portrait is one-sided. Gibbon calls him "brave Constantius" and a "generous soldier" (Vol. 3, Ch. 33). Others see that Constantius "possessed some of the traits of sound statesmanship" (Oost, p. 145), though these qualities were evident in his years as a general, not his seven months as emperor.

147 Descriptions of the mosaics and the building of the church of St. John in Ravenna depend on Oost, pp. 273–75.

148 "The summa of a life." Hodgkin's own, highly sympathetic, summation is worth quoting: "Upon the whole issue, without palliating her alleged share in the judicial murder of Serena, or denying her ill-success in the training of her children, one may plead for a favourable verdict as to the character of Placidia. Her love for Ataulfus, her grief at his death, her brave endurance of the insults of his murderer, long ago enlisted me on her side; and now, after carefully reading all that her detractors have to urge against her, I look upon her still as the sweetest and purest figure of that dreary time" (Vol. 1, Ch. 19).

149 Placidia was partly responsible for Honoria's behavior, and she probably knew it. Honoria and Valentinian had been too young to remember their father Constantius; they knew him only from what their mother told them. Constantius was a buffoon;

but Athaulf was a gallant man, a *real* man, though a barbarian. If a foreign marriage had worked out so well for her, then why not for Honoria, too?

150 The ancient historical source omits Valentinian III, either as an oversight, or because he disapproved of the reburial of Theodosius in the family crypt.

151 The idea here expressed is Oost's, p. 291.

152 Vol. 1, pp. 263–64. Note that Bury's quote begins "Her own sarcophagus," which I have changed to "Galla Placidia's own sarcophagus" for clarity. Hodgkin is quoted from Vol. 1, Ch. 19. Charles Dudley Warner, *Saunterings* (1872), and Ferdinand Gregorovius, *Wanderings in Italy* (1856–1877), are available online.

CHAPTER SIX

153 "In a letter dated April 23." I have modernized an older translation found in the multi-volume *Nicene and Post-Nicene Fathers*, Second Series, Vol. 12. Text available online.

154 "Two weeks earlier, on April 7." Gregory of Tours, *History of the Franks* (sixth century), is the source.

155 Jordanes's extensive account of the Battle of Châlons is found in paragraphs 184–218 of the *Gothic History*. All quotations are based on Mierow's translation.

156 Jordanes's nineteenth-century editor, Theodor Mommsen, believed that Priscus underlay the account of the campaign in Gaul. There is solid ancient evidence for this claim as well. In Book 1, Ch. 17 of his *Ecclesiastical History*, Evagrius Scholasticus (sixth century) writes: "During those times arose the celebrated war of Attila, king of the Scythians: the history of which has been written with great care and distinguished ability by *Priscus the rhetorician, who details, in a very elegant narrative, his attacks on the eastern and western parts of the empire*, how many important cities he reduced, and the series of his achievements until he was removed from the world" (Walford's translation, 1846).

157 Vol. 3, Ch. 35.

158 Edward Creasy's judgment, as expressed in *The Fifteen Decisive Battles of the World* (1856). Text available online.

159 "Semimythical king Merovech." Gordon, p. 204.

160 We know that Priscus was in Rome and saw the young Frankish prince (since he tells us so), but the claim that this occurred *in 450* is more tenuous. We *do* know that Maximin was in Rome at this time delivering letters to Pope Leo; since we know that Priscus also visited Rome at some point, it is logical to place both of them in Rome together. See R. C. Blockley, *The Fragmentary Classicising Historians of the Later Roman Empire* (1981), p. 82. The phrase "peach-fuzz" is my loose paraphrase of Gordon's "a lad without down on his cheeks."

161 Bury's suggestion, Vol. 1, p. 291n.

162 "The king of the Visigoths, Theodoric." This is the grandson of Alaric, not to be confused with Theodoric the Great—the more famous of the two, an Ostrogothic king who succeeded Odovacer as king of Italy and is remembered in medieval poetry as Dietrich.

163 There is no surviving legend about Gaiseric's daughter-in-law, though the Goths told similar stories (which Jordanes relates): for example, the story of Ermanaric's brutal killing of his wife, whom he suspected of unfaithfulness, and of the attempt to avenge her death.

164 On Gaiseric's possible role in bringing about the Gaul campaign, see Frank M. Clover, "Geiseric and Attila," Historia 22 (1973): 104–17. Clover analyzes the scant evidence and concludes that Jordanes's account is credible, backed up as it is by Priscus and other circumstantial evidence. Geiseric is a variant spelling of Gaiseric.

165 Priscus is quoted from Gordon's translation, pp. 106–06.

166 "Nobody knows why the Eastern army stayed anchored." Rumors of intrigue and bribery have circulated, peddled by all the usual suspects (Procopius et al.). Some have alleged that general Aspar (who was an Arian Christian) was secretly plotting to assist his fellow Arian Gaiseric, and bribed Basiliscus to halt his advance. There is no hard evidence of this, however.

167 Speculations can be found in all the usual treatments: Gibbon, Hodgkin, Bury. On the name of the battle: Bury notes that it "has been vulgarly known as the battle of Châlons, because some of the sources (Jordanes, Hydatius) vaguely describe it as fought in the Catalaunian Plains, an expression which probably denoted nearly the whole of Champagne." Bury believes that the battle was fought nearer to Troyes than to Châlons, ancient Durocatalaunum (Vol. 1, p. 293n). Edward Creasy (1851) gave the battle marquis status as one of the "fifteen decisive" battles of the world. Bury is among those who disagree. "The battle of Maurica," as he stubbornly calls it, "was a battle of nations, but its significance has been enormously exaggerated in conventional history. It cannot in any reasonable sense be designated as one of the critical battles of the world. . . . The battle was fought when [Attila] was in full retreat, and its value lay in damaging his prestige as an invincible conqueror, in weakening his forces, and in hindering him from extending the range of his ravages. . . . If Attila had been victorious," Bury concludes, "there is no reason to suppose that the course of history would have been seriously altered" (Vol. 1, p. 294). (A modern treatment by Arther Ferrill, The Fall of the Roman Empire [1986], reaches a different conclusion.) The reference to "generations of French colonels" is a standard trope in the modern historical literature, and it must rest on some evidence, though I've never seen any.

168 Once again, Evagrius Scholasticus (cited earlier) gives compelling witness to the ex-

tensive history that Priscus wrote of Attila's campaigns against the East *and* the West. Though I characterize the attribution of this passage to Priscus as a "hunch," it does rest upon reasonable evidence, even if the claim cannot be proven conclusively.

169 The account that Gibbon attributes to the hagiographical literature is also found in Gregory of Tours (539–594), *The History of the Franks*. It's unclear why Gibbon disregards Jordanes's account.

170 Bury's phrase, Vol. 1, p. 250.

171 The phrase, which comes from Plutarch's *Life of Marcus Brutus*, has had a considerable life in Western culture. Gibbon calls Boethius, author of *The Consolation of Philosophy*, "the last of the Romans whom Cato could have acknowledged as a countryman." Cassiodorus has been honored as the last of the Romans and the first of the Italians. Francis Bacon called Justinian the Great, the "last of the Romans." Pope Gregory the Great (died 604) has been so described for his deep roots in ancient Roman culture.

172 Vol. 3, Ch. 33.

173 Oost notes that the court poet Merobaudes "offers no hint of the real nature of the relations between his hero [Aetius] and the imperial family, but it is a fair assumption that if Placidia had disliked and distrusted Aëtius before, she now hated him with a cold hate which she doubtless transmitted to her son and which Aëtius' undeniable services to the Empire in Gaul did nothing to assuage" (239). This is all assumption, and not necessarily the best assumption either.

174 "A remarkable convergence of interests." My conjecture is based on the marriage alliances.

175 "As Attila rightly believed." An overanalysis? Perhaps, though it does offer a narrative explanation for the strange inconsistencies in what the soothsayers said, what Attila believed, and what actually happened.

176 "Heroism like this is Greek." We're on thin ice, since heroism like this is also Germanic, as *Beowulf* shows us. Priscus is a possible source for this literary depiction of the heroic ideal, though it could just as easily have been pasted into the text by Cassiodorus or Jordanes.

177 The most extensive discussion of Monsieur Bonhomme's discovery is in Hodgkin, Vol. 2, Ch. 3.

178 I don't want to leave the impression that a lot has been found; in fact, it's amazing that more has not been uncovered from one of the greatest battles ever fought on European soil. The information about Napoleon III comes from an article by George Clause, "The Civilian Environment around the Camp at Châlons," available online at www.napoleon.org.

179 "June 20, 451." Bury's meticulous reconstruction of this date is widely accepted. See Thompson, *The Huns*, p. 154, for a summary of how this conclusion has been reached.

Incidentally, it's been calculated that Halley's Comet reached its *perihelion* (the point closest to the sun) just four days later, on June 24.

180 This is the conclusion of Thierry, Vol. 1, p. 185.

181 Discussed by Thompson, *The Huns*, p. 155.

182 The details are examined by Clover, "Geiseric and Attila," p. 109.

183 "The delegates were restless." A surprising figure pops up in the voluminous documentary records of the Council of Chalcedon. In a list naming those in the imperial corps around Marcian is a certain Vigilans, whom A. H. M. Jones (Vol. 1, p. 584) identifies as Bigilas, the unlucky translator we followed in earlier chapters. What *he's* still doing on the imperial payroll is anybody's guess.

184 This problem (or challenge) has been variously described. Alfred Whitehead spoke of a "climate of opinion" that must be reconstructed for an age. The German philosophers of history described this as a culture's *Weltanschauung*, or "worldview." In literary theory, Hans Jauss described the "horizon of expectations" that writers and readers negotiate on opposite sides of a text.

185 The translated passages from St. John Chrysostom are taken from the multi-volume works of the *Nicene and Post-Nicene Fathers* (available online). The homilies are cited in the following order: XXVII on the Acts of the Apostles, XVI on the Acts of the Apostles, and two passages from XIII on Timothy. I've modernized the translations and added italics for emphasis throughout. These homilies would have been delivered from the pulpit of the Megale Ekklesia, the "Great Church," the original Hagia Sophia, which was burned by rioting mobs in 404 when Chrysostom was sent into exile for criticizing the Empress Eudoxia. The church was subsequently rebuilt by Theodosius II, burned again, and then magnificently rebuilt in the sixth century by Justinian the Great. This church, the Hagia Sophia, is still standing in Istanbul.

186 "The Pardoner's Tale," ll. 293–96. *Deyde*, died; *bledynge*, bleeding; *ay*, always; *lyve*, live. An *exemplum* is a topical "example," a commonplace illustration in the homiletic literature concerning some vice or virtue.

187 This is the Mierow translation again, though the italics are mine, and I have substituted the word "obstructed" for Mierow's "hindered," so as to draw out the obvious parallels with John Chrysostom.

188 Note what Sir Thomas Browne had to say about this practice in classical sources: "There is scarce any philosopher but dies twice or thrice in Laertius, nor almost any life without two or three deaths in Plutarch. Which makes the tragical ends of noble persons more favorably resented [i.e., represented] by compassionate readers, who find some relief in the election of such differences" (*Hydriotaphia*, Ch. 3).

CHAPTER SEVEN

189 Details can be found in Andrew Thompson, "Malaria and the Fall of Rome." Available online at www.bbc.co.uk/history.

190 Mark R. Hughes, deputy director of the National Center for Human Genome Research, as quoted on www.faseb.org.

191 Valentinian's *Novella* dated January 31, 451, indicates that Italy was suffering from a severe famine in the winter of 450–51.

192 Vol. 3, Ch. 35.

193 Some two hundred sarcophagi were discovered in Concordia in 1873. Discussed in R. Lanciani, *Pagan and Christian Rome* (1892), Chapter 7 (available online). It's impossible to connect these artifacts dogmatically with Attila's invasion.

194 "Theodor Mommsen." Cited in 1902 by the Nobel Committee as "the greatest living master of the art of historical writing, with special reference to his monumental work *A History of Rome*." Mommsen's edition of Jordanes is the standard Latin text.

195 Maenchen-Helfen's phraseology, p. 132.

196 The story of Maenchen-Helfen hand-delivering his manuscript is related by his editor, Max Knight, in a foreword to the edition of *The World of the Huns* (1973).

197 From Maenchen-Helfen's "Preface," p. xxiii.

198 Much of the documentary evidence cited can be found in Maenchen-Helfen's own presentation of these arguments, pp. 129–41.

199 Vol. 3, Ch. 35.

200 But Thompson persists (*The Huns*, pp. 158–59); he claims that "the Hunnic cavalry could easily have been checked in mountain warfare" (Prosper's old falsehood), and that, after Aetius "recovered from his astonishment," the general's options had been whittled down to one: "to take Valentinian with him and abandon Italy altogether." Thompson voices what other historians have only dared to imply about the redoubtable general: "Rarely in history has a statesman been caught so completely off his guard as was Aetius in the spring of 452." And yet, as we've seen, this cannot be true.

201 Thompson's misunderstandings (p. 163) are based on the usually reliable Otto Seeck. Italics are mine in Thompson's quote.

202 Occam's (1285–c. 1347) phrase in Latin, *Pluralitas non est ponenda sine necessitate*, seems tailor-made for this little textual problem, where entities have multiplied without reason. Occam's name is also spelled Ockham.

203 A strong inference, I believe, which Maenchen-Helfen locates (pp. 129–30) in the letters of Leo to Marcian in the spring of 451.

204 "As Thompson glibly claims," p. 159. Maenchen-Helfen's reply, p. 135.

205 The plot keeps reproducing itself like a virus. The typical choice is to plant the seeds of the Honoria affair in some imagined prior relationship between the two in Rome.

206 Emperor Aurelian (270–75) constructed massive walls around Rome that bear his name, and were later fortified by Emperor Honorius in the early fifth century. However, these walls were not nearly as effective as Constantinople's defenses and never managed to keep out any army that was determined to get in.

207 Jordanes ¶ 222.

208 Jordanes ¶ 157–58.

209 Galla Placidia was among the nobility who had been carried away by the Visigoths, and she may have witnessed the disasters that afflicted Alaric in southern Italy.

210 The theory behind this book assumes that Priscus knew more than the surviving fragments of his history tell us—but not that he knew *everything*.

211 Vol. 1, p. 295n.

212 "Anonymous Valesianus." The main source for the events surrounding the deposition of Romulus Augustulus in 476 (in which context this piece of information about Odovacer's father, Orestes, is related).

213 A recently published historical novel by Boris Raymond, *The Twelfth Vulture of Romulus: Attila and the Fall of Rome*, points an accusing finger at Orestes and attributes to him patriotic motives for killing Attila. I've not read the book.

214 Otto Seeck, in particular. The Constantius tombstone is discussed by Maenchen-Helfen, pp. 102–3, and Thompson, p. 298.

215 Jordanes ¶ 223.

216 The translation of Prosper and (later) of the Anonymous Life of Leo are based on the translations in J. H. Robinson's *Readings in European History* (1905), pp. 49–51. Text is available online.

217 Paul the Deacon's account of Leo and Attila is discussed by Maenchen-Helfen, p. 141, where the relevant scholarship is cited.

218 Claimed by Leo in Sermon 84 that he delivered in 455. Discussed by Maenchen-Helfen, p. 141.

219 As cited by Bury, Vol. 1, p. 295n.

220 Maenchen-Helfen, p. 141.

221 This one detail seems to refute Maenchen-Helfen's skepticism about the Honoria affair. Maenchen-Helfen is almost alone among scholars in believing that the affair was nothing more than Byzantine gossip. That wouldn't account for the highly specific detail about Herculanus, a validating detail in the narrative. One would expect something far more general, such as "Honoria was married off to an old senator." Instead, we get the very name of a senator who was elected consul in 452.

222 Mommsen's surmisal is logical but unattested in any ancient source.

223 Alexander Haggerty Krappe, "La légende de la naissance miraculeuse d'Attila, roi des Huns," *Moyen Âge* 41 (1931): 96–104.

224 Bury summarizes these details in Vol. 1, p. 294.

225 "Widespread dissatisfaction." Maenchen-Helfen notes cautiously that "although we have no evidence of unrest among his German subjects or among the ruling group of the Huns, we may safely assume that the former were more heavily exploited than ever and the latter grew increasingly dissatisfied with the king who failed to provide them with booty and gold" (143).

226 History provides an interesting analogy in the person of Napoleon. Recent forensic evidence has demonstrated that Napoleon was probably murdered. Analysis of hair samples shows high levels of arsenic in his system. Just as the ruling elite of the Western and Eastern Empires wanted Attila dead, so also Napoleon declared of himself, in his will, that he would "die before my time, murdered by the English oligarchy and its hired assassins." Like Attila, Napoleon was the target of frequent assassination attempts. After Napoleon's death, numerous rumors circulated as to the real circumstances—much as the rumors that floated around the Empire in the time of Attila. A contemporary publication, the *Observer*, noted in June 1816 that "it is truly ridiculous to read the contradictory accounts with which the newspapers are crammed respecting Napoleon. . . ." The *Observer* went on to note how some accounts depicted Napoleon as drinking two bottles of wine at breakfast, while "the fact is that there are very few men more temperate than he in the use of wine." This is reminiscent of a central contradiction in the Attila accounts. The eyewitness account of Priscus shows a man who was temperate in drink and food—Spartan in his tastes— who is nonetheless described in other accounts as dying after riotous feasting and drinking. (Summarized from David G. Chandler, "Death and the Emperor," *Folio*, Autumn 2002.)

227 A question asked by Klaeber, "Attila's and Beowulf's Funeral" (1927), p. 258, who cites a similar instance in the Old English Chronicle in which the woman (quite naturally) screams.

228 Amédée Thierry, Vol. 1, pp. 218–19. The translation is mine.

CHAPTER EIGHT

229 "*Strava*." The details are covered minutely by Maenchen-Helfen, who concludes that "here and there a feature seems to have been misunderstood or misinterpreted" in the ancient record (277). Slaying the laborers so as to conceal the tomb is one example. Maenchen-Helfen writes: "To kill the laborers who buried the king was an inefficient means to prevent the robbing of the tomb, for thousands must have known of it. Besides, who killed the killers?" (278).

230 "Over the body, too." I've transposed the order. Jordanes lists the funeral hymn first and then describes the *strava*.

231 Adapted from Mierow's translation of Jordanes. Some philologists, such as Kluge (1911), have attempted to "reconstruct" the supposed "Germanic original" underlying the poem—a ridiculous enterprise, as Maenchen-Helfen points out, p. 277.

232 Thierry, Vol. 2, p. 291.

233 *New York Times*, Monday, Oct. 6, 1975, p. 10:3.

234 *Science Digest*, April 1975, pp. 16–17.

235 *The Academy*, Sept. 12, 1874, p. 304, cols. 2–3.

236 "Fishermen's stories." Ildikó Ecsedy, "The Oriental Background to the Hungarian Tradition about 'Attila's Tomb.'" *Acta Orientalia* 36 (1982): 129–53. See also Géza Komoróczy, "Attila's Grave and Burial: A Legend in Light of New Publications." *The New Hungarian Quarterly*, pp. 159–64. In 1920 *The Times* (London) reported yet another discovery of Attila's grave in the bed of the Arauka River near Nagy-Szent-Miklos: Dec. 6, 1920, p. 12, col. D. Once again, the fantastic claim never materialized. An interesting pattern, however, begins to emerge in all these stories: The search for Attila's grave is closely linked to the rise of Hungarian nationalism in the nineteenth century.

237 See Donald J. Ward, "Attila, King of the Huns in Narrative Lore." In: *Attila, the Man and His Image*, ed. by Franz H. Bäuml and Marianna D. Birnbaum (Budapest 1993), pp. 43–44.

238 Vol. 3, Ch. 35.

239 Letter CXXVII (to Principia). Text is available online.

240 "Myth of their invincibility." This is not uniformly true, despite the limiting of my description to the "Roman nobility." There were statesmen, just as there were churchmen, who understood that Rome was falling. Still, the description holds well for most of the later emperors in the West—certainly for Valentinian III, though definitely not for Majorian (457–61).

241 First published in English in 1939, *Mohammed and Charlemagne* has been one of the most influential modern treatments of late antiquity. The central idea of the book is often simply referred to as "Pirenne's Thesis."

242 Hodgkin, Vol. 2, p. 314.

243 Note Oost's brief discussion of this account, p. 301n.

244 Vol. 3, Ch. 35.

245 There's good reason to believe that this happened, as Eudoxia's daughter had been betrothed earlier to Gaiseric's son, Huneric.

246 We can't prove that this is the same Thraustila; my judgment that he received sanctuary in the East is an extrapolation from the limited set of facts we have. John doesn't explicitly state a connection between the two Thraustilas. He may *imply* a connection,

however, in that both men are described by a common phrase, "man of reputation."

247 Prosper of Aquitaine is quite believable on this point, as he was a resident of Rome.

248 Vol. 3, Ch. 35. Of course, "fabulous" here means that he tells "fables."

249 The emperor's daughter, Placidia, went on to marry a senator named Olybrius who ruled briefly as Western emperor in 472.

250 "Strange irony." Thompson's phrase, p. 171.

251 Gibbon first noted that an ancient source, the Anonymous Valesianus, specifically draws a connection between Attila's secretary and the father of Romulus Augustulus. Vol. 4, Ch. 36.

252 But R. C. Blockley, *The Fragmentary Classicising Historians*, dates the text of Priscus to c. 476.

253 We can't trace Edecon's career, post-Attila, with the same kind of certainty. We know that the father of Odovacer was a certain Edeco, but we don't know if this was the same Edeco(n) from Attila's court. That identification was first suggested by Tillemont (1637–98), was endorsed by Gibbon, and is still followed by many historians. Maenchen-Helfen is among those who doubt the connection. Most historians are agnostic on the point, believing that the evidence is not conclusive one way or the other.

254 The fate of Romulus after his settlement in Campania is unknown, although it has been suggested that he might be the Romulus to whom the Ostrogothic king Theodoric wrote circa 507–11 concerning a bequest made to a certain Romulus and his mother.

255 For the possibility that Ernach was a mercenary in the Eastern army, see C. A. Macartney, "The End of the Huns," *Byzantinisch-neugriechische Jahrbücher* 10 (1934): 106–14.

256 Ample textual evidence points to this parallel—the confusion of the names in manuscripts, the sharing of legendary details, etc. See Babcock, pp. 46–51.

EPILOGUE

257 The *Plerophoriai* of John, cited from Wortley's translation, *The Byzantine "Beneficial Tales."* Text is available online.

258 The details of Marcian's death are reconstructed by Brian Coke, "The Date and Circumstances of Marcian's Decease, A.D. 457." *Byzantion* 48 (1978): 5–9.

259 Pulcheria, incidentally, had preceded Marcian in death in 453—just a few months after Attila died. She left her considerable fortune to the poor, "a bequest which Marcian, to his eternal credit, faithfully carried out" (Norwich, *Byzantium: The Early Years*).

260 "An inventory of the city's monuments." A. Cameron and J. Herrin, trans., *Constantinople in the Eighth Century: The Parastaseis Syntomai Chronikai* (1984).

BIOGRAPHICAL INDEX

This is not a comprehensive list of proper nouns in the text, but a list of the dramatis personae *who play a role in the narrative. The names of scholars—ancient and modern—have not been included.*

Aetius, Western Roman general (c. 390s–454) and *de facto* ruler in the West during the first half of the fifth century. Acquainted with Attila from his youth, Aetius would become Attila's main foe, defeating him in 451 at the Battle of Châlons. Aetius was assassinated by Valentinian III in 454.

Alaric, Visigothic king who sacked Rome in 410.

Ambrose (c. 340–97), bishop of Milan.

Anatolius, patriarch of Constantinople during Marcian's reign.

Arcadius, emperor of the Eastern Empire (395–408). Son of Theodosius the Great and father of Theodosius II.

Ardabur (died 471), Eastern general and son of Aspar.

Aspar (died 471), the most powerful general in the Eastern Empire during much of the fifth century.

Athaulf (died c. 415), Visigothic king who succeeded Alaric. First husband of Galla Placidia.

Berica, a Germanic chieftain in Attila's court. Traveling companion of Priscus and Maximin on their return trip to Constantinople in 449.

Bigilas, Eastern Roman diplomat and translator. Bigilas was central to the plot to assassinate Attila in 449.

Biographical Index

Bleda, older brother of Attila, co-ruler of the Huns from 435 to 445. Most likely assassinated by Attila.

Boniface, powerful Western general and arch-enemy of Aetius. Died in battle against Aetius in 432.

Chrysaphius, a eunuch and advisor to Theodosius I. Chrysaphius was behind the failed plot to assassinate Attila in 449. He was a Eutychean heretic and was executed by Marcian and Pulcheria when they came to power in 450.

Chrysostom, John (the "Golden-Voiced"), patriarch of Constantinople (died 407).

Constantius, Western Roman and Attila's first secretary. Crucified by Attila and Bleda.

Constantius, Western Roman and Attila's second secretary at the time Priscus and Maximin journeyed to Attila's court in 449.

Constantius III, Western general and, briefly, co-emperor in the West (421). Second husband of Galla Placidia and father of Honoria and Valentinian III.

Dengizech, son of Attila who died fighting the Eastern Romans in 469.

Dioscorus, bishop of Alexandria, declared a heretic and deposed by the Council of Chalcedon in 451.

Edecon, a top lieutenant and diplomat in Attila's court. Edecon conspired with the Romans to assassinate Attila in 449, but reneged on the plan. Edecon is probably the father of Odovacer, the chieftain who deposed Emperor Romulus Augustulus in 476.

Ernach, Attila's youngest and favorite son.

Eslas, a senior Hunnish diplomat sent to Constantinople in 449.

Eudocia, daughter of Valentinian III and wife of Huneric the Vandal.

Eudoxia, wife of Emperor Arcadius and the target of much of John Chrysostom's sermonizing.

Eudoxia, wife of Valentinian III and daughter of Theodosius II.

Felix, Western general murdered at the instigation of Aetius in 429.

Gaiseric, Vandal king from 428 to 477. The most talented of all the barbarian chieftains, Gaiseric led his troops from Africa and sacked Rome in 455.

Galla Placidia (c. 388–450), daughter of Emperor Theodosius the Great, mother of Valentinian III and Honoria.

Gaudentius, son of Aetius who was betrothed to Valentinian's daughter Placidia.

Gundahar, Burgundian king (died 437). Remembered in medieval German poetry as Gunther.

Heraclian, Western Roman military officer who assassinated Stilicho.

Heraclius, Western eunuch who assisted Valentinian in assassinating Aetius.

Honoria, daughter of Galla Placidia and sister of Emperor Valentinian III. Honoria sent her ring to Attila in an apparent marriage proposal.

Honorius, emperor of the Western Empire (395–423). Son of Theodosius the Great.

Huneric, son of the Vandal king Gaiseric.

Hyacinthus, eunuch sent with Honoria's ring to Attila. Executed by Valentinian III.

Ildico, Germanic maiden and the last wife of Attila the Hun.

John the Usurper, pretender emperor in the West who was defeated in 425 by forces loyal to Galla Placidia and the Theodosian House.

Leo, bishop of Rome (440–61). A central figure in both the theological and political problems of his day, Leo met Attila face-to-face in 452 and persuaded him to abandon Italy.

Leo the Butcher, Eastern emperor who succeeded Marcian (457–74). "Butchered" Aspar and his family in the palace in 471.

Marcian, emperor of the East Roman Empire (450–57).

Maximin (died 452), Eastern Roman ambassador under Theodosius II and Marcian. Friend and traveling companion of Priscus.

Merobaudes, court poet in the West who wrote flattering poems for both Aetius and Valentinian III.

Mundiuch, father of Attila and Bleda.

Octar, Hunnish king and uncle of Attila and Bleda. Co-ruler with Rua until Octar's death in 430.

Onegesh, Hun "prime minister." The second-ranking official after Attila; the brother of Scottas.

Optila, Germanic mercenary in the Western army who participated in the assassination of Valentinian III.

Orestes, Roman-born official in Attila's court. Father of Romulus Augustulus, last Roman emperor in the West.

Petronius Maximus, Roman senator and ill-fated emperor who succeeded Valentinian III.

Placidia, see Galla Placidia.

Placidia, daughter of Valentinian III, betrothed to Gaudentius.

Plinthas, Eastern Roman diplomat who negotiated with the Huns in the 430s and 440s.

Priscus, Greek historian (died c. 470s) on whose eyewitness account much of our knowledge of Attila rests.

Pulcheria, sister of Theodosius II, wife of Marcian.

Rua, Hunnish king (died 434), uncle of Attila and Bleda.

Rusticius, Eastern Roman translator who accompanied the Roman diplomats in 449 to Attila's court.

Scottas, a high-ranking official in Attila's court, brother of Onegesh.

Serena, wife of Stilicho and foster mother of Galla Placidia.

Singeric, Visigothic king who succeeded Athaulf.

Stilicho, Germanic general who served the Western Roman Empire and was slain in 408.

Tatalus, father of Orestes.

Theodoric, Visigothic king who died at the Battle of Châlons in 451.

Theodoric the Great, Ostrogothic king in Italy (died 526), patron of the writer Cassiodorus.

Theodosius, infant son of Galla Placidia and the Germanic chieftain Athaulf.

Theodosius I ("the Great"), last emperor of a unified Roman Empire (379–95). Upon his death, Theodosius left his two sons in control of the Empire: Arcadius in the East and Honorius in the West.

Theodosius II, emperor of the eastern Empire (408–50). Son of Arcadius and grandson of Theodosius I.

Thorismud, son of Theodoric, who became king of the Visigoths upon his father's death at Châlons in 451.

Thraustila, Germanic mercenary in the Western army who participated in the assassination of Valentinian III.

Valentinian III, emperor of the Western Empire (425–55). Son of Galla Placidia and grandson of Emperor Theodosius the Great, Valentinian murdered Aetius in 454 and was himself assassinated the following year.

Wallia, Visigothic king who succeeded Singeric.

Zerko, a Moorish dwarf at Attila's court.

INDEX

Page numbers in italic indicate illustrations.

INDEX

INDEX